The Mind of the Artist

The Mind of the Artist

Personality and the Drive to Create

WILLIAM TODD SCHULTZ

OXFORD
UNIVERSITY PRESS

OXFORD
UNIVERSITY PRESS

Oxford University Press is a department of the University of Oxford. It furthers the University's objective of excellence in research, scholarship, and education by publishing worldwide. Oxford is a registered trade mark of Oxford University Press in the UK and certain other countries.

Published in the United States of America by Oxford University Press
198 Madison Avenue, New York, NY 10016, United States of America.

Library of Congress Cataloging-in-Publication Data
Names: Schultz, William Todd, author.
Title: The mind of the artist : personality and the drive to create /
William Todd Schultz.
Description: New York, NY : Oxford University Press, [2022] |
Includes bibliographical references and index.
Identifiers: LCCN 2021033674 (print) | LCCN 2021033675 (ebook) |
ISBN 9780197611098 (hardback) | ISBN 9780197611111 (epub) |
ISBN 9780197611128
Subjects: LCSH: Artists—Psychology.
Classification: LCC NX165 .S33 2022 (print) | LCC NX165 (ebook) |
DDC 701/.15—dc23
LC record available at https://lccn.loc.gov/2021033674
LC ebook record available at https://lccn.loc.gov/2021033675

DOI: 10.1093/oso/9780197611098.001.0001

1 3 5 7 9 8 6 4 2

Printed by Sheridan Books, Inc., United States of America

Contents

Acknowledgments

My deepest thanks are to Josh Shenk and the Beverly Rogers & Carol C. Harter Black Mountain Institute (BMI) at University of Nevada, Las Vegas, where I was so fortunate to be a Shearing Fellow from 2016 to 2017. BMI is where these ideas came together. This is a Vegas book.

Eternal thanks and love, also, to the Denton family, who gave me a place to live in Boulder City, and to John L. Smith. Sara and Sally will be in my heart forever (Fremont, too). I hope I can say I am an Honorary Denton.

My fellow Fellows at BMI were a delight and an inspiration: David Morris, Gabe Urza, David Ulin, Hossein Abkenar, Jane Barnes, Malena Morling, and most of all, Yelena Akhtiorskaya, with whom I talked over the subject of art as therapy, among so many other topics. Drew Cohen, Kellen Braddock, Michael Ursell, Cindi Reed, Jennifer Dreher, Stephen Bates, and Maritza White were also helpful friends to me from day one.

Deep gratitude to the Corporation of Yaddo, a magical place, and to my fellow artists-in-residence in July and August of 2021.

Amanda Fortini has been immensely kind in so many ways, impossibly generous with her time and ideas and editorial acumen. I am also grateful for Walter Kirn's counsel. His writing is an inspiration, as is his brilliance.

Thanks to the sublime Kuwaiti painter Shurooq Amin, who got so many ideas churning, and whose courage has been an inspiration.

Early on, people sat for interviews, as I was getting started, or read drafts of chapters. These include Hilary Hodge, Hannah Mickunas, Lisa Onstad, Stephanie Lawrence, Kaitlyn ni Donovan, Ana-Maria Gavrila, Asia Argento (a supernatural presence in my life and brilliant artist), Michelle Cameron, Dan P. McAdams, the late Scott Timberg, members of the Society for Personology, Natalie Johnson, students in my Mind of the Artist and my Personality courses at Pacific University in Forest Grove, Oregon, Craig Bartlett, Natasha Kline, my agent Betsy Lerner, and Karyn Marcus.

For the past 10 years I've been blessed to work with Abby Gross at Oxford. She's a dream editor, no matter the project. I cannot express how grateful I am for her sanity and clarity and sense of perspective. More recently, Nadina Persaud and Katharine Pratt have been excellent caretakers of the work.

Endless love, today and to infinity, to Theresa, Adrienne, Henry, and Shar Deisch.

Introduction

> I do not believe in illusion, the great vacillator. My painting carries within it the message of pain.
>
> —Frida Kahlo

> When you get your heart broken, you've got all the time in the world to write about it: how it feels, what the temperature was that day. When you're happy, the last thing you want to do is slow down and write a song, unless it's "Zip-a-Dee-Doo-Dah."
>
> —John Prine

> He abstracted himself from the mean and actual world. He drove his mind into the abyss where poetry is written.
>
> —George Orwell

> You can play a shoestring if you're sincere.
>
> —John Coltrane

> I accept chaos. I'm not sure whether it accepts me.
>
> —Bob Dylan

For 25 years I've researched and written about artists. I've read biographies, artists on art, art critics, critics of art critics. I've interviewed artists (some famous, some not), poured over diaries and journals and books of letters, discussed interpretations of art with artists, lived with artists, lectured on artists, taught classes on artists and the artist mind. I've gone from a callow romantic notion of the artist as a basically touched and incomprehensible limit case to where I am now, a belief in

The Mind of the Artist. William Todd Schultz, Oxford University Press. © Oxford University Press 2022.
DOI: 10.1093/oso/9780197611098.003.0001

the idea that while making something out of nothing might seem magical, it is a knowable process, at least in outline. I should say: I've always believed the *meanings* of art could be scrutinized and understood; what I wasn't sure of, initially, was whether or how *the ways in which the art got made* might be probed with success. These are two different things—deriving meaning and the work itself, the craft, the shaping.

I'd be pleased to call this book the Sum Total of What I've Learned, but the fact is, I'm still learning. I'm still finding new stuff out. Really, it's where I am now, where my thinking has taken me.

One of the first questions to interest me about art was whether it did the artist any good making it. I knew a lot of artists were troubled or tortured or just plain vexed. I was suspicious of the idea of art as therapy. I did not buy it, nor did any artist I ever spoke with (including three last night, here with me at Yaddo). This raised additional questions. Why make art? It's so difficult in so many ways. Is the torture in the artist or in the process? Does art require frenzy, as Nietzsche said it did, or is frenzy incidental? What are the goals—egoism, beauty, fame, validation, self-expression, money, satisfaction in a job well done, a tonic for boredom, self-entertainment?

There's a worry important to address right away because it's common and it may cross your mind as you read, if it hasn't already. It is this: *It's impossible to generalize about the mind of the artist because artists are so different and they work in different media.* The same could be said, I suppose, for the mind of any profession or activity—scientists, accountants, roofers, jockeys. I don't believe there is one artist mind. I'd be an idiot to do so. But I *do* believe there's a basic profile that, with minor exceptions, gets at an essential sameness. Psychology creates general pictures of, say, schizophrenics or racists or happiness. I'm after the same thing here: the typical qualities of mind, personality, and life experience that prime creativity. Will there be outliers? There will. But that's always the case. To put it differently: This book isn't about individual difference, but group-level sameness. There truly is an artist type, in other words, and I will describe its features.

Here's an example: the poet Sylvia Plath (whom I discuss in more detail later). She started writing at age 8. She was an academic superstar, a roaring success. Her bumblebee expert father Otto died when she was a child, from an illness he seemed to take no action against.

Her mother, Aurelia, was clutching, overidentified with her daughter and her daughter's life. (Plath wrote a poem about her titled "Medusa.") She married a poet, Ted Hughes, and their relationship was intense and challenging. Suicide was a constant lure, for reasons she connected with the loss of her dad. She moved to England, where she had a hard time fitting in while raising two small children. In terms of her work, she started by writing finely wrought, technically successful but mannered poems that left her feeling dissatisfied, as if something vital had not been accessed. There was a series about her father, the "bee sequence." There were stories, a novel. She assiduously kept a journal. Then, feeling isolated, deeply troubled, and at times beset by fever, in a state qualifying as psychotic, she wrote the poems that made her name—the *Ariel* poems—in a spasm of weeks. This work she recognized as genius. She wrote to her mother to say so. Finally, while still in the midst of these poems, work so unexpected and raw and unforeseen, she committed suicide, some say by accident, some say on purpose.

From this short paragraph numberless questions arise. She took to writing so young—was she a born writer, a born artist? What was the impact of the loss of her father, an event she pointed to ominously? Did it spur her to write more, or did it play no significant role? What about suicidal feelings? Can causes be isolated? Did writing about suicide, a common subject for her, worsen the feeling or help her make sense of it? How important was the Hughes relationship vis-à-vis the poems she made? In contrast with Plath, he was famous before they met, important, formidable, intense. She had a breakthrough that she did not survive. What mysterious process got her to that point; how did she make the leap? Can it be argued that the cost of genius was death? Are the two connected, or are they entirely separate outcomes, foolish to align?

In sense I'll elaborate on later, Plath was born to write. It was part of her personality. To put it crudely, it was in her. Trauma, external to her, determined subject matter, specifically in relation to her father's death. Because of the nature of her personality, her mind was organized in ways that made a breakthrough possible. The way her mind worked allowed, finally, for access to inner raw materials that she shaped into poems the likes of which she almost did not recognize. They came in torrents, bursting forth. She wrote through fever and madness and pain and loneliness, in winter months when England was freezing. To some, art may seem like an escape, a balm, a separate place to go, apart from the troubles of the world. It was not that for Plath, and I don't believe it's that for the majority of artists. It was more a reminder. Not a flight but an immersion. Writing genius poems of suicide did not make Plath less suicidal. Writing poems about her dead father, or about her mother's "eely tentacles," did not dispatch her grief. This wasn't art therapy.

In Plath the primary elements of this book are encapsulated.

Art starts with personality. We know that for sure now. It is a settled fact. It's based in decades of persuasive scientific research impossible to discount and obtuse to dismiss. In the past, writers (myself included) have theorized as much, working iteratively and inductively, guessing, speculating, finding promising commonalities. We don't have to guess anymore. It's clear. At the start of this book I'll tell you all about personality and art, and features of personality that will reappear. For now, let me say this. There are particular, largely heritable personality tendencies that predict creativity and creative achievement. These constitute the settled facts I mentioned. Are they "in" every single artist who ever lived? No. As I say, there are outliers. But do they capture something essential, a common factor? They do, yes. You'll be reading all about them. And if you are an artist, odds are good you will see them in yourself.

Personality is relatively static. It's who you are. It's your way of being. But types of personality give rise to, or make more likely, types of mental states. The states are the outgrowth. They come and go, but some do so more than others, precisely because of who you are. You tend to go into particular states your personality sets you up for. If you're high in a trait called neuroticism, you go into states like anxiety, vulnerability, depression. If you're high in a trait called agreeableness, you go into states like trust, empathy, friendliness. States of mind are intimately connected to creative process. Mental states make art more or less doable. Every artist knows this. They can't always describe it. They feel at the mercy of it. It's hard to predict or steer. But they know it. There's this need to get into a feeling, a mood, a receptive frame, a vague encompassing atmosphere. You can tell when you're in it, and when you're in it everything comes easier. It's about how your mind is arranged, about access, fluidity, loosening, surrender, surprise, discovery. It's not like you go insane, but you partake of, with purpose, certain crazy-feeling processes. A lot of the apparently insoluble mysteries of art have to do with exactly this—the making of it. The *how* not the *why*. Again, science points the way. We know a surprising amount about these mysteries. They are not actually indescribable. More deeply, they wind up circling back to personality. The two can be connected: traits and states. They work together, and they go a long way toward deciphering creativity's most fundamental ingredients.

Then, from the outside, there's trauma. Here things get less clear but not unclear. Not every artist is traumatized, and not every trauma victim becomes, *ipso facto*, an artist. Yet trauma is gripping. It jars and focuses. It becomes obsessive. It draws the mind to it. Plath kept returning to her father. She kept writing poems like "Daddy," about what his death did, what it meant. He intruded, a restive poltergeist. In the biographies of artists, research shows a prevalence of early loss. The loss can take forms. For many, it's repeated, symbolically and imaginatively, in the work (as it was with Plath). Precisely why loss might mobilize creativity is fascinating to parse. Way back when, it was the subject of my PhD dissertation, on the writer James Agee. Most likely, what loss does is recommend a subject matter, one especially complicated, insistent, irrepressible, and raw. Also, tenacious—it keeps coming, pressing, it keeps volunteering itself for inspection. I've written a lot about loss-afflicted artists. The loss is like a song they can't stop hearing. In the art, they don't make it go away or mute it; they replay it, they pay attention to it. In other words, they return to it, with paint, words, music, photographs. Again, there's the question of therapeutic potential. Is the repetition salutary? The answer I've arrived at is this: maybe sometimes, but not as a rule. Dreaming is a decent analogy; art's like dreaming while awake. Do trauma dreams undo pain? They shape it. They express it, contain it. Some may present it beautifully arranged. It's still there, in a different form. There are times it's more trauma, not less.

One last topic, age-old, is art and madness. It's another question I get into. This idea, alarmingly popular, that *many or most* artists are mad is wrong. I realize it's ubiquitous, but ubiquity, in this case, obscures truth. Most of the time, making art is torturous, but not for exotic reasons. The reasons are mundane. For one thing, art is hard.

Orwell called writing books a "horrible, exhausting struggle," a "long bout of some painful illness." No one "not driven on by some demon" would do it, he said. It's grueling, grinding work. It's maddening because you never know how it will go or what you will produce. One day's masterpiece is another day's mediocrity. You can't summon the muse. There's no guarantee it arrives. People like the work or hate it or, worse, feel nothing about it. They also, more confusingly, like what you don't in it or about it. There are scores of examples of a person's most embarrassing, unsatisfying work achieving a popularity that becomes terrifying. Plath called her famous novel *The Bell Jar* a potboiler and published it under a pseudonym; in contrast, many haven't read the *Ariel* poems. Kurt Cobain mocked and mostly despised the song "Smells Like Teen Spirit," but if Nirvana did not play it, the crowd would riot. So, art can be crazy-making, for sure, but not because the artist is crazy.

In instances where an artist *does* come across as insane, often the culprit turns out not to be mental illness, but trait- and state-based factors alluded to before. I devote a chapter working out what I mean by this. What's confusing, but actually simple on its face, is that styles of personality and the mental states they give rise to *resemble* and are mistaken for signs of disorder. There's a family resemblance, but you are not your brother. I feel equipped to parse this conflation because I worked for more than 20 years on a locked inpatient psych unit. I've seen a lot of terrible madness. I know what it does and what it feels like. In a state of, say, extreme depression, you can't think, you can't act, you're in misery. No sparkling ideas come; no art gets made. It's the same for mania or schizophrenia. You can't focus, you may be delusional, you follow pointless tangents, you can't sleep or rest. A little of what *looks like* but isn't madness sets the stage and opens doors in the artist mind. Madness is a closing. It scatters all your resources. The only thing you think about is being mad and how to make the madness stop. You aren't planning your next novel or your next symphony. You aren't planning anything.

A good portion of this book is devoted to telling artist stories, from John Coltrane to John Lennon, from Francesca Woodman to Frida Kahlo, with plenty of others in between. Any time I get into the specifics of research findings or theories, I show how they apply in real artists' lives. I try making the abstract concrete. Of course, art and artists have been around forever. There are numerous ancient examples, such as Sophocles and Homer. I can't survey all this terrain. My cases are of two sorts: artists I know and/or interviewed, and mostly 20th-century writers, painters, musicians, comedians, and photographers. This is perhaps a limitation. I omit great portions of the field, and I spend more time on some media than others. I can't see a way around that. Intrinsic to the articulation of a general profile is just that, it's generality. It will fit most artists, but not all, and not in every respect. Even with famous 20th-century artists, a few seem anomalous. For instance, Elvis Presley. He wrote almost no songs. There was trauma, but it happened at birth: his twin Jesse was stillborn. The average artist, research tells us, is "disagreeable"; Elvis was self-destructively compliant, obedient, and eager to please, as his manager, Colonel Tom Parker, appreciated. The average artist, research tells us, is open to experience, hungry for it, restless for the shock of the new; Elvis liked things simple. He made a home to hide away in. He was more an interpreter than a maker. If you look hard enough, exceptions appear. But that's the point: You need to look hard. Most of the time, what you find is sameness, and that is what the research points to: sameness perfused with a smattering of individual differences.

The first stop in all this is personality, what I call the unifying glue of the artist mind. As I said, a generic type exists. Let me tell you what it is.

1
Traits, States, and Stories

How does one get to be an artist? How does one get to be anything at all? It's not as if we come into the world with preset destinies, or do we? And if we do, what's baked in, what's learned, and what's a product of circumstance? Jackson Pollock started by painting Jungian archetypes in what are called his psychoanalytic drawings. He moved on to Picassoesque figurative work, as in "Guardians of the Secret" and "Moon Woman Cuts the Circle." Then, one otherwise average day, he threw a canvas on the floor. He became, miraculously, Jack the Dripper. What he'd done was so unforeseen, so puzzling, legend has it he turned to his partner Lee Krasner (herself a painter) and asked, "Is this art?"

Or take Miles Davis. At a gig, Herbie Hancock played a wrong chord. The effect was dissonant, embarrassing. But rather than stopping, or hesitating, or somehow calling attention to the miscue, Davis rolled with it, veered, made order out of chaos. He took his solo in a different direction. He accepted, instantly, the path deflection.

Creative moves like these can seem inscrutable, they can seem like magic, divinely inspired. You are in a state of possession, but by what? Maybe it's a mindset you go in and out of. Maybe it's a readiness, an openness to forces, to new ideas, always there. Maybe it's a product of where you are, the time you live in, the people you surround yourself with. Is it possible to reverse-engineer? Can you follow the path backward?

Yes, you can.

It all begins with personality, a word we take for granted. Our goals, our beliefs, our preferences, our habits, our drives, our tendencies, how we manage our thoughts and feelings, even our days, our time—all these grow, bit by bit, out of personality. Personality drives them, brings them to coherence. It's the same with creativity. Your personality sets you up to be creative. It's a scaffold.

The Mind of the Artist. William Todd Schultz, Oxford University Press. © Oxford University Press 2022.
DOI: 10.1093/oso/9780197611098.003.0002

Theories of self approach the concept from countless angles. Some see it as a repertoire of learned behavior. Some see it as a reflection, the sum total of how others perceive us. Some see it as a constellation of memories. Some, like Freud, see it as a disguise, a coded representation of hidden urges. None of these theories is wrong, per se. Each captures a component of the picture. But now, after decades of research, personality scientists have come to agreement, at least on the subject of building blocks, the bottom layer of who we are.

Personality starts with *traits*, simple compounds we capture in language with words like shy, belligerent, outgoing, ambitious, and friendly. By sifting and simplifying, or what is called, with fancier terminology, factor analysis, all such adjectives, thousands upon thousands, reduce to five dimensions, the so-called Big Five. These dimensions (the dimensions are the traits) reveal the *why* behind creativity as well as the *how*, the ways in which creativity functions. This is the power of personality. It accounts for the why and the how. It's the secret sauce.

You come into the world with baked-in motivational units. One of these units, in particular, primes creative behavior. It's called "openness to experience," or "openness" for short, and it's the focus of this book. Others, the remaining four traits, have slighter impacts that are also important, especially in combination. By "baked-in" I mean you are born this way, to a degree. There is no serious debate any longer. We now know that half of personality difference is inherited. You have default settings, default "programs." But 50% is not 100%. You've got flexibility. You're steered, but you can take the wheel. It's a paradox. You are (1) at the mercy of personality and (2) personality's sovereign, supervisory master.

Traits are dichotomous and comparative, so you'll be high or low in them, or more commonly, near a midrange percentile rank. But ignore middle scores. They aren't the core you. They don't get at your most powerful urges. What you really want to know is which of these Big Five dimensions you express *in extremis*. The extremes show you at your most flagrant, personality-wise (for instance, 70th percentile or above, and 30th percentile or below). If you're massively shy, for instance, that dictates a lot of what you think and feel and do. Midrange shyness is immaterial, safely passed over.

One more thing to know: traits cause adaptations. They give rise to habits that solidify. The habits aren't the same thing as the traits, however. They are side effects of the traits, and you develop them without consciously trying to. Say one of your traits sets you up to be anxious. You might drink to self-medicate. You might worry a lot, think negative thoughts, predict gloomy life outcomes. You either cope or coexist with your traits. Traits plot a course, and you adjust. Some adjustments are happy and productive, and some come at a price.

So, what are these Big Five traits and how can you notice their workings, their expressions, in yourself and your day-to-day life, creative and otherwise?

One is neuroticism (N; or what some prefer to call "dispositional negativity"). It's not strongly connected to creativity, despite what a lot of people believe. That is, creatives aren't notably likelier to be neurotic, studies show. N includes a lot of negative emotion—anxiety, depressed mood, anger—as well as self-consciousness and vulnerability. N is the personality foundation behind a range of mental disorders. If you are high N, you're at risk for anxiety and mood problems; you are also inclined to abuse substances. N correlates with so-called personality disorders, too: everything from narcissistic to borderline to dependent personality. Usually, there's a reluctance to call any of the Big Five traits bad. They tend to be presented neutrally. With N that makes little sense. It is clearly less than ideal to be high N. High N sets you up for a lot of difficulties down the road. You can learn to cope, but it's as if, saddled with N, you start the race 20 yards behind everyone else. Life is struggle, worry, and fragility for high N individuals. Because creativity requires, at minimum, a degree of fearlessness, a belief in the value of your self-expressions, neuroticism gets in the way. It's an obstacle. Neurotic people fear risks. Creativity is risky, by definition.

Then there's extraversion (E), which presents like N's antithesis. At the center of high E is positive mood. Extraverts are happier. In that sense they start the race 20 yards ahead, assuming happiness is the flag we're racing toward. The findings on E and creativity are mixed—there's no powerful correlation between the two. It's not a hindrance; it's not a speed bump. Extraverts are perpetually on the go, looking for excitement. They come into the world starved for stimulation, so they constantly try upping their arousal level. Part of this is accomplished by being around people—going to parties, concerts, events. If you were a class clown, voted most popular or high school president or most likely to succeed, odds are good that you're an extravert. People want to be around you. Your personality is infectious. You're a charismatic leader, accustomed to being the center of attention. In terms of mental disorder, E inoculates you. You're a lot less likely to be depressed or anxious. Your capacity for pleasure is sky high. Neurotics recoil in fear. Extraverts go forth exuberantly. Neither is the prototypical artist type.

Conscientiousness (C) and agreeableness (A) are all about efficiency, order, friendliness, and sympathy. As it turns out, both link up with creativity in ways that, initially, seem hard to parse. If you often feel like the adult in the room, the measured organizer who gets along, softens conflicts, plans, and works humbly in teams, you may be high C and A. Like extraversion, high C protects you against anxiety, depression, and substance abuse. The high C person gets things done on time. She walks the walk. She can be counted on. High A suggests honesty and cooperation.

Last is openness (O), creativity's holy grail. It's the nucleus, the hub, of everything creative. *In the history of psychology, no variable of any kind, no process, no mechanism, no tendency, no diagnosis—nothing—predicts creativity and creative achievement as strongly or as consistently as openness.* Pointing to artists who are low in openness is a difficult job. They don't seem to exist. The question for us is how openness *works*. For starters, it's outrageously heterogeneous. More than any other trait, it peels off in countless directions. It correlates with IQ. It predicts a need for sensation. It's associated with radical politics. It encourages drug experimentation, a thirst for self-altering experience. Those high in O are more mystical, more curious, filled with feelings, less likely to repress, addicted to shock and awe. They get bored easily. They want what's new and spine-tingling. Most of all, what they do is create—invent, discover, expand, and redefine.

Any attempt to get to the bottom of creativity has to go through openness. There's no other credible path. Creativity isn't only openness. Other factors play important roles. But openness is the star. It's the difference between a strong, forceful push and a nudge. Openness is the strong, forceful push.

The Big Five Factors and Facets

Extraversion (happy, high energy, enthusiastic, dominant). Facets: warmth (comfortable around people), gregariousness (loves large parties), assertiveness (takes charge), activity (always on the go), excitement-seeking (wild and crazy), positive emotion (radiates joy)

Agreeableness (trusting, modest, people-pleasing, conflict-averse). Facets: trust (believes people are basically moral, with good intentions), straightforwardness (does not cheat), altruism (makes people feel welcome), compliance (can't stand confrontation), modesty (dislikes talking about self), tender-mindedness (interested in other people's problems)

Conscientiousness (orderly, disciplined, rule-abiding, dependable). Facets: competence (completes tasks on time), order (does things according to plan), dutifulness (keeps promises), achievement-striving (works hard), self-disciplined (carries out plans), deliberation (avoids mistakes)

Neuroticism (fearful, self-conscious, nervous, impulsive). Facets: anxiety (lots of worrying), angry hostility (often in a bad mood), depression (often down in the dumps), self-consciousness (easily embarrassed), impulsiveness (does things that one later regrets), vulnerability (easily overwhelmed)

Openness (loves art and beauty, curious, adventurous, fantasy-prone). Facets: fantasy (enjoys wild flights of fancy), aesthetics (sees the beauty in a lot of things), feelings (feels emotions intensely), actions (prefers change and variety), ideas (enjoys thinking about things), values (more likely to embrace radical political beliefs)

Now, say you took a test (there are several online), and scored 99 in O, 97 in A, 96 in E, 63 in C, and 40 in N. You'd now have a solid sense of your broad makeup. You're sky high in O, A, and E—that is (1) you love art and beauty, you're curious, you like to think and reflect; (2) you're super-friendly and warm and modest—you get along with people; and (3) you tend to be happy and enthusiastic and sociable. Because your scores cluster near the mean for C and N, you can set those results aside. They aren't powerful components of who you are. You aren't especially organized, and you don't have problems with anxiety or insecurity.

Broad trait scores are macro. We want to get micro, we want the details. Here's how that works. Scores on traits are a function of scores on six trait "facets." It's the combined lower level facet score that makes up the trait score. Take neuroticism. It's composed of anxiety, depression, anger, vulnerability, self-consciousness, and impulsivity. These are its six features. You may be mainly impulsive and angry—that's one version of neuroticism. You may be anxious and vulnerable—that's a different version. There are 30 possibilities—the five broad traits multiplied by their six micro manifestations. These personality configurations give rise to the habits and adaptations mentioned before. It can get complex. But if people are anything at all, if artists are anything at all, they are complex. The details make us. We're the same (say, we have the same overall O score), and we're different (we have facet scores that are unique).

Let's look at a particular example to see how everything comes together—traits, states, and stories—with openness as a driving factor.

The writer Truman Capote, most famous for his masterpiece *In Cold Blood*, the inventive "nonfiction novel" about the murder of a farm family in Kansas, grew up in Monroeville, Alabama. From day one he was an odd bird. Effeminate, beautiful, fragile-seeming but, in fact, tough as nails, a bit of a natural shit-stirrer. As a kid he was a dreamer, a fantasist. He saw endless possibilities where others saw few. He'd plan and organize carnivals for neighbors and friends, elaborate Halloween costume galas. He loved telling ribald stories, and claimed to have written his first around age 8. As an author he met with precocious success, winning the O. Henry Award for the short story "Miriam," then publishing a heralded novel *Other Voices, Other Rooms*, followed by the novella *Breakfast at Tiffany's*. Through his career, Capote wrote in every possible mode: plays, film scripts, reportage, profiles, short stories. He claimed to have inaugurated a new form with *In Cold Blood*—fact-based fiction. Clearly, this was a person with a boundless imaginary impulse, restless to create, committed to aesthetic discovery. He liked to say he had a thousand perceptions to the average person's one. His head was full, his sonar exceptional. In short, blazingly open.

But Capote was also disagreeable and neurotic—contrary, provocative, and scalding in his judgments, yet anxious, fearful, and vulnerable. He took sinister pleasure in running other writers down, and with his last book, the unfinished *Answered Prayers*, a scandalous tell-all, he roasted friends—mostly rich white socialites he referred to as his "swans"—who then quickly blacklisted him, erasing him from their lives forever. He pretended to be unfazed by this, but secretly he was crushed. He never got over the rejection. He died alcoholic and drug-addicted and more or less alone, in the arms of a rare friend who did not reject him, Joanne Carson, Johnny Carson's ex-wife. He'd booked a one-way ticket, to Los Angeles. His plan, it seems, was to die there.

It was his openness that pushed Capote to create, to write, to make art of a high order. But the added spices were low agreeableness and high neuroticism. They also lent shape to the fictions, directing themes and contents. At the facet level there was anxiety and anger and vulnerability (N), low humility and antagonism (A). These, mixed with his driving O, made for his personality framework. They were Capote's baseline orientation, the fundamental components of who he was and why he did what he did, creatively and otherwise.

But you cope with your traits, too. You adjust. Traits cause adaptations, and adaptations settle into habits, patterns that repeat. For Capote, the chief pattern was being creative, writing, imagining new prose forms, pushing himself to maximize his built-in gifts. This sprang from openness. Openness steered him, produced the requisite qualities of mind. Because he was neurotic, Capote drank. It helped to fend off anxiety. It quelled demons. It worked, at least for a time, and so it became habitual. Partly because he was neurotic, he feared rejection. His sense for the possibility of anyone leaving him was fine-tuned, super-sensitive. In fact, he would abandon friends and lovers preemptively, at the first sign of relationship distress. Bridges got burned. Confidantes got axed. In addition to all this, he was disagreeable; he habitually, impulsively lashed out. He used a scorched-earth strategy. He shared nasty opinions freely. His judgments were blunt and scalding.

This is how it works for anyone. It's the same for you as it is for Capote. Everything artistic starts with openness, with one's score on that preeminent, creativity-enhancing trait. It's the art-making impulse, the instinct to do art. Surrounding traits fill in the picture, especially those at extremes. Take your combination of extreme scores, blend them together, and what you get is the basic you.

There's one last step: narration. As you watch yourself do what you do, you construct a self-theory, a matrix of self-perpetuating scripts. These three levels dynamically intersect, inform each other, and interact. Traits lead to states and habits of mind; stories tie everything together into a coherent, interconnected bundle.

Capote, for instance, told one story over and over. It was the leitmotif of his life. In a tidy, densely constructed package, it summarized who he was. It could be that we all do this. Cling to one story that says it all. Repeat it as need be. First, to remind ourselves of its centrality. Second, to fill others in efficiently.

In Capote's prototypical scene, he's 3 years old. He's somewhere in the South, possibly New Orleans. In certain versions he's with his mother, in others both his mother and father. Whatever the case, he's locked in a hotel room. He's left terrified and alone as his parents party long into the night, forgetting about him, not caring about him. In reality, Capote actually was abandoned, repeatedly, and raised by spinsterish aunts. His childhood he characterized as a "total absence of love." No one was ever consistently responsive and available. He was made to fend for himself. He was forced to be self-sufficient. He managed, but with damage, a residue of ongoing anxiety, fear, and anger, exacerbated by native neuroticism. Openness made him a storyteller, and the stories he told—as in *Other Voices, Other Rooms*, where a boy, Joel Knox, searches vainly for a father—repeated his lovelorn history, the failure to find the care he craved. Joel never does locate his dad. Or, he does, but the dad is a disappointment, a mute, brain-damaged invalid who communicates by tossing tennis balls down the stairs. So, this modest script packs a wallop. It represents the signal fact of Capote's early life—being discarded and treated as if he did not matter.

Stories are the top floor of the personality system. We can't *not* tell them, as decades of neuroscience research makes clear. They may be veridical—that is, hewing to real facts—or they may fanciful, what researchers call "false memories." They can also be, and probably usually are, a mix of truth and fiction. The function of the story is to explain yourself to yourself and to others. We don't introspect and locate traits. Traits are abstract, inferred potentials. You can't look inside and inspect your openness or neuroticism. What you *do* see is what traits make happen, their visible manifestations. These get woven into narratives. It's actually disarmingly simple. You watch yourself behave, then you tell a story about it. Capote was a writer, so his stories assumed dozens of forms, and they came in waves, spread over novels and the rest of his corpus. You don't differ from Capote. Your stories may be less plentiful, but they still organize, or constellate, the sum of your experience.

What we have is a three-step process, a chronology of personality layers. There's more to personality than just this, but it's the guiding framework common to everyone.

In Chapter 3 I zero in on openness in all its majesty. First, however, we need to examine ancillary factors. There are surprises in store. Nothing drives art like openness. But on the fringes, in the afterglow of other tendencies—agreeableness and conscientiousness—we meet with additional creativity prerequisites.

Our question is: What does the science say about traits and art? What is the ideal trait-based portrait of the artist mind?

2

Trait-Based Origins of Creativity

Artist stereotypes abound, and as with other stereotypes—car salesmen or college professors—some seem valid, some don't. There's the undeniable genius, the pure, true, born artist. The fragile, needy, oversensitive brooder. The strange prodigy. The prolific grinder. The immoderate, reckless, self-destructive drug addict. The sensitive poet. The self-absorbed depressive. There's even the fake artist, the poser, the wannabe.

Some scholars work toward a sameness, defining core artist qualities. Others argue irreducibility—total, unfathomable uniqueness. Indeed, aside from art itself, what could Beyoncé and Amy Winehouse have in common, or Kurt Cobain and Lil Wayne, or Nabokov and Frida Kahlo? For the purists, any attempt to get at a typical artist mind—how it's formed, how it works—is doomed. Too many artists of too many stripes, too many media, they say; take the art on its own terms. View it, hear it, read it, *absorb* it, but leave personality out, leave the life of the artist out. I always feel there's something protective about this mindset, as if the idea of sameness is somehow leveling and ruinous, destructive of the creative product. That hasn't been my experience. (See the Epilogue, in which I explore these ideas more.)

We can have our cake and eat it too. We can appreciate art for art's sake, for its formal beauty (what Susan Sontag called "erotics of perception"), yet analyze how it gets made, what motivates it, the personalities of the artists behind it. Two realities apply here, and they aren't contradictory. We can't know *everything* about artist personality or the intricacies of artistic process. But that does not mean we can't know *anything*. We can know a lot. We already do, in fact. The research has been done. The job, now, is to sift through it, identify what's known, and craft a general portrait.

I start with a contrast, the average scientist versus the average artist. From there, I focus on the trait-based roots of creativity, including detailed discussion of the exact Big Five profiles of two real, living,

The Mind of the Artist. William Todd Schultz, Oxford University Press. © Oxford University Press 2022.
DOI: 10.1093/oso/9780197611098.003.0003

accomplished creatives, Kuwaiti painter Shurooq Amin and American writer Walter Kirn.

Contrasting Artists and Scientists

In 1998, in what was then the most large-scale, searching study of its time, Gregory Feist conducted a meta-analysis of 29 studies of artists and 26 studies of scientists, all published between the years 1950 and 1995. "Artists" were defined as students majoring in or studying art, or anyone earning an income through writing, painting, photography, cinematography, dance, music, or poetry. "Scientists" showed talent in science, or majored in it, or worked in scientific careers. What Feist examined was the strength of correlations between personality and artists (vs. nonartists) and personality and scientists (vs. nonscientists). Not all studies made exclusive use of Big Five inventories. Even so, what we get, after the different findings are assessed and combined, is a concrete, unusually thorough picture of the personalities of artists and scientists, and how the two orientations compare and contrast.

Let's start with artists. Just as expected, openness (O) is the glue, the invariant artist personality style. Low O predicted low creativity, high O maximum creative potential. But conscientiousness (C) factored in too. Artists were less cautious, controlled, orderly, reliable, rigid, conventional, and socialized. So, low C correlated with high creativity—a so-called negative association. Correlations for the other three traits (extraversion, agreeableness, and neuroticism) were weak—meaning, no significant findings. In terms of the Big Five, creativity was all about low C and high O, in Feist's review, a sort of messy, disorganized curiosity plus fine-tuned aesthetic sensibility. Reliably creative but unreliable, in short.

Other findings round out the picture. Artists were more conflicted, impulsive, nonconformist, rule-doubting, independent, and unconcerned with obligations or duties. They were radical, egocentric, sensitive, serious, and tough-minded.

Results like these confirm a stereotype: the messy, radical creative. That's good, because we can't assume stereotypes to be true. Here, however, science supports the myth. It's not in the eye of the beholder; it's in the artist herself, part of her personality DNA. According to tabulated results of these 29 studies, artists *really are* norm-doubting and nonconforming. They *really are* open and imaginative. They *really are* impulsive, aloof, and serious.

Expanding on these results, Feist presents what he believes to be a defining principle of creative activity: Being an artist means spending time apart from other people. You can't write a novel or poem, or paint a painting, or compose a symphony in the raucous company of others. *Solitude is the norm; loneliness the principle.* You sit in a room by yourself and make things. You isolate. You focus attention and energies inward. David Bowie, whom I discuss later, is a prime example. He said two things of interest: (1) that all his work was about isolation, and (2) that he needed isolation to create. Another example is writer Patricia Highsmith. In a 1978 interview with Mavis Nicholson, she speaks of how she "deliberately isolates" herself. "I don't like much social life, I don't like going out to dinner... I need my evenings. I love my evenings... I don't like other people around me, I like to walk around the house quietly, I like to daydream... If I'm in the house alone, everything gets solved."

Artists separate themselves on purpose, Feist suggests, based on an intuition that apartness is essential for the work. Even "observed levels of hostility in creative people," Feist says, "may be a defense of their creations against others who either inadvertently detract from time spent creating or who criticize or misinterpret [a] heretofore novel solution or product." Doubt and skepticism from others are a bane of the artist's existence. In response, creatives tend to be stubbornly independent. As Feist puts it, "submissiveness and expressed creativity make unlikely bed partners."

The ideal artist is audacious and aslant. One needs to be those things in order to embrace uniqueness, a capacity for saying something new, something fresh and inventive, something off-putting, weird, or provocative. The alternative is conventionality, or noncreativity.

Now, let's contrast this with the scientist side of the personality picture.

First off, as Feist notes, there's institutional support for noncreative science. Most studies aren't revolutionary. Truly creative scientific breakthroughs are rare. So, in terms of personality and science, one might imagine a dogged technician. And in fact, that's exactly what we get. Most scientists, *precisely unlike artists*, tend to be high C: higher on conscientiousness and controlling of impulses. They are careful, cautious, fastidious. They also turn out to be low O and low in extraversion

(E)—conventional, rigid, and socialized; deferential, reserved, and introverted. They "like to work in settings where tasks and expectations are clearly defined." They show a "strong drive to do well."

We're left with two extremes: the generic artist and the generic scientist. But what about *creative* scientists, the Einsteins, Darwins, Freuds, and Newtons who *do* become revolutionary? Here, the extremes converge in specific respects. More creative scientists tend to be high E yet also high O. In other words, more ambitious, outgoing, open-minded, confident, expressive, flexible, and intelligent.

What findings like these reveal is that, no matter the creative endeavor, openness sets the stage. It's the engine behind differing creative modes. Creative scientists and artists depart from each other in terms of extraversion, probably for the reason mentioned before. Art demands solitude. Science, in contrast, can be, and usually is, collaborative, a group process.

The Vain, Dishonest Creative?

Feist's research unearthed one overlap: Both creative scientists and artists are open and norm-doubting. Yet unlike creative scientists, artists actively reject group norms. They care less about making a positive impression. They achieve by flouting rules, not by going with the crowd. Some of this relates to conscientiousness, as Feist discovered. But it calls to mind another Big Five trait too: agreeableness, or the lack thereof.

These are the six facets composing agreeableness (A): trust, morality, altruism, cooperation, modesty, and sympathy.

Agreeableness

Facets:

Trust (does not suspect hidden motives, trusts what people say, believes people are basically moral)
Morality (does not cheat, does not use others, sticks to rules)

Altruism (takes time for others, does not look down on others, likes to help others)
Cooperation (is easy to satisfy, does not hold grudges, does not yell at others)
Modesty (dislikes talking about self, considers self to be an average person, does not have a high opinion of self)
Sympathy (values cooperation over competition, suffers others' sorrows, likes soft-hearted people, thinks about the needy)

Those who are high A get along. They are conflict averse. They don't blow their own horn. They don't dominate over others. They follow, contentedly.

Not everyone's agreeableness is equal. As always, it comes down to where you land on the facets, and which of the six contributes the most force and thrust. For some who are high A, modesty plays a key role. For others, it's cooperation.

According to a 2011 study that splits agreeableness into two distinct halves, artists aren't less forgiving, gentle, flexible, or patient, but they do score significantly lower on measures of "honesty" and "humility." What this means is that artists may be agreeable in some ways, yet decidedly disagreeable (on average) in others.

The "honesty-humility" facet gets to the hostility Feist identified in creatives, but it also goes beyond it. It contains four elements: sincerity, or a tendency to be genuine, especially interpersonally; fairness, as in avoiding fraud and corruption; greed avoidance, or disinterest in wealth and luxury; and modesty, meaning lack of arrogance and a tendency to view oneself as ordinary and unspecial.

In some ways, the fact that artists score low on honesty-humility is unsurprising. To be low is, partly, to be arrogant, pretentious, and immodest; maybe not hostile, as Feist found, but a little full of yourself, vainglorious.

Back in the 1970s, psychologist Abraham Maslow, famous for his hierarchy of needs and the concept of "self-actualization," which stood atop that hierarchy, outlined what he named a "Jonah complex." Some people, Maslow said, shrink back from destiny, deny it, and refuse their talents, their possible greatness. Others ask, "If not me, who? Someone has to be great. Why can't I be?" They feel touched. They feel special. They feel gifted, and they proceed accordingly.

Bob Dylan exemplifies this second set of attitudes (the Jonah complex's opposite). He describes his career in terms of destiny. When asked about his songs—how he wrote them, where the imagery came from—he says he has no idea. He calls the process "black magic." He's a sort of vehicle, a conduit. The song-making is outside his control. This train of thought in artists is not uncommon. The art is a visitation. But it highlights a sense of specialness. It's you through whom the visitation comes to fruition. You've been singled out. At least, that's how Dylan feels: chosen.

One can be a modest artist—no doubt. The type exists. One can toil quietly, advocate humbly on behalf of one's gifts. In most contexts, these tendencies are charming, lovable, laudable. But as research shows, in artists they are rare, and they may impede success. In fact, in this 2011 study, the only dimension rivaling low honesty-humility with respect to prediction of creativity was openness.

Most artists don't literally declare, "I am a genius." Some do, though, and that's not always a bad thing. I've talked already about Capote. His famous line was, "I am an addict. I am an alcoholic. I am a homosexual. I am a genius." John Lennon, another example, was cagier on the subject, but not uncertain. He said he never forgave his mother for not treating him "like a fucking genius." "I used to be coy about it," he said. "Either I'm a genius or I'm mad, which is it?"

We saw before how Plath called her *Ariel* poems "genius" in a letter to her mother. Photographer Diane Arbus never announced her genius, but she felt she had "a slight corner on things," as she put it; she believed there were subjects no one would see unless she, and she alone, photographed them.

Then there's Kanye West, one of the most cocksure geniuses of all. He told Jimmy Kimmel, "For me to say I wasn't a genius, I would just be lying to you and to myself." Here, the last detail is telling. Privately, he knows he's a genius. He knows, also, that saying so isn't socially acceptable. But rather than fake a humility that's false, he comes right out with it. "No matter how many people tell me, 'Stop believing in yourself! Stop seeing what you can do! Stop affirming what you're gonna do and then completing that in real life.' That's the improper way to do it. I refuse to follow those rules that society has set up."

There's a narcissism intrinsic to creative work. It's not "narcissistic personality disorder" narcissism; it's not about exploitation or lack of empathy. It has more to do with a sense of specialness and a feeling that rules don't apply. Even artists with no notoriety, no tangible accomplishments, have to sense, at some basic level, a uniqueness, a capacity for anomalous expression. You can't make art without feeling there's something in you that sets you apart. Cyril Connolly describes this sense in the opening paragraph of *The Unquiet Grave,* a book composed, mostly, of aphorisms and musings on life, psychology, and art. The wish, ordinarily buried, is to make a masterpiece. You may not say it. You'd disavow it if anyone suggested it to you. You keep it secret. But it's there. No one aims for what Connolly calls, in a lovely phrase, "iridescent mediocrity." Work in some disciplines, for instance science, *can* be mediocre yet lead to tenure, promotion, and a modicum of fame within one's field. Art can't. Or, truly successful, truly shattering or awesome art can't. Art doesn't work that way. Mediocrity is the kiss of death. It's what every artist fears, more than anything else.

Rising above mediocrity, creating something truly powerful requires, for one, talent, but also perceptiveness, ambition, originality, and, maybe most important, an extraordinary commitment to self-expression, sometimes against formidable odds. Making something deeply distinctive is lonely and grueling and typically thankless. And indeed, a hot topic of discussion among writers, and probably also painters, photographers, and playwrights, is, *Why do I do this*? *Why not just stop?* It's also hard, art is. Lennon, for one, went on and on about the difficulty of writing a single good song. The reasons that artists persevere are many and individualized, but one has to be, *because I, alone, can say what must be said; because I, alone, possess the necessary perceptions and insights*. Several of my friends are writing novels now, and each is autobiographical. Most people don't sit down and tell fictional stories about their life. Doing so puts you in the 1%. It's an extremely unusual enterprise. To undertake it requires firm belief—in your talents, in your exceptionalness. At root, art is not a humble act. It's announcing, *I have something to say that you will want to hear about, something no one else is saying, at least not in the way I'm saying it*.

Besides scoring low in humility, artists also tend to score low in honesty, or sincerity and fairness. For instance, they might use flattery to get what they want—a gallery showing, a gig, a fellowship—or pretend to like someone, or laugh at jokes they don't find funny.

If artists really are, on average, less honest, as well as less modest, if they fudge facts, embellish, exaggerate, pretend—these are par for the course. Their métier is fantasy; their job is to go beyond facts, to present alternate realities. A certain disrespect for fact is built into creative enterprises. This isn't dishonesty per se, but a capacity for invention. Artists make things up, after all. They are honestly dishonest, faithful first and foremost to the imaginary worlds they represent.

The lesson in all this is clear, and it's one that Dylan, West, Lennon, Plath, and Arbus all recognized. Art demands confidence. As Arbus said, you need to feel you have a special corner on things, an ability to see and express what other people miss, a fresh insight, a new take, a novel perception. No one likes braggarts. But art is a kind of bragging. It's the assertion of a gift, a gift you need to assert. The takeaways would be these: Don't get in your own way. Don't shrink back meekly. Be bold. Be audacious. Accept your powers.

The Neurotic Creative?

No artist stereotype is more routinely expressed than the "tortured artist," although the nature of the pain is rarely defined. It's left vague. The Big Five includes no torture-focused variable. Torture is too broad an experience. It might be obvious. It might be subtle. It can be short-lived. It can also be chronic. Sometimes, rarely, it may veer into mental illness. There is neuroticism, however, one particular torture form. High N means proneness to negative mental states: anxiety, anger, depression, and vulnerability.

In a 2009 article, "The Bright Side of Being Blue," this vulnerability to neuroticism and its afflictions was reduced to thinking too much, worrying, regarding neutral or benign situations negatively. You see the dark side; you see problems; you overanalyze, all regardless of what's actually happening. You can't help it. It seems to be outside your control. The authors go on to say that because neurotics ruminate, because they dwell on self-created problems, they also tend to be more creative in generating unexpected solutions. They obsess, and their obsessions bear fruit. They grind their way to original insights.

On one hand, the idea makes sense. Obsession is the artist's friend. You dwell, you ruminate, you don't let go until you break through. It's a moment-by-moment challenge. What's the best next paragraph, what's the proper verb, what's the ideal photographic angle, the most pleasing palette, the smoothest chord change? These are all problems, creative problems, and in the course of creativity, they need to get solved, over and over again. You keep hammering away until you end up with something you're happy with. It serves you to be a brooder.

But are you a *tortured* brooder? Are anxiety, sadness, anger, and vulnerability consistently, reliably associated with creativity? This is a question we can answer, at least in terms connected with neuroticism and the circumscribed "torture" it implies. According to studies, high N does *not* predict creativity. There is no correlation. Divergent thinking, problem-solving, intelligence, everyday creative behavior, self-assessed creativity—none of these correlate with neurotic tendencies. *Artists are not more neurotic.*

So, is the tortured artist a myth? Not entirely. Again, it's a question of what is meant, exactly, by torture. Artists do tend to be disorganized in their thinking. They feel more, and more intensely. Their inner life is chaotic. All these facts and findings we examine later, in coming chapters. But it's worth noting, now, that just like low humility, chaos serves creativity. It's a benefit. Artists make use of their chaos-torture. It's more material to shape, to order, to express.

Neurotic torture isn't key to artist experience—we know that for sure. But a different form of torture derived from the trait of openness may be. That's something we know for sure, too.

The Happy Artist?

One trait remains, extraversion, with its core element of happiness, and if we compare qualities of the average extravert with qualities of the average artist, the fit seems off. Extraverts aren't lonely. They don't seek out quiet isolation. They tend to have high hedonic capacities. Primed for pleasure, they find it everywhere—like pleasure-seeking missiles. Extraverts are solid, composed, secure, enthusiastic, and positive in their outlook.

For all the extraverted Justin Timberlakes out there, one can point to farragos of Amy Winehouses. She, for instance, suggested fame would make her "insane." Possibly it did. There were times she thought it did. In the least, she found it difficult to contend with. Artists like Winehouse need to perform. It's how their art gets expressed. But that doesn't mean they like it. At a basic level, it's their job. A similar rule applies to fame. We tend to think, understandably, that famous people enjoy being famous. Yet a lot of artists seem temperamentally unsuited for it. Fame puts them at odds with who they are, personality-wise. Elvis Presley is one example. Kurt Cobain is another. On one hand, part of them wanted fame. On the other, it turned out to be unnerving, more than they bargained for.

In Feist's meta-analysis, extraversion was not correlated reliably with artistic creativity (though it was with the scientific form). Some studies showed a slight negative correlation, some positive, but most wound up being simply null—no connection. We've already seen that a certain antisocial aloofness characterizes most creative lives, so on balance, extraversion would constitute interference. Time spent with people is time lost to making art. You need to preserve your energy. You need aloneness in order to imagine.

Two Cases: Shurooq Amin and Walter Kirn

Now we've assembled an initial, trait-based template for how artists live, who they are inside, their basic personality makeup. Here's what research shows to be the ideal setting: (1) exceptionally high openness, (2) glaringly low conscientiousness, and (c) a disagreeableness characterized by low honesty-humility.

Remember, traits themselves are broad personality descriptions. If we want to get specific, we need to look at facets, the subtler components. The best way to do this is by unpacking real cases—real creatives and their Big Five scores—and seeing how the results do or don't confirm the profile of the typical creative.

I contacted two very different artists—painter Shurooq Amin and writer Walter Kirn—and asked if they'd complete a Big Five inventory. Both agreed, totally unreluctantly (a fact itself suggesting high openness, or at least a willingness to disclose). I'm not claiming to prove a hypothesis here. The goal is more modest: to use these artists as test cases, and to see how facet scores affect the making of art.

Shurooq Amin

Shurooq Amin calls herself a "hybrid." She was born in the East, her father a Kuwaiti, her mother a Syrian. But she studied in the West, in England, where she focused on Ekphrasis. She's got Western sass and self-belief. She's committed to empowering women. She's forceful, tough, proud, sexy, and uncompromising, a protest against the role she's expected to play in stultifying, rigid, and male-dominated Kuwaiti culture.

Her life was riven by a central trauma. When she was young, her beloved father collapsed and died before her eyes. He had always encouraged her drawing and the bolder parts of her personality. She sees her art, now, as linked with this loss. At her website— https://www.shurooqamin.com/bio.html—the first image is a shot of her with her dad. On her forearm she's tattooed the date of his death. It serves as a reminder. She sees it constantly as she paints—the origin of the drive to create.

Her art is a deliberate, thinly veiled assault on what she sees as false pieties of the Arab world: religious hypocrisy, gender relations, double standards, the divisions of public and private lives. She's clear about her work being for "the masses." The paintings are messages. They don't obscure what she wants to say. "For me," she says, "the Arabian gulf is my child, and I'm treating it by exposing its negatives. I see things that upset me, that create a sense of injustice in me, and I use art as my weapon to respond. I open a dialogue about issues my society claims to be taboo."

It's a risky business. In Syria, in 2011, for instance, a protest singer named Ibrahim Qashoush was murdered, his vocal cords severed. Amin, too, has faced backlash. In 2012, her show "It's a Man's World" was promptly shut down, the work labeled obscene, blasphemous (her latest show, from 2020, was shut down too). Kuwaiti authorities charged her with violating laws related to iconography. Her children's friends called her a "whore" and a "witch." Other artists condemned her for "opening Pandora's box." Authorities settled for the bland term "unpatriotic."

From a Western perspective, it's hard to see what the furor was about. These were beautifully drawn paintings of men being men, doing the things men do—smoking, gambling, drinking, ogling women. There's no sex. There's no raunchiness. In most of the images the males are faceless, their features a white Phantom of the Opera–type mask. Miniaturized figures sit around them, women in suggestive poses, men engaged in understated intimacies. Likely the chief offense involved Amin's depictions of females, many of them self-portraits. She sits crowned in a chair, holding a daisy chain of robed males. She pries open her son's astonished eyes. She sits on the floor of her upside-down bedroom. With painted nails she plucks away at small, scurrying, white-faced boys.

The anonymity—faceless men, women in veils—is intentional. Amin explains, "We are brought up to be two-faced. To have a private and a public life. So, when you have your mask on, you are free to be yourself. . . . The veil—it frees and empowers the women. It's not about being submissive and invisible. Being invisible is a good thing because it means freedom. With a veil, women can go wherever they want and do whatever they want and fuck whomever they want, and no one will know. Whereas, I get the Scarlett Letter treatment because I don't wear a mask."

Knowing, now, a little about Amin, the question is the role played by personality, and how it shaped her boundary-breaking, her courage, her subject matter, her violation of societal taboos. Luckily, we have her exact Big Five test results. We can compare them to the general artist findings. We can also place them in individual context.

No surprise: Her openness score is 99. Precisely what we would expect.

Shurooq Amin Openness Scores

Overall score: 99
Facet scores:
Imagination (high fantasy proneness), 83

Artistic interests (love beauty, aesthetically sensitive), 87
Emotionality (awareness of feelings, expressive of feelings), 75
Adventurousness (prefers change, easily bored), 98
Intellect (curious, loves ideas, likes to think, enjoys puzzles and brain-teasers), 83
Liberalism (challenges convention, rule-flouting), 98

The liberalism facet of openness denotes a "readiness to challenge authority, convention, and traditional values." It represents hostility to rules, sympathy for law-breakers. On it, Amin scores 98. This makes obvious sense given her transgressive art, her exposures of hypocrisy. Her adventurousness score, denoting boredom susceptibility, is also 98. This is a plus. It drives her to push into new territories, to keep growing and changing, to find new expressions.

Agreeableness is low, the score 37. Two facets leap out. The morality facet score is 12. This shows a guardedness, a belief in the inevitability of social deceptions. Strikingly, the modesty score is 1, which suggests overt arrogance. These facets together describe low honesty-humility. They jibe precisely with the aforementioned artist findings. To make the art she does, to face off against social censure, Amin's firmness, her self-belief, has to be high. There's no other way. "I have unfaltering vision," she says, "unfaltering courage and conviction in my role as an Arab artist. . . . I have no problem dealing with any resistance that comes my way. Fear will not stop me from what I feel I need to do." To some, this may read as vanity, a high value placed on personal perceptions. But it's necessary, it's a prerequisite. "I'm changing minds slowly, one at a time," says Amin. "In time, I think I'll win." Audacity clearly serves her.

At this point, Amin's fit with the average artist profile is good. But as any individual artist will, she departs from it, too. Her extraversion score is 99. That's unusual. Yet it also makes sense. For instance, the assertiveness score was 99. This means she speaks out, she takes charge, she's a leader. She's not averse to saying what she feels. Excitement-seeking is 99. She seeks thrills and takes risks. Given the nature of her art—its audacity, its riskiness—these findings seem predictable. They may not square with most artists, but they do with her.

She's low on neuroticism, with a score of 18. Could she make such strident, outspoken art and live in fearful self-consciousness and vulnerability? No. She needs inner strength and security. She needs, as she put it, "unfaltering vision."

Finally, conscientiousness is high (86), another way in which she departs from the usual artist template. She's very low in cautiousness, however, despite her overall C score. She lets rip without concern for consequences. Again, she says what she thinks. She's not overly deliberative. She makes decisions quickly.

The engines behind Amin's art are two: early loss combined with the scaffold of a powerful personality. Her father saw her talent. He believed in her. He knew she had a gift. After his death she foreclosed on a future, riding high in the faith he'd bestowed on her, painting in honor of his memory. But she also possessed, partly by nature, a perfect set of basic tendencies. She's as open as can be, with a score of 99. But she's low in agreeableness—modesty in particular—and low in neuroticism, which sets up fewer inner obstacles impeding her drive to make provocatively message-oriented art. With slight deviations, she's a perfect type. She's practically textbook.

Walter Kirn

In 2014, writer Walter Kirn wrote a profile of himself for the *New York Times*. It featured a staged photo of the author looking vaguely hostile in front of a pickup in Montana, ready either to start another book or kick the reader's ass (or both). The whole thing was a spoof, yet few caught on. Friends messaged Kirn saying the "writer" of the piece had been unkind (apparently, they missed the byline). This is a fair summary of who Kirn is. He's always operating on several levels simultaneously, and he shows no concern for whether they line up or make sense. He keeps a journalistic distance. In his head, he's taking notes, wondering what he can use later. This applies to people who know him, and it applies to Kirn too: Walter Kirn finds Walter Kirn unpredictable. And he likes it.

He's been called a literary badass, frank and captivating. His range is capacious. He grew up in Minnesota, and for a good part of his early life he was raised in Mormonism, his father having spontaneously converted. He went to Princeton and Oxford. He's written in virtually every form: poetry, memoir, novels, plays, stories, journalism, book reviews, and opinion pieces on everything from liberalism to QAnon. Two of his books, *Thumbsucker*, about a Mormon kid with the titular compulsion, and *Up in the Air*, about a lonely, disconnected businessman intent on compiling air miles, were made into major motion pictures. A memoir, *Blood Will Out*, which he wrote in 18-hour bursts over 4 months, concerns a psychopathic, murdering conman pretending to be a Rockefeller. Kirn met the guy and bought his lie, a failure of judgment that serves as the book's focus. This turned out to be a crazy-making exercise. For months after, Kirn was post-traumatic. He trusted no one. He saw impostors everywhere. He carried around a basically paranoid mindset. In time, he concluded, "we are all impostors to ourselves" and that impostor narratives entice because, reading them, we experience "the terrible thrill of self-invention, of trading who we are for who we might be."

In the 2014 self-profile, Kirn says he brims with an "outer confidence that can be intimidating at times to those unused to brash, creative types . . . indifferent to the niceties of literary image." He says, "a writer who isn't writing is asking for trouble." He says his prickliness and flashes of arrogance disguise a basic insecurity, a longing for approval. In a way, these are self-ratings of personality. The creativity points to openness, the confidence to extraversion, the insecurity to neuroticism, the "indifference to social niceties" to low agreeableness. But again, as with Amin, we are lucky, because we have Kirn's actual Big Five scores. He took the test not once, but twice, over the span of 2 days. Results did not differ (they rarely do, especially after such a short length of time).

By now, the first finding should be obvious: openness 96, with a 98 in adventurousness, a 92 in artistic interests, and a 96 in imagination.

Walter Kirn Openness Scores

Overall score: 96
Facet scores:
Imagination (high fantasy proneness), 96

Artistic interests (loves beauty, aesthetically sensitive), 92
Emotionality (awareness of feelings, expressive of feelings), 63
Adventurousness (prefers change, easily bored), 98
Intellect (curious, loves ideas, likes to think, enjoys puzzles and brain-teasers), 88
Liberalism (challenges convention, rule-flouting), 55

He enjoys novelty, variety, and change. He's curious, imaginative, and creative, just as we'd expect him to be. The score on liberalism is average. He's averse to rote, knee-jerk beliefs. Psychological liberalism and conservatism aren't identical to political affiliation, but they do incline people toward actual political parties. Kirn's score shows his party commitments to be unclear. This fits. He's not a joiner. He tends toward an unstable iconoclasm. His opinions are unpredictable.

As with Amin, agreeableness is low, at 24 (Amin scored 37), and in the same ways: low modesty (11; Amin was 1), low morality (13; Amin was 12). The artist profile strikes again. Both cases fit the pattern. What do they tell us? Reject the Jonah complex. Be the badass that's in you. Embrace audacity. Accept your artistic destiny.

With Kirn, the prototype match is closer still, as he also shows low conscientiousness, with a score of 8. Duty is low, at 9. Cautiousness is particularly low, at 1. Shurooq Amin, our painter, scored 86 on conscientiousness, but for the duty facet, she scored just 27. Low duty scorers find contracts, rules, and regulations confining. Low duty signifies unreliability. These people may not turn things in on time, but what they produce is worth the wait ("late but great"). They aren't lazy slackers, just undependable.

Despite what he said about his insecurity and need for approval, Kirn is average in neuroticism (55), but in line with the self-disclosing, self-interrogative nature of most of his work, he's low in self-consciousness (9). He's not sensitive to what others think of him. He's not nervous in social situations. This frees him up to expound, something he does frequently—and brilliantly—in interviews and elsewhere. He's not constantly worrying about being judged.

Extraversion is high for Kirn, at 97. For Amin, it was also high (99). This marks the two of them as outliers vis-à-vis general findings on the artist type. Both are assertive and excitement-seeking. For artists high in E, benefits accrue. They are seen as charismatic. People are drawn to them and want to be near them. Since people generally like them, they are primed, also, to like the work. They come to it with positive, enthusiastic feelings.

What we've got, now, is a powerful, scientifically validated personality prototype for artists, a recipe for the trait-based roots of creativity. Who you are, at a basic level, your inclinations, your tendencies, what you value, what turns you off, the ways in which you conduct your day-to-day life—all these predict creative potential, they shape the mind toward greater fecundity. Art always seems so mysterious, so exotic. We feel, at first, mostly because we are told this over and over, that it's ungraspable. In fact, despite prevailing uncertainties, the personality picture is pretty clear. We saw it in the general findings, we saw it in the artists profiled.

Openness is the one indispensable. It's the lynchpin. Added to this are (1) a stimulating mental messiness, a comfort with chaos (associated with low conscientiousness), and (2) boldness, audacity, high self-regard, belief in your gifts, and a talent for invention, an ability to go beyond accepted facts (associated with low honest-/humility, as measured by agreeableness scores). This, in a nutshell, is "the creative."

There's more to come, though. So far, we've only scratched the surface of openness. We need to take a deeper dive, into the murk of the trait, so that its usefulness gets clearer. One particularly critical detail is this: Openness changes how you think, how you take in and process information. And just as openness does, these styles of thinking also predict creative achievement. We need to know what they are.

We're clear on the Big Five. Now we zero in on the Big One, and the question of how openness lifts the lid off creativity and creative process.

3
The Unifying Glue

It was 2009. I was writing a book about photographer Diane Arbus, an investigation into the sources of her creativity, her fascination with sex and "human oddities" and "freaks." To that point, I'd known her in the ways I could: through her pictures, first and foremost; through words on paper (her own and those of others); and by talking to people who'd been in intimate contact, for instance her therapist, Helen Boigon. I'd been turning Arbus inside out, assembling a portrait, a sketch, of this fierce, serious artist, this seeker of the sordid and nasty and perverse, this risk-taker and adventurer, this psychic explorer. I saw Arbus in all these ways. I felt as if I were coming to know her, to understand what she was like.

Then I heard her voice, in a newly released 25-minute lecture. It was a line drive to the forehead. I no longer knew where I was. Fierceness came through not at all, nor did seriousness. Arbus was flirty. She joked. The audience adored her. They were rapt when she was quiet, charmed when she said anything goofy or strange. It was like stand-up. Arbus registered as daft, coquettish, inappropriate, unprepared, improvisational.

But there was something else, something most important. She started out with a long, sighed, "Ahhhh." Then: "This is my favorite part because I never know what I'm going to say." She went on like this, rambling, thinking out loud. There were pauses, awkwardly long thought-filled silences, more jokes, anecdotes, sudden turns, detours, digressions, confessions. It was not a lecture. It was a collage of thought, an explosion in a word factory. Arbus flipped a switch and followed her mind wherever it took her. She didn't analyze, she didn't explain. There was no point or moral. It made sense, and it didn't.

I thought back to what Arbus' mentor Lisette Model had said about her: "You can see her schizophrenia in every picture." Actually, in no way was Arbus a schizophrenic. She just wasn't. Yet hearing her speak,

The Mind of the Artist. William Todd Schultz, Oxford University Press. © Oxford University Press 2022.
DOI: 10.1093/oso/9780197611098.003.0004

she seemed undeniably weird. There was a primitive quality to the workings of her mind. A disorganization. An absence of anchoring.

One could approach these qualities psychiatrically, like Model did. An assortment of clinical terms might be leveled: loose associations, nonlinearity, tangentiality, derailment. Psychiatric jargon. Signs and symptoms. Markers of deep disorder. But these are labels, shorthand descriptions, names for sets of behaviors. They don't and can't explain anything, they weren't *made to* explain anything. All they do is shackle Arbus, label her, and stick her in a box.

In fact, there's no need to get clinical. We don't have to assume. Doing so wouldn't get us anywhere interesting. There is another way forward. We can focus, more neutrally, on *personality*—the structure of Arbus' thinking, the motivations behind it. What's clear from this angle is that her free-wheeling, loosey-goosey style expresses an underlying trait: openness. It's not that she was crazy. It's that she was open. Her talk wasn't a side effect of some wide-ranging clinical syndrome. It was her.

Openness

Facets:

- Fantasy (imaginative)
- Aesthetics (interested in art)
- Feelings (emotionally excitable)
- Actions (adventurous)
- Ideas (curious, inquisitive)
- Values (liberalism)

Correlates with IQ score, divergent thinking, and verbal score on SAT

Correlates with sensation-seeking, low repression, need for experience, loose boundaries, need to think and reflect and analyze

Correlates with desire for self-altering experiences, including meditation, experimental drug use, group encounter sessions

Correlates with belief in esoteric, dubious phenomena such as astrology and the existence of ghosts
Does not predict marital adjustment, but if husband high O, more long-term marital satisfaction; if wife high O, more sexual satisfaction
Between friends, correlations on O scores highest of all the Big Five traits
High O partners engage in problem-focused coping. High O parents are more emotionally expressive and warm, less insistent on obedience and deference to authority
At work, high O people generate ideas, promote discussion, synthesize team efforts. High O predicts low organizational loyalty, less goal clarity, attraction to tasks that are changeable and investigative in nature
High O people root for the underdog, tolerate out-groups, prize uniqueness and originality, and show less ethnic prejudice, racism, homophobia, and prejudice against people with mental disabilities
In the US, highest O in Washington DC, followed by New York, Oregon, and Massachusetts. Lowest O in Alabama, Alaska, Wyoming, and North Dakota.
O positively related to favorable attitudes toward legalizing marijuana, abortion, and same-sex marriage

In some ways openness is just what it seems to be. You aren't closed-minded. You aren't buttoned up. You're not stiff or timid or uptight. You want to feel. You want experience. You get bored a lot so you do what you can to spice up your life. Your mind is a little unhinged, like Arbus' was, but productively so, in a way that feeds creativity. You share what's inside you. You're loose, unguarded. It's a "damn the torpedoes" attitude.

But the question of how these things relate to art is more complex. If you're open, you're driven to express yourself. Why? How does art, of all things, satisfy thirst for experience? You're alone. You're writing or painting or playing guitar. You're not sky-diving or bungee-jumping. You're sitting with your own mind. You're focusing internally. There's no audience, no applause. What's so thrilling about creating something? What makes it irresistible?

Openness, like the rest of the Big Five, affects every aspect of mental life. But remember, traits are abstract potentials. We infer their existence from what people say and do, how they behave. What we're more interested in are the habits of mind they give rise to. These involve ways of thinking, feeling, and behaving. So far, I've described openness generally. What we do now is get into the details.

The Motivation and Structure of Openness

Openness has two broad aspects that influence creativity more or less directly. One is ***motivational***. It makes you do things. It's a push, a preference, a set of needs. If you're open, you are driven to be that, to express that portion of your personality.

You need novelty and variety, what I called earlier the "shock of the new." You need "cognition"—you like to think, to analyze, to examine, to reflect, to process information. It's not something you do because it's required, an assignment for school or a job. Rather, it's a source of enjoyment. It gives you pleasure. Sometimes this manifests as random Internet browsing, or idle and superficial curiosity; but it can also take the form of potent, focused attention on particular topics or experiences in which you lose your sense of time or self. You get absorbed.

There are people with high needs for closure. They seize on the first plausible answer then freeze their views. This is the opposite of openness. If you're high O, you resist conclusions. So, it's a hybrid attitude. You don't quickly settle, you don't run with the first solution. But when you get to a place that feels promising—a type of engagement, a subject, an emerging path—you lock in, and the world drops off.

Jackson Pollock is a good example. He wasn't content with his first solution, the representational, Picasso-inspired work he'd been producing, or the attempt, informed by Jung, to dredge up and symbolize archetypes. He kept searching. He wanted something else, something unexplored. With the canvas on the floor he felt inside the painting. He was in a state of oneness or what psychologist Mihaly Csikszentmihalyi has called "flow."

Another is children's writer Roald Dahl, most famous for his book *Charlie and the Chocolate Factory.* He believed there were two sides to writers of fiction. The first was the public face, "that of an ordinary person like anyone else, a person who does ordinary things and speaks an ordinary language." But there's also a "secret side," what the artist does alone in his workroom. "I slip into another world altogether, a world where imagination takes over and I find myself actually living in the places I'm writing about at that moment. I myself, if you want to know, fall into a kind of trance, and everything around me disappears. I see only the point of my pencil moving over the paper, and quite often two hours go by as though they were a couple of seconds. . . . I float back in time. . . . I become totally absorbed in what I am doing."

Open people need cognition, they need to think and imagine; they also need, just as strongly, experience. This comes in different forms. O predicts thrill and adventure-seeking, disinhibition, a feeling of understimulation. There's a different trait containing these elements, and it was introduced in the 1970s by Marvin Zuckerman. It's sensation-seeking, and it correlates strongly with O scores. Openness is more than sensation-seeking—a lot more—but if you're a sensation-seeker, openness covers that tendency. You like spicy foods, for instance. You like to travel. You drive fast. You are sexually adventurous, with multiple sexual partners. You prefer arousing music, surrealistic paintings, art that's discordant or suffused with unpleasant themes (death, violence, despair). You're also drawn to any experience that's self-enlarging, mind-expanding, or consciousness-raising. You'd be open to trying LSD, for instance. You're up for group meditation, encounter sessions, micro-dosed mushrooms, spiritual drugs like ayahuasca—anything disruptive of the status quo, anything promoting change from within. You habituate quickly. You move on to the next thrill, the newest "same old–same old" antidote.

As it turns out, causality may work both ways with LSD. In a 2011 study published in the *Journal of Psychopharmacology*, people completed Big Five inventories—before and after 8-hour LSD sessions. For those who reported stronger LSD mystical experiences, postdose openness score rose immediately and stayed higher 14 months later, with the strongest effect obtained for the O facet of fantasy-proneness. Tellingly, no changes occurred with respect to any other of the Big Five traits. This is a finding at odds with received wisdom. It suggests traits might be less stable than believed. Chemically induced mind expansion reverberates, keeping the mind expanded many months later.

One short example: When I interviewed Arbus' therapist, I was interested, naturally, in what she'd learned about Diane, her take on Arbus' psychology, the sources of Arbus' art. Some of what she told me was unexciting. There weren't a lot of revelations. In the therapy itself, hot-button topics seemed to be avoided or ruled (by Arbus) out of bounds. On the subject of needs, however, Arbus said one thing over and over. It was vague but consistent: *She needed experience.* She couldn't live without experience, intense, disorienting, psychically challenging experience. The "freaks" she took pictures of were born with their trauma, she said. As the cloistered daughter of a rich New York furrier, she manufactured hers. She remedied years of privation, doing, in effect, what she was never allowed to, experiencing modes of life denied her. Her art was disturbing and provocative, full of the "nasty" images she was shielded from. She hunted subjects down, a pursuit that took her to porn sets, freak shows, morgues, twin conventions, circuses, bedrooms, and dressing rooms of cross-dressers and strippers.

Her art was a lot of things, driven by multiple motives, as all art is, but what remained constant was this quest for strangeness, sensation, a need to go places—dark and dangerous places she'd never been told about, never been shown. The same urge permeated her life. One project was a sort of shame-erasing. She'd force herself to sleep with the ugliest partners she could find. She'd masturbate in front of open windows. She'd seek out orgies, parties organized by swingers. She faced fears. It was self-engineered exposure therapy. Intentionally, she took on more than she felt she could handle. There was no special point, her therapist told me, no esoteric, secret agenda. She just wanted to feel.

Arbus' high openness preselected her themes for her. How she shot what she shot was as least as important as the image itself. She was a boundary-pusher, and the pictures a kind of proof—she called them a "stain"—that she'd been to these scary places, that she'd seen what her openness drove her to see.

Openness Motivations

- Need for cognition (to think, reflect, analyze, make sense of, integrate, learn)
- Need to know (high and relentless curiosity about a range of subjects plus low need for closure)
- Need for experience (sensation-seeking, experience-seeking, thrill- and adventure-seeking, high tendency to get bored)
- Need for novelty, change, newness
- Need for self-altering experiences

Openness Structure

- Breadth of consciousness (being interested in more things, diversity of interests and talents)
- Depth of consciousness (more associations, more awareness, more access to inner life, including feelings)
- Low repression (more comfortable with mental contents others might find odd or offensive or outside the norm)
- Looser boundaries, both inner and outer
- More permeability (low filtering of sensory experience)

The other half of openness is ***structural***, a matter of mental organization. When psychologists talk about "structure," they mean inner processes, mechanisms, thought-patterns, coping tendencies. Egocentrism—the inability to take someone else's perspective—is a mental structure. Freud's superego—our internalized sense of conscience, of right and wrong—is a mental structure. High O shapes your mind. It's your psyche's interior decorator. It arranges how you think, how you feel, how you perceive, and how you go about making sense of the world.

First, high O consciousness has more breadth. You're interested in more things. Your work—whether it's art, philosophy, science, or psychological theory—exhibits topical diversity. You're not a satisfied specialist. Your intelligence proliferates, sparking this way and that. David Bowie, for instance, was a musician—of countless styles—but also an actor, a producer, a painter. Carrie Brownstein was a riot-girl rocker in the band Sleater-Kinney. Then she started acting, in *Portlandia* and *Transparent*. Next she wrote a memoir. Kanye West veered from music into fashion. It comes down to wide interests, a non–self-limiting attitude. Any form or style you've mastered gets old quickly, begins to feel stale. This basic boredom provokes a readiness for change.

Breadth relates to feelings, too. What you get with neuroticism is interesting. There's more negative affect, but not less positive affect. In other words, positive affect is not negatively correlated with N. It's similar with extraversion, which correlates with positive affect, but not negative. Openness is a different story. In terms of feelings, you are more excitable. Your range of affect is wider. You have heightened access to emotional experience. N means negative emotion, E means positive emotion, and O means emotionality. You enjoy feeling. Feelings don't scare you. In fact, you want to feel more. You also want to understand where your feelings come from, how to make sense of them, how to cope with them, how to express them authentically.

You like to imagine, to fantasize. You get lost in daydreams. You come across as distractible, internally preoccupied. In some ways the world inside your head holds more interest than the world outside. You vividly visualize scenarios, you make things up, you identify with characters in novels and movies. For high O people, fantasy is a reality just as real as the world of objects. It can take over. It's a constant lure.

Consciousness has added depth, as well. You make more associations, especially nonobvious ones. If someone asks you to list uses for a brick, you're off and running. You don't stop at three. You come up with a dozen. Associations fire more freely in open than in closed individuals. Your natural, adaptive filter is porous. You don't inhibit thoughts, you disinhibit them. You go toward irrelevant info, you take in stuff others regard as meaningless. You're a sort of meaning-finding machine.

This affects how you literally *see* things. One 2017 study induced an experience of "binocular disparity"—two different images sent simultaneously to each eye. To deal with this visually, most people alternate between stimuli: seeing one, seeing the other, switching back and forth. Some, however, blend the images or, in technical terms, "mix the percept." They take in two things at once. They see more of what's presented to them. This "mixed percept" experience is strongest in those who are open. There's a heightened receptivity, a tendency for permeable information-gathering.

The term "permeability" is key. It applies to what's outside—how stuff gets in. It applies to what's inside—how much access we have to our psyche. Some people come across as compartmentalized. They are Christian, but they hate homosexuals. They call themselves a feminist, but they vote for Trump. They keep beliefs separated. Their minds are parallel universes. It's a tendency we all have, on occasion. We block out discordant, contradictory info. But if you happen to be high O, you've got fewer, less firm, boundaries, plus more complex and differentiated moral and political attitudes. There's a test you can take online, Hartmann's Boundary Questionnaire. It consists of 164 questions and includes items such as, "My feelings blend into one another," "Either you are telling the truth or lying, that's all there is to it," and "At times I feel happy and sad all at once." Results on this test relate strongly to openness scores. Your boundaries are looser. Experiences, ideas, associations, feelings, attitudes—they all blend together.

Still More of What It Means to Be Open

You can think in terms of motivation. You can think in terms of structure. These are the broadest expressions of the openness concept. But there's more, too.

For instance, O correlates with IQ. On average, open people are smarter, in the limited ways IQ measures "smartness." That is a fact, but it's a small part of the story. You can be very smart and very uncreative.

O means love of mystery, complexity, and ambiguity. The impulse is "referential mania"—everything means more than it seems to, with hidden aspects. Generic happy endings, one-note interpretations, simplifying reductions—none satisfy the high O person. Openness is constant inquiry. If this sounds messy and torturous, it is. The silver lining is that there's more to work with. With most things, there's an easy path—the mapped line—and a path you make by walking, a path all your own. The open person takes the latter. It's corny, but true. The choice goes back to motive: a need for experience, high boredom susceptibility.

Scales exist for measuring eccentric perceptions and dissociative experiences—in other words, unusual beliefs, in things like magic or past lives, and the ability to tune out from what's around you, to enter trance-like states. These correlate with openness. The world becomes pliable. Not only are open people fantasy-prone; they are also experientially oceanic, spreading out mentally to gather in what's around them. They tune out to tune in.

Openness has its *sensory* side, too, evidenced by the findings related to "mixed percept." It correlates with something called "sentience." Being high in sentience means you notice more—smells, sounds, sights, tastes, the way things feel. You also remember sensations, believe them to be an important part of life. Trait adjectives capturing sentience include observant, aware, sensitive, sensuous, perceptive, responsive, noticing, and alive to impressions, the opposite of detached, numb, or unobservant. So, being open isn't just letting more in. It's also about recognizing, noting, and being touched, transported, or overcome. There's research on the sense of wonder—that tingling feeling we've all had of hair standing up on the back of our neck. That's related to high O. It's a surprisingly specific finding, but it makes sense. To be O is to be a sensualist. You can't be touched if you filter out impressions.

It's helpful to compare O with its opposite, the so-called authoritarian personality, outlined by Theodor Adorno, whose goal was to capture the personality markings of Fascist susceptibility. Authoritarians are black-and-white thinkers, with a firm, absolute sense of right and wrong, particularly moral right and wrong. They detest "soft-mindedness," the world of subjectivity, of complexity, ambiguity, and imagination. They do not value art. They do not value philosophy. They are sexually repressive and judgmental. They believe in things like the public punishment of homosexuals. They are power-obsessed, revolted by signs of weakness. They assert dominance, a supernatural order in which the strong prevail. They lack sympathy, their credo being "you get what you deserve." All these characteristics comprise what O is *not*. They also comprise what creativity is not. To be authoritarian is to be closed. It's a fear-based orientation, whereas openness is growth-based, an attempt to enlarge the self by inclusion.

It is obvious what all this has to do with creativity. To be open is to be replete. Just as validly, the trait could be called "fullness." Everything is a little more immediate, more accessible, more poignant. The more that's in you, the more passing through, the more you notice, the more you feel, both highs and lows, the more directions your thought takes, the more you have to draw on, work with, and shape.

In a talk titled "The Ruthless Intimacy of Fiction," novelist Philip Roth looked back on his 31 books, after deciding he wasn't going to write anymore, or as he says, after he'd lost the urge to describe his past. At one point he turns to the "heart of the task to which every American novelist has been enjoined," listing, in effect, the traits of the artist: A passion for specificity. A need to discover what's arresting and evocative. A focus on what most people would consider mundane. An aversion to generalization. A "scrupulous fidelity to the blizzard of specific data." An uncompromising attentiveness. A "lubricious sensation." A "multitudinous intensity of polarities, polarities piled shamelessly upon polarities," to the point where the artist becomes a "theater of one."

These are the lyrical descriptions of a writer who spent his life trying to make sense of what he did, and most crucially, why he did it. But if we boil them down to an essence, they are openness, they capture artistic attitude and temperament. Roth was what I've been describing: full, replete. And he used his supercharged experience to create a supercharged body of work. The books came out of what he so vividly remembered.

It comes down to a frame of mind. Noticing more. Paying attention. Not cutting off feeling. Repressing as little as you can. Freeing the mind to wander and drift in what seem, at first, to be pointless or odd directions. Staring down fear. Eschewing easy answers, cliché, simplifications.

But this book isn't only about concepts. It's also about how the concepts are embodied, and to see them embodied, we have to look to artists who embody them. The stories aren't always happy. Openness, because of its chaotic qualities, puts demands on the mind. It can make you seem crazy (a subject I come back to later). Think of the following as openness case studies, examples of how openness drives and organizes the mind of the creative.

Let's begin with Coltrane.

John Coltrane's Openness

Coltrane, born in 1926, was a modern jazz god, if not its supreme deity. In 1966 he told a Japanese interviewer he hoped, one day, to become a saint. This was in line with his vision of music, which he saw not as an end in itself, but a means to enlightenment. This was a theme of his career: musical expansion as spiritual development. He refined the music, and the music refined him.

From the beginning, Coltrane possessed a relentless curiosity. His father, a preacher, died when he was a child, so Coltrane was raised by his mother, who instilled religious principles of living and exposed him to the church. Musically, he started on alto sax, then turned to clarinet, then to the flute, and after some time in the Navy, played juke joints and bars to make money. At this point it was all R&B, a form he might have reimagined had he stayed with it. But like everyone else in the scene, he discovered bebop, eventually gigging with Dizzy Gillespie.

It was quickly apparent to those around him that Coltrane was an innovator. Sax player Jimmy Heath says, "He had this sound similar to Charlie Parker, but he didn't play as many cliches as other people did around that time." Wayne Shorter adds, "It seemed as if he was playing a saxophone as if it was not a saxophone," using his instrument as pianists or violinists do, pushing it to new expressions. "He attacked problems. He wanted to know everything that was possible," Heath explains. The two spent hours in the library where they listened to Stravinsky, among others, imagining how classical idioms might energize or widen jazz arrangements. But Coltrane was keen to learn about all music—Japanese, South African, Indian, anything. He never stopped being a student. His appetite to know was legendary.

Excursions like this and others led to what jazz critics later called "Coltrane changes," a mode of composition and technique composed of dense, rapidly changing chords with complex extensions, as in "Giant Steps," which many call a test piece for musicians. Pianist

Tommy Flanagan played on the record. His sense was that the songs didn't "resolve as you would expect most progressions to logically resolve." It was "logical for Coltrane," Flanagan says, "but totally different for the time." A key was open structure, organized around a scale or mode, or two to three alternating, repetitive chords (as in "So What?" by Miles Davis). From there, the playing progressed at the soloist's discretion. Coltrane deliberately chose this direction to go in, according to Jimmy Heath. He was "more daring, freer; he felt fewer ties to the harmonies."

He'd played with Gillespie and Miles Davis by then, and learned still more from Thelonious Monk, but in 1960 Coltrane went his own, iconoclastic way, forming a quartet devoted to experiments in modal structures. As a prime example of what he was up to, a documentary, *The World According to John Coltrane*, offers his take on *The Sound of Music* song "My Favorite Things." It's breathtaking (and worth an immediate listen). He plays all over and around the tune in "sheets of sound," slyly brushing against the melody, almost boringly sampling it, and then, for far more extended periods, lashing off into musical unknowns. He takes the song apart, then remakes it, over and over—destruction and creativity. It became, as the film's narration explains, "a hypnotic Eastern dervish dance." And also, almost inexplicably, a hit.

Avant-garde composer La Monte Young provides one of the more musically sophisticated descriptions of Coltrane's method, a blend of minimalism and "fixed constellations of tones" on which he superimposed "very interesting mathematical permutations." In Young's view, Coltrane refined this process through, on one hand, exposure to Indian classical music and, on the other, intense study of Eastern traditions of modalism. Added to this was simple, unexotic hard work. From an early age, Coltrane was tenacious. All he ever wanted to do was play.

Miles Davis explained, "I liked Trane but we didn't hang out much once we left the bandstand because we had different styles. He would go back to his hotel room to practice. It was almost like he was on some kind of mission. He was only really concerned about playing his music and growing as a musician. That's all he thought about. He couldn't be seduced by a woman's beauty because he had already been seduced by the beauty of music, whereas for me, after the music was through,

I was out the door seeing what pretty lady I was going to be with that night. . . . He could play real fast and real loud at the same time and that's very difficult to do. . . . It was like he was possessed when he put that horn in his mouth."

Drummer Rashied Ali recalls visiting Coltrane before gigs, in his dressing room, where "he'd always be playing, just like a prize fighter warming up"—actually "sweating from warming up," constantly "*pressuring* the music."

Day by day Coltrane's quartet rose in prominence, but he was restless. He wanted the new. It was classic "boredom susceptibility," a hallmark feature of high O persons. As one band member put it, "He was always trying to be better than he was. Anything he'd done became obsolete the next day. That was the mentality he had."

His music got more and more spiritually focused, more religiously preoccupied, and also less like music. Some felt Coltrane experimented too much. In liner notes he documented what he called a spiritual awakening that led to a "richer, fuller, more productive life." He'd asked to be given the means to "make others happy through music." This was granted, he said, "through His grace. ALL PRAISE TO GOD." Critics found Coltrane's next move less than magical. They called the music "anti-jazz," "willful ugliness," "gobbledegook," "deliberately destructive," "nihilistic," and "grotesque."

For Coltrane, the final artistic departure was part of his constantly evolving investigation into ancient sciences of sound. He met Ravi Shankar. He looked into how musical structures mapped specific states of consciousness. This led him back to the church sounds he grew up on: congregants lapsing into trances, speaking in tongues, shrieking, wailing, and crying. He made his instrument do the same. An idea he had, and it's a little hard to get one's head around, was that repetition engraved a series of patterns—pulsations or oscillations—in the nervous system of the listener, vibrations the brain learned and responded to at deep, automatic levels. Music was the universal structure. It was meditative. It pulled you in, and you soared with it.

But it wasn't necessarily peaceful, at least not on his last, posthumously released record. "Om" is hard to categorize as music at all. It's noisy, chaotic, and formless, a tossed-salad symphony of chanting, bells, horns, and recited passages from the Tibetan book of the dead.

It can't be listened to with pleasure. It's a musical acid trip, possibly by circumstance, maybe by design. Coltrane was taking LSD as he made the "Om" record. This was new for him. When he'd played with Davis there were periods when he lapsed into heroin addiction. In fact, Davis fired him for nodding off during solos. Heroin is death of consciousness. It's oblivion and nothingness. It's turning off the inside world. LSD is turning the inside world on. It's a magnification. Fans talk about "Om" as if it's the LSD record. Maybe Coltrane was trying to capture musically what acid felt like, how it altered perception, transformed mental structures. Maybe the drug made music-making disorganized and sloppy. Or finally, perhaps LSD had nothing to do with "Om" at all. Coltrane's sound always tended toward loosely organized chaos. On "Om" he might have done away with the organization. "Om" could signify the emptiness of form (or the form of emptiness).

Trait theorists asked Coltrane experts and biographers to rate his openness. This was done by filling out standard Big Five measures based on what they—the experts and biographers—knew to be true of him. His score was off the charts (no surprise). This can't prove anything, strictly speaking; ideally, we'd need Coltrane himself to complete a Big Five inventory (as Kirn and Amin did in Chapter 2). But the finding does cement what one can already easily see based on the set of characteristics I've been describing: Coltrane is a classic case. He's got it all, from originality and creative daring, to musical risk-taking, to boredom susceptibility, to drug use, to mind expansion, to restless curiosity, to endless spiritual pursuits. One thing consumed him above all, as Miles Davis recognized clearly: perfecting his art and taking his sound to places no one had gone.

John Lennon's Openness

From an early age, people like his aunt Mimi, who raised him, were calling Lennon amazingly inventive. "I was always hip," Lennon says. "I was hip in kindergarten."

He felt different. He figured there might be something wrong with him "because I seemed to see things other people didn't see. I thought I was crazy or an egomaniac." He felt poetic, intuitive, and psychic.

His visions seemed "hallucinatory." He came to believe, as he put it, that "my imagery and my mind wasn't insanity, that if it was insane, I belonged in an exclusive club that sees the world in those terms. Surrealism to me is reality. Psychic vision to me is reality. Even as a child. When I looked at myself in the mirror or when I was 12, 13, I used to literally trance out into alpha. . . . I would find myself seeing hallucinatory images of my face changing and becoming cosmic and complete." As a Beatle, Lennon smoked marijuana for breakfast. He took LSD hundreds of times, as if to tune into the mental surrealism that set him apart as a child.

He liked to draw and doodle, and he was good at it. He went to art school, as did so many English rock stars. He wrote and published nonsense verse, of the *Jabberwocky* variety.

Emotionally, Lennon was all over the place. It's clear he repressed almost nothing, especially after the Beatles. He was gratuitously, promiscuously open, inclined to share the contents of his mind, no matter where they took him. His anger, too, was legendary. In the early Beatles years, he kicked in the face a fan who'd climbed on stage. He also beat up close friend Stu Sutcliffe, so savagely that recent biographers suggest the beating may have had something to do with Sutcliffe's death (this is very unlikely). He talked in interviews about bitterness, depression, insecurity, neediness, loss. But he was incredibly witty, hugely funny. In large part it was this sense of humor that endeared fans to the Beatles early on. He was goofy, playful, infantile, silly—psychologists call this "regression in the service of the ego," and it's another quality correlating with openness, according to research.

Like Coltrane, Lennon was spiritually restless. In the song "God" he listed all the things or people he did not believe in—Krishna, the Buddha, Jesus, and so on—but that's not to say he didn't try most of them out first. There was the meditation phase in India, primal scream therapy, LSD, weed—anything that altered consciousness.

He was spiritually and artistically restless. As everyone knows, the Beatles went through several phases—from straight R&B early on, to Revolver, to Sgt. Peppers, to the Abbey Road medley. Post-Beatles Lennon made bizarrely experimental music with Yoko Ono, recorded an album of rock and roll standards, stripped everything down on "Plastic Ono Band," and returned to straight pop on "Double Fantasy."

Other songs—"Working Class Hero," "Give Peace a Chance," "Woman Is the [N-word] of the World"—expressed difficult political beliefs. It's impossible to say where Lennon might have gone with his songwriting had he lived, but his range was wide. He craved the new, constantly reinventing himself and his sound.

Most observers of the time felt his politics were naive or exhibitionistic, but there's no doubt he was creative about them. He staged the bed-in for peace. He tried what he called "bagism"—interviews with a sheet over his head.

His look even morphed. There was the mophead phase, the fat phase, the hippie phase, the skinny phase. At one point he took off on a walkabout, his 14-month long "lost weekend" in which he left Yoko—it was her idea. He got nothing done. He drank like a frat boy. He fought in bars. He was a mess on purpose. Then he came home and transmogrified, snapping into a stay-at-home, bread-baking dad.

There's one fact about Lennon that's glaring, and it leads outside the openness orbit. He was also high in neuroticism (unlike Coltrane, according to the biographers who rated him). Lennon seemed to know this. It was one of the reasons for the primal scream therapy—to get the negative emotion out, once and for all. He was self-conscious, insecure, anxious, vulnerable, and definitely angry. One way his neuroticism expressed itself was in relation to Yoko. He could not function without her, he said. He insisted on symbiosis: What I say Yoko says, what Yoko says I say. As a test of independence and self-sufficiency, the "lost weekend" was a failure. All Lennon did was beg to come back. What it showed was that he could *not* be on his own. It underscored his lack of an autonomous self.

Francesca Woodman's Openness

Photographer Francesca Woodman makes for an interesting case because, on one hand, she seems so plainly high O—a "capital A artist," as one of her friends put it. Yet she also came from an artist family with, in her father's words, "a remarkably aesthetic attitude towards life." Remember, these traits are baked in. Of all the Big Five, openness has the highest heritability—57%. That leaves 43% unaccounted for, however. So, it's natural to ask, as Woodman's father did, if her art was by choice or by nature. What made her so "capital A?"

There was no childhood trauma for Woodman. She didn't lose her father, like Coltrane did. Her parents didn't abandon her, as Lennon's did repeatedly, and Capote's; nor was she doing things like doubting her sanity by "trancing out into alpha" at ages 12 and 13. But she was quietly creative. She liked dressing up and role-playing, imagining identities for herself, as she did later in her photographs. She also had a quirky attraction to mythology and flamboyant fictional characters. These aren't particularly exceptional characteristics, but they point toward an early fantasy-proneness and a desire to lose oneself in make-believe worlds, both high O tendencies.

Her family kept a home in Italy, where she'd be dropped at museums with a sketch pad. Hours passed as she crouched in front of paintings, most of costumed women, whose look she studied and drew. Her brother summed up a family attitude toward Francesca: She was "aloof, determined, and special." She stood apart, she dedicated herself to creative pursuits, and she seemed like a clear original. The practice was to leave her delicately alone. No one wanted to bug her. No one wanted to interfere with whatever happened to be running through her amped up, highly personal imagination. At the same time, the stakes were high. There could not be much doubt about what was expected. Her mother made this plain, saying she had no interest in nonartists. She'd simply "hate them." To put it starkly, it was art or annihilation. And the family was competitive. You didn't just have to be good in your own way. You had to be *really, really good.*

Contingent love, competitiveness, a comparative sense of value—these cause feelings of falseness and emptiness, as a child works to be what others expect of her rather than who she truly is (psychologists call this an "as-if personality"). It's a catch-22: secure love by being someone else, or risk hate by being what you are. This isn't a rare predicament for gifted kids, or really, for anyone. A new book on opera diva Maria Callas, written by Wellesley psychology professor Paul Wink, paints a similar picture. Her unhappy, ambitious mother forced her into singing at age 13 and ran her ragged. Callas was her mother's narcissistic extension (and to Wink in his book, a narcissist herself). All along she felt as if she'd rather be a piano player, or even more, an actress. But she had no choice. Her mother withheld affection. Callas learned, day by day, that singing elicited responsiveness. She sang for her love.

When Woodman was 16, her dad gave her a camera, and everything fell into place. It was as if she'd been handed a key to a door she didn't know was there. Instantly she was "on fire to do photography," said her father. It made immediate sense. She found a purpose and held on. But these weren't dreamy pictures of trees or pets or sunsets. They were shots of Woodman herself, almost all of them, nude and faceless, "liberated in the act of addressing herself," her brother said. The family took the nudity in stride. It wasn't something they worried about. It was art. But friends found the pictures scary, eerie, creepy. They were shocked. And in context, it would have been shocking. This was a 16-year-old girl accepting no limits. It's not as if she built up slowly to a particular subject matter. She dove in, with abandon. Thinking in terms of openness, art just seemed to be in her. But not just any art. What she was doing was risky, bold, daring. It was instant total exposure. She wanted to be seen and to dictate the terms of the seeing. It sometimes came across as desperate. At minimum, it was obsessive.

There wasn't anything accidental about it, either. It's tempting to think of Woodman as a loosely organized dreamer working by instinct. But she wasn't that at all. She was hugely ambitious. Her ideas were clear. She never did anything by chance. When accidents came, she took advantage. She saw the art in them. Once a truck dumped flour on her street. She carted the powder back to her room, spread it across the floor, then, with great deliberation, formed outlines of her naked body. She'd lie in the dust, carefully step up and out of it, and shoot the results. Chance got her going. But skill, planning, and imagination helped her make the most of it.

In 1975, Woodman ended up at a place she seemed destined for—the Rhode Island School of Design, or RISD. She would have been surrounded by ambitious, creative kids, each with a sense of specialness, just like her, each hot to make art. But even there, in that charged-up setting, peers saw her as a "rock star," her concepts beyond the level of the class. She stood out, in other words, in a place where doing so couldn't have been easy. You can trace this to a native creative disposition. You can trace it back to her family, too. Painter friend Robert

Kushner said her sense of herself "depended on how quickly she could equal her parents as an artist, and it wasn't fast enough for her."

One shot is interesting for what it might reveal about sets of motives. It's with Woodman and two female friends. The friends are nude; Woodman alone wears shoes and knee-length stockings. Each holds in front of the face a picture of Woodman's face (Woodman does this too). The same face picture is tacked to a wall, hanging bodyless. This fourth face was adventitious, a spur of the moment decision. One woman failed to show for the shoot. Woodman stuck the picture there as a sort of eerie placeholder—and it worked. A boyfriend sees the shot as a kind of "fuck you." He'd been sleeping around, as had Woodman, as had a lot of students at the school. His belief is that Woodman stuck her faces on the faces of other nude women as a way of addressing his unfaithfulness, as if to say: You may be with other girls, but I'm there too; I'm the one you really want; they are all me.

When friends and family describe Woodman's personality, the same words and phrases show up: "She never hid herself from others"; "she had a very open, simpatico personality"; "everything she felt was intense"; "all her relationships, with men and women and herself, were intense"; "she had her skin inside out, there weren't a lot of layers, there wasn't any protection"; "she had a very fragile interior." The absence of repression, the intensity of feeling, the self-exposure, the permeable boundaries—this is openness, the picture of a flagrantly open type. She was needy, too. Needy to be seen and validated. Needy for approval, attention, and love. Needy to be recognized. Friends recall "incessant sexual attempts to the point where it didn't mean anything." More openness possibly, more need for experience. And despite her obvious brilliance, she kept doubting. She scrutinized her motives. She worried her art was about herself for all the wrong reasons (she does not list what these reasons were). It made her feel alone. "We began to wonder about self-preoccupation," her father said. "It was a little excessive." Her mind, she said, scared her, more than "real things" did.

After college Woodman moved to New York but couldn't fit in. She was ambitious and determined. She made one call every day—to a gallery, to dealers, to anyone she thought might help her get a toehold. It was a grind, she didn't like doing it, but she felt she had to—she felt her talent deserved it. Nothing tangible materialized. She was getting nowhere. And the mismatch—between what she believed about the value of her work and the lack of response to it—drained and depressed her. Eventually—and this is something artists confront—she found she simply had to make a living; she had to support herself. Yet as friends said, "she didn't fit into any job." She got jobs—such as photographer's assistant—but all they did was increase her distress, a distress that was growing, becoming more noticeable. Some of this probably had to do with Woodman's openness. If you're open, you don't like structured, clearly goal-driven tasks. You prefer to be more investigatory, more idea driven. So the world of work was going to be a challenge no matter what. It called for sets of tendencies Woodman didn't naturally possess.

At some point she tried antidepressants, but she took herself off them. It's not clear why. Maybe they weren't working. Maybe she did not like the side effects. Her initial suicide attempt occurred in her apartment (the means, to my knowledge, has not been described). She was 22. The fire department had to break in the door. Eerily, she assessed it in what seem like artistic terms. She tried to do it, she said, "as neatly and concisely as possible." In its wake she stopped taking pictures, a fact people found alarming because it seemed like giving up. For several months her family lived in terror. Someone had to be with her constantly. "We seemed to be able to do nothing to help her," her father said. "And things just unraveled."

In the end, after several minor setbacks (her bike was stolen, for one), she jumped to her death from a building.

Openness doesn't cause suicide. There are no correlations. It doesn't increase the likelihood of suicide attempts. In fact, those who are high O seek out therapy as a function of their interest in understanding themselves, their joy in digging into and getting to the bottom of things. But we also know high O brings complications, including, according to one study, a risk for depression.

Here are some of the challenges—not insurmountable—that come with exceptionally high O:

- Unclear identity and unstable goals
- Excessive fantasizing and daydreaming
- A nonconformity that interferes with vocational success (as with Woodman)

- Disconnectedness from social groups because of a fiercely idiosyncratic personal reality and a desire for self-expression that interferes with the formation of relationships
- An overabsorption with feelings and subjective states to the detriment of clear thinking about external reality

A scale was created to measures these qualities of super-high O called the Experiential Permeability Inventory. It includes odd and eccentric beliefs (when I wish for something hard enough, I can make it happen); unrestricted sense of self (I refuse to change my personal style of living so that I can fit in); less rigidity (I don't follow a daily routine); and less superficiality (I am interested in learning about people). At root, the scale is about problems with adaptation centering on "how well an individual can balance external pressures with internal emotional drives." In other words, the degree to which one *accepts reality*.

So, depending on how high you are in O—your exact score—certain challenges may (or may not) materialize. Take Lennon. His reality was psychedelic. Or Woodman, who had a hard time fitting in, adjusting to real-world demands.

Chapter 4 provides a close, inside look at how openness brings about inner chaos, a state many artists point to as part of their creative process. Openness makes your mind more creative. It's also a little destabilizing. *Deliverance* writer James Dickey described these polarities. On one hand, he says, the excited, deep, associational style of mind promises, for artists, "earthly paradise." But there are times, occasional times, one also desires "relief" from qualities of lived inner experience that Dickey calls "a hell."

4
Chaos Rainbows

You find it hard to control your thoughts. At work you get distracted by daydreams. You see patterns and connections where there are none. You often feel happy and sad at the same time. You confuse fantasies with real memories. You have urges to do something shocking, or to break and smash things. Accidents, you believe, can be caused by mysterious forces. There are times you get a feeling you may possess magical powers. You like doing the opposite of what people suggest even though you know they are right. As a child, you lived in a make-believe world much or most of the time, and you spent at least half your waking day imagining. If you want to, you can finish or change a dream after it's over. You blend visual images together instead of seeing them separately and sequentially. You don't filter information coming at you from outside, even stuff that's irrelevant to whatever you happen to be focusing on.

These mental qualities sound like something from a diagnostic manual. They sound, in fact, like prodromal symptoms, the beginning stages of schizophrenia. They aren't. They are the artist mind. Each of these statements is an item taken from questionnaires measuring aspects of creativity and creative accomplishment. But they don't just correlate with creativity. They also correlate with openness. Our question, now, is: What makes this style of mind emerge, and why is it so conducive to new and different ways of shaping experience?

In the psychology of old, traits and states were seen as separate processes, two different types of phenomena. That's why I learned in college, in fact. Traits were static (always there), states dynamic (ever-changing). Traits were durable, impervious to context; states episodic, they came and went. Anyone could go into any state at any time, whereas traits were more person-specific, with borders and limits.

The reality is more interesting. Traits incline you toward states. They make states more or less probable. States, then, aren't disconnected

The Mind of the Artist. William Todd Schultz, Oxford University Press. © Oxford University Press 2022.
DOI: 10.1093/oso/9780197611098.003.0005

entities. They come for a reason, and a reason is personality. Who you are is why you think and feel and perceive as you do.

Let's take one particular mental state: chaos. What does it mean to have a chaotic mind, a chaotic inner life? It means a lot of the things referred to in the opening paragraph. A capacity for irrationality. A willingness to forsake logic. A reluctance to follow rules. A commitment to fantasy, a belief that fantasy is part of reality. A comfort with messes, with jumbled thoughts and feelings, with uncertainty, with disorder and disorganization. A desire to suspend belief sometimes, and to let the mind wander. A talent for accessing child-like experience, for stepping outside adult concerns.

We tend to think of chaos as just that—chaotic. It's bad, destabilizing, something to be avoided. On occasion, these reactions—an instinct to recoil—might seem valid. Useless chaos is unhelpful. With artists, however, it's a different story. Chaos is key. It delivers the raw material. It's the portal. It is *useful.*

The philosopher Nietzsche, for instance, believed in creative frenzy. To him, chaos birthed dancing stars. Francis Bacon arrived at the same conclusion. "Deeply ordered chaos" was how he described his art. Saul Bellow called art "the achievement of stillness in the midst of chaos." To Paul Cezanne, being creative meant living in "a rainbow of chaos." Henry Miller called chaos "the score on which reality is written." Then there's collagist Romare Bearden, who phrased the question most directly: "The artist confronts chaos. The whole thing of art is, 'How do you organize chaos?' "

Notice how, in most of these quotes, what's being described are two seemingly opposed qualities. Chaos then stillness. Chaos then reality. Chaos then organization. A chaos rainbow. The question really is as Bearden laid it down: How is chaos shaped, how is disorder ordered?

You might think artists alone knew the answer. You might think you could ask them and they'd tell you. It's not that easy. They usually have no idea. They know what they are doing, but they don't know how they do it. It's as much a mystery to them as it is to us. I mentioned Bob Dylan earlier. He believed his early songs came out of a penetrating magic. He couldn't say what this magic was or how it came to possess him, how he put it to words and music. Looking back later, he doubted he could write such songs again. The secret was lost to him. Other times meanings come long after the fact. Capote reread his first novel *Other Voices, Other Rooms*, and he was embarrassed by how transparently autobiographical it was. He'd missed that fact before, and he found his ignorance "unpardonable." Grammy-winning songwriter Aimee Mann told me something similar. Now and then her songs got clearer to her years down the line. She'd have a Eureka moment: Wow! So that's what this song was about.

This chapter reconstructs a frame of mind artists themselves have a hard time describing. We need to define the components of the chaos, its inner geography. From there, questions center on the shaping, the organizing, the ordering. Aimee Mann said something else to me. In contrast to Dylan, she didn't like the idea of art as penetrating magic. She thought it was incomplete. What it left out, in her view, was the work, the discipline, the apprenticeship, the learning. Most of this chapter is dedicated to chaos and its roots in personality. But chaos alone isn't enough. Creativity is *making something*. Chaos is a means to that end, the making. How you use chaos is just as important as finding ways to stay open to it.

Here is a simple example. We know that one of the six facets of openness is "fantasy." You have a vivid imagination. You love to daydream. You get lost in thought. You indulge in wild flights of reverie. There's a measure of fantasy proneness called the Creative Experiences Questionnaire (CEQ). It includes items such as, "When I think of something cold, I actually get cold"; "I am never bored because I start fantasizing when things get boring"; "Sometimes I act as if I am somebody else, and I completely identify myself with that role"; and "Many of my fantasies have a realistic intensity." Fantasy-prone people don't stay on task, their mind veers off, they make errors. The need to fantasize, in other words, gets in the way. It's a sort of interruption. It's chaos in the system.

As expected, the trait of openness correlates with fantasy proneness. The two go together. There's more. Fantasy proneness correlates with creativity. One study, for instance, found those high in the fantasy proneness state to be better storytellers.

What emerges, then, is a triangular relationship. Openness produces chaotically creative states of mind. What these states toss up into consciousness is art's raw materials. There's an activation, followed by a synthesis. Mental contents get arranged.

The Chaos

Cognitive Disinhibition

Apple founder Steve Jobs had a simple take on creativity. He said it was just "connecting things." And since doing it seemed so dull, so ordinary, it made him guilty when anyone asked about it. All he could say was that he saw something that seemed obvious after a while. He connected experiences and "synthesized new things." Two processes are at work here: (1) soaking up what the mind offers you, and (2) forming unexpected linkages.

There's a theory about minds wandering and how this wandering invites creativity, and it revolves around something called cognitive disinhibition, which itself revolves around—no surprise—openness. Here's how it works:

Humans automatically filter information, and we do so unconsciously. It's an evolved adaptive mechanism, a screening tool. We don't know we do it. We just do. It happens beneath the threshold of awareness. The process goes by the fancy-sounding name of "latent inhibition" (LI). We inhibit what we take in. We focus in order to get things done. We avoid distraction.

Except, some people are less inclined to this than others. Some don't focus. Some don't avoid distraction. Their filters are porous, their barriers against stimuli thinner. For these people, latent inhibition is reduced. Stuff that may be irrelevant to the task at hand—perceptions, mental images, memories, thoughts, fantasies, or partially processed material—injects itself into awareness. They get sidetracked. They go off on tangents. They feel, in some cases, overstimulated.

Reduced LI seems to have one of two main outcomes. For some, it's destabilizing, overwhelming. There's too much going on in the mind, and the mind unravels. You lose your bearings. You can't think straight. But for people like Jobs, reduced LI is a gift, a positive. The less you filter the more you notice. Noticing more widens the field of perception. It's very basic. And artists, of course, are noticers.

At root, it's a lot about relevance judgments. If your relevance threshold is strict, info gets excluded. You see and think what you need to. You find out nothing new. If your relevance threshold is loose, info gets included. New patterns suggest themselves, as do new metaphors, new connections. It's straightforward. LI is limiting, reduced LI is stimulating. LI is closed, reduced LI is open. Novel associations never come from blocking out sources of information.

For Pollock, a trowel might have seemed irrelevant. But he picked one up and splashed paint with it. Lennon wrote nonsense songs—"I Am the Walrus"—full of irrelevant lyrics. Woodman scooped up irrelevant powder in the street and made photographs with it. David Bowie fixed an irrelevant bottle cap to the bottom of his shoe so he could keep time while playing the song "Heroes." In fact, art generally is about letting irrelevance in or making irrelevance relevant.

But we don't need to speculate or pile up case study type examples. We can look to the science, the research findings. What they show is this. First, compared to a noncreative high IQ control group, high IQ creative achievers had significantly lower LI scores. They filtered less, they screened out less. Second, *eminent* creative achievers—those who'd sold a novel or published poetry, or who'd had a gallery showing, or who'd composed music and gotten it recorded—were seven times more likely to have low rather than high LI scores. So, LI doesn't just predict creativity. It predicts creative success. This last fact is almost unbelievable. What could it mean? Probably that success is related to newness, and that newness comes from the "boring," "obvious" process Jobs called "combining things." It's a homely takeaway—"combining things." It's disappointingly unromantic. But for many, it's the key to creativity, creativity's definition: making connections others have missed. And since you can't connect what never gets in, *art is enhanced potential for connectivity*.

One last detail. I said before that openness could be called "fullness." It fills you up. There is more contained in the mind. And since reduced LI is also about being full, its correlation with openness makes sense. The basis for the correlation revolves around fantasy and creativity, but also "ideas," another O facet. The meaning of "ideas" isn't instantly clear. What it captures, based on items in Big Five surveys, is (1) liking complex problems, (2) enjoying thinking about things, (3) easily handling lots of information, (4) reading challenging material. Tendencies such as these move you outside the envelope, away from simplicity and conventional wisdom.

This takes us back to Jobs. For him, facts were pliable. He'd bend them to fit the purpose at hand. He had what his coworkers called a "reality distortion field." At first, it seemed like lying. He'd assert something—say, a detail about world history—with no regard for the truth of the assertion. To others and to himself, he willfully defied reality. He'd reverse himself, too. If particular lines of argument failed to persuade, he'd advocate others. He'd throw people off by adopting their position as his own. He'd say an idea was crazy, then a week later call it great. Jobs' biographer Walter Isaacson sums it up this way: "It was as if Jobs' brain circuits were missing a device that would modulate the extreme spikes of impulsive opinions that popped into his mind." Exactly. The device Jobs was missing, or that he purposefully overrode, was the filter. He set things up so that more opinions and more "facts" popped into his mind. He allowed for irrelevancies and connected them.

Schizotypy

The word schizotypy looks forbidding. It's not even clear how to say it. Plus, any term with "schizo" in it triggers automatic negative associations. But labels don't have intrinsic value. They are only names. And it turns out, schizotypy can be, for some, a powerful plus.

Therapists see schizotypy as a set of experiences lying somewhere along the schizophrenia spectrum. A diagnosis exists called schizotypal personality disorder, including odd beliefs, magical thinking, unusual perceptions, eccentric behavior, and social anxiety. There's a related disorder referred to as schizoid, which focuses more on relationships or the lack thereof. Schizoid persons prefer solitary activities. They lack close friends. They come across as cold and detached, indifferent to the opinions of others.

Artists aren't more likely to have these disorders, but interestingly, one openness facet, *fantasy*, predicts schizotypal personality. Artists are fantasists (obviously) and so are schizotypal individuals. Both have strange beliefs, perceptions, and thoughts. The key, shared characteristic is oddness. Jobs, with his reality distortion field, had odd ideas. Lennon championed psychedelic truths he discovered by taking hundreds of doses of acid. But he used the frame of mind as a means to an end: acid-soaked lyrics. Coltrane tried acid too, and some say it shaped his final record, "Om." Jobs, Lennon, Coltrane—they *made* themselves schizotypal. But it didn't undo them. It facilitated creative formulations.

This form of facilitation seems to be more the rule than the exception, according to dozens of studies looking into links between schizotypy and creativity. As with fantasy proneness and cognitive disinhibition, to be high in schizotypy is to be, in several ways, more creative.

Schizotypy is measurable through the use of a questionnaire called the O-Life, which, like so many of these questionnaires, is available to take online. It has the following five components:

1. Cognitive disorganization (you don't control your thoughts, unrelated thoughts creep into your mind). Here again, irrelevancy is welcome. It's a stimulant.
2. Impulsive nonconformity (you're impulsive, you overindulge, you do not think before acting, you like taking drugs that produce strange effects).
3. Unusual perceptions (unreality excites you, you're drawn to mysteries, you feel things like "evil presences").
4. Introvertive anhedonia (you don't go out, you don't talk to people, you like to be alone, you feel less pleasure).
5. Isolation (you feel lonely or empty, you get the sense that life has no purpose).

Since the label schizotypy tends to be seen as implicitly pathological, some recommend replacing it with the more clinically neutral term "apophenia," which means to detect patterns or connections where there are none, to see more than is there.

In 2014, a clever study appeared in the *British Journal of Psychiatry*. It zeroes in on these ideas, and it does so by applying them to a group of artists not often focused on: comedians. Five hundred twenty-three stand-up comics were compared to 364 actors. Each group filled out scales measuring unusual experiences, cognitive disinhibition, introvertive anhedonia, and impulsive nonconformity. Both the comics and the actors scored above average on the scales, but comedians turned out to be especially high in cognitive disinhibition and impulsive nonconformity. They think outside the box (especially the female comedians, an interesting wrinkle), and they flout rules; they don't fit in. A comment from one subject is on point: "Comedians train their brains to think in wide associative patterns. This relates to joke-writing where the word 'bicycle' brings up a picture of a bicycle in the mind of a non-comedian, but for the comedian it's like running a search on the internet—everything pops up, from images of fat people riding bicycles naked and getting chafed to the fact that Lance Armstrong has only one testicle."

Jerry Seinfeld offers additional insights. Seinfeld, maybe more than the average comedian, works jokes hard. As he told Marc Maron for the podcast *WTF*, all he cares about is the laugh, nothing else. It's all about the laugh and only the laugh. When starting out, he had a revelation. You couldn't simply improv new material, test it out on the fly. You had to write. You needed to commit 2 hours every day to crafting, and meticulously revising, jokes that delivered the laugh. Comedians were writers, Seinfeld realized. You had to assemble mounds of material. You needed a solid 60 minutes, all of it working, all of it funny. There was something else too: rage. Seinfeld resists calling it that; he tells Maron he prefers words like irritation. In either case, he's describing the feeling of something gnawing at you, bugging you.

For the *New York Times*, Seinfeld disassembles a joke he wrote about Pop Tarts, of all things—but that's Seinfeld's shtick, he writes (he says) about dumb stuff that, because it's so dumb, seems funny. First, Pop-Tarts just grabbed him. The sound of the words, the one-two punch, the consonants. He likes to count syllables, he says, like one does in songwriting, where words have to fit melodic lines. But then, his mind went everywhere, and he let it. Pop-Tarts became a stimulus in a word-association test—he surrendered to streams of consciousness. Finally what he came up with—and he worked the joke for years—was this: Kids discovering Pop-Tarts were chimps playing with sticks in the dirt. It's an odd connection. We don't think Pop-Tarts then think chimps. But Seinfeld did. He found a weird simile, and made it comedy.

Simile—how things resemble other things—is key. It's a microcosm of creative process because, when it works, it's about bringing together what hasn't been connected before. It's also about unusual perception. There are countless examples, of course, but let's take one detail from the Aimee Mann song "Goose Snow Cone." She's looking at pavement under snow. What it suggests, to her, is an "origami crow." Her mind makes a creative leap. She sees past what's there. Joni Mitchell, in the song "Harry's House/Centerpiece," sees downtown taxis as "yellow schools of fishes" and women in Bloomingdales with "credit card eyes." Helicopters land "like dragonflies on a tomb." We could all locate favorite similes in songs, poems, novels, or anywhere. What they show is the same. Two unrelated perceptions get combined. We encounter new realities.

This is where everything comes miraculously together into a single, blended creativity matrix. Schizotypy, or apophenia, according to various scientific studies, correlates with cognitive disinhibition, the loosening of filters. Both form part of the same basic way of experiencing the world. They are not two separate things. They are one. They co-occur more often than they stand alone.

Moreover, just like cognitive disinhibition, schizotypy is correlated with creativity, verbal and visual, with one caveat: Desiring isolation, being introvertive, lacking a capacity for pleasure—these do *not* predict creativity. They don't make you more creative, according to the studies.

Finally, and this is what I meant when I called openness creativity's glue, cognitive disinhibition and schizotypy, according to research, both spring from open personality. They are states of mind, mental inclinations, deriving from openness. The relationship between these variables, then, is triangular: schizotypy correlates with cognitive disinhibition, cognitive disinhibition correlates with openness, schizotypy correlates with openness. What seem like three independent elements are in fact a blended unity, a gestalt.

If we put these characteristics together—loose thinking, connectivity, strange perceptions, and so forth—they capture the chaos we started with at the beginning of the chapter. They describe a mind thoroughly receptive. There is little to no censorship, no sentry posted at the gates of awareness. Impulse is welcome. There's a talent for, a commitment to, nonconformity. Artists know all these things intuitively; they know about the chaos rainbow, the chaos prerequisite. Now there's science to back it up. The science proves the artists correct. The chaos is real; the chaos truly is connected with creativity and creative achievement.

"Openness" as nucleus

Projections include:

- Reduced latent inhibition (less filtering of experience, porous filters)
- Fantasy-proneness (a love of imagining)
- Cognitive disinhibition (free-flowing, uninhibited, irrational thinking)
- Schizotypy (disorganized thinking, unusual perceptions, impulsive nonconformity)
- Loose boundaries, both inner and outer
- mixed percept (blending of sensory information, seeing things all at once, combined)
- Low repression (in touch with feelings, wishes, unconscious materials)

The result of all of this, for artists, is a STIMULATING CHAOS.

We have to take this chaos seriously. It's not some romantic notion. It is fact. What we are talking about, really, isn't some variety of madness, but *method*. These mental qualities, spiraling out of openness, are creativity's accelerant. If we graphed them out, the picture would be of a slightly lopsided, inverted U. Too little chaos equals less creativity; too much and you wind up so disorganized that making or shaping something becomes impossible. The right amount is what you need. You need an alert, productive anarchy.

For centuries, artists have taken stabs at describing what this chaos feels like, the forms it takes in the mind, the conditions in which it seems to occur, and also how to evoke it. Arthur Rimbaud, for instance, advocated systematic derangement of the senses, required, he said, for visionary art. He talked about studying your own awareness, testing it, inspecting it, making the mind into a monster. Discover the unknown, he suggested. Accept and understand it. Then, after searching and exhausting yourself, "preserve the quintessence" of what you've found. It's not clear he had this sort of mind to begin with. But he pursued it, sometimes via intoxicants. He latched onto it as his method, his personal theory of how art happens.

Another example is writer Jack Kerouac, best known for his novel *On the Road*, which became—to his annoyance—a bible for the Beat Generation. Many seem to regard Kerouac as some sort of carefree, free-wheeling, hitch-hiking, Tokay wine–guzzling bohemian. Proud hero of hippies. Father of the summer of love. He wasn't these things. He was a watcher, a loner, a brooder, the opposite of a joiner. He had no interest in movements. He just wanted to write down his life in a series of books and then, before he died, insert all the real names and, as he said, die happy (he never got around to inserting the real names).

But along the way he did, early on, outline a method. It's like Rimbaud's, who Kerouac read and called a "deranged seer." The key was spontaneity. Kerouac titled what he came up with "Essentials of Spontaneous Prose," a handbook for writers. The starting points were visions, a word he used in book titles—*Visions of Cody*, *Visions of Gerard*. Reality was a mash-up for Kerouac. He made no distinction between fantasy, facts, memories, dreams, images. He was "cognitively disinhibited." He filled himself with "unusual perceptions."

With your personal vision before you, you write without consciousness, you write in semi-trance, Kerouac said. Do not censor. Allow your subconscious to admit whatever it chooses. Don't begin from preconceived ideas. He continues: Don't "afterthink" to improve or "defray impressions." Write from the "jewel center of interest in subject of image at moment of writing [sic]." Write excitedly, swiftly, without pause, without thinking of "proper words," with no selectivity of expression. Follow the "free deviation (association) of mind into limitless seas of thought." As with jazz musicians—whom Kerouac adored—seek undisturbed flow of "personal secret idea-words." The best writing, Kerouac said, felt like a fist coming down on a table. It banged and shocked.

Kerouac took speed to get into this headspace. Speed quickened the work, which Kerouac insisted had to come rapid-fire, without blockades. Speed erased what he called the "beclouding of consciousness," the editing, censoring, second-guessing mind.

He claimed not to do any shaping or polishing. He claimed what he unloaded had, automatically, its own "deep form." Who knows what the truth is. He didn't start with spontaneous prose. He came to it over time. It was in the Zeitgeist, a Zeitgeist he helped to construct.

Clearly, not every writer works like this, and some dismissed the results of Kerouac's method. They felt he should have shaped more, done more selecting of incidents and details. Maybe he took his method too far, but what he said about permeability, flow, access, and disinhibition squares with what science says about the artist mind. In fact, *flow*—Kerouac's main attraction—is a creativity buzzword. All artists have felt it. All artists recognize what it means. They seek it avidly. It's the juice of invention. In flow you feel free, you don't edit, you don't censor, the words and images come, unrestrictedly, in a way that seems unbidden. Flow is the magic Dylan talked about, and like Kerouac read Rimbaud, Dylan read Kerouac.

Being Less Conscious

There's a lot of basically false talk about artists being "right-brained," as if the key to genius requires turning off one's boring, logical left hemisphere. But in 97% of people, the right brain can't talk. It can't make words. It's got its specializations, but speech isn't one of them. No words means no poetry, no novels, no plays. If you're a writer, the last thing you want to do is turn off or even turn down your left hemisphere. It's your word factory.

Even so, there's merit in these right brain cliches. What they really pertain to is consciousness and the part played by higher, so-called "executive functions" in the making of art.

A lot of what we've been talking about so far involves bypassing consciousness, or at least relaxing its supervisory hold over mental contents. This is what Kerouac meant. The state to get into, he said, was trance. Disconnect to disinhibit. Switch off the editor. Be impulsive. Think less. "Fish as far down as you want," he suggested.

When you fish far down you're in the deep water and you run into archaic, unprocessed material as well as older, less rational ways of working with it. Think of it as surrendering to chaos or giving up what you thought you needed, but don't. It's funny, neuroscientists and philosophers haven't yet figured out the reason for consciousness—why we have reflective awareness—but we do understand, better than before, the mind's unconscious. It's the automatic brain. It never stops working; it works when you sleep. It's the layer you take for granted, the layer under the layer you control and steer and aim like a flashlight.

We have two minds. These minds aren't the right brain mind and the left brain mind. They're systems, system 1 and system 2. In the old days, Freud referred to these as primary and secondary processes.

Let's start with some examples. If I want to make pesto, or unclog a drain, or replace a fan motor, I need to think. I need to think a lot, actually. I need to be hyperconscious of what I'm up to. Consciousness, *explicit* consciousness, is essential for tasks like these. Awareness can't be bypassed. There are clear steps, an order in which to do things. If I deviate from that order, I go astray. This hyper-explicit awareness, an awareness through which I filter out irrelevancies distracting from the task at hand, is system 2 consciousness. System 2 is the Mr. Spock style of thinking. It's slow, deliberate, focused. If I tell you to pay attention, you activate system 2. What's system 2 good at, what's it made for? All the expected stuff. Filling out a tax form, locating someone in a purple sweater, attending to a single voice in a loud room, telling someone your phone number, assessing the validity of a complex argument, searching memory for the title of a song you just heard on the radio.

System 1 is the other mode; it's what we've been exploring in this book, the chaos. It's rapid, effortless, automatic. It's not what comes to mind when we think about thinking. In fact, it's thoughtless. Even animals make use of it. It helps us orient to sudden sounds, complete phrases like "bread and . . . ," detect hostility in a voice, read words on large billboards, drive a car on an empty road. If you see 2 + 2 = ?, you respond immediately. You don't consciously choose 4, you blurt it out. System 1 is also irrational. It thinks globally and jumps to conclusions. It's careless. For instance, if I tell you a bat and ball together cost $1.10, and the bat costs one dollar more than the ball, you'll say—wrongly—that the ball costs 10 cents. (The correct answer is 5 cents.) Snap judgments serve us well some of the time—we've evolved to make them. But they get in the way, too. They are pushy and falsely authoritative. It's system 1 Trickster-Coyote mind versus system 2 Mr. Spock.

When it comes to art and creativity, the rushing, loose, irrational, free-wheeling system 1 is not some sort of impediment. It's not a limitation or a negative. It's a positive. Artists see it, rightly, as natural, inevitable, and helpful. It's acknowledged and deliberately elicited. It's the mode you try getting into. Songwriter Paul Simon was asked if he thinks about what songs ought to say. "No, not anymore. . . . In fact, I try *not to think* what a song should say. I'm interested in what I find. . . . I like to discover it rather than plot it out. So I let the songs go this way and that way and this way and whatever way it is. 'Oh, that's interesting,'" Simon starts to realize. "'Never mind that, that's not so interesting.' *You want your mind to wander*, and pick up words and phrases and fool around with it and drop it."

James Taylor's reflections are just like Simon's. The songs "come through me," he says, "and I wait for them to show up. *It's not a controlled process. I don't have much direction over it. It's always happened as a kind of subliminal thing* that just occurs. The main thing is to give myself enough time to let that thing happen. It occurs as if it's delivered on your doorstep."

It's the same for Joni Mitchell, who speaks of "stirring the process up" and somehow "making the head jump." She says she works with "*the chaos that the contemplative mind-thing dishes up*. You watch it and steal from it."

Diane Arbus said, "I don't press the shutter, the image does, and it's like being gently clobbered." Painter Lucien Freud lets his paintings "finish themselves." Hemingway felt it was a mistake to think about his stories after he'd left them for the day because to do so "would damage [his] ability to write" them. "You must not worry about it before you start nor when you stop," he told himself.

What's notable about these reflections is the lack of top-down, higher-mind direction. You surrender. You wait. You watch. It comes or it doesn't. You never know. It's unpredictable. It's passive then active, not the other way around. You hope the chaos tosses up something usable. You can't even summon it because if you try too hard, you mess the process up.

If I want to do my taxes, I sit down and focus and think hard and do them. I don't wait for any chaos. It's very system 2, very top-down. Yet here's Bruce Springsteen on his *creative* process, which works antithetically: "I don't really sit down. I rarely have a subject where I sit down and say I really want to write about this or that. Usually when I do I don't do it very well or it ends up feeling forced or contrived." He continues: "I'm going on instinct, and that's a wide open game. I'm following all kinds of paths and all kinds of roads. . . . You pull something that doesn't exist out of the air. . . . You're mining, and you hit a vein, and then you go with that, and then it dries up."

For such a subtle, nebulous inner experience—pulling things that don't exist out of the air, waiting for the contemplative mind-thing to dish up chaos or drop something on your doorstep—the unanimity of artist description is surprising. All these people are saying the same thing: It's irrational, it comes, I can't explain how, I stay patient, I stay out of the way, and I grab it if I can. Brain science has looked at this in the manner it can, at the apparent workings of system 1, and the findings square with these first person accounts. One study, for instance, wired rappers up to a functional magnetic resonance imaging (fMRI) test. They were divided into two groups: improvisers creating words and rhymes on the spot, and a second group whose task it was to recite already finished, typed-out lyrics. Both did so over the same eight-bar musical track.

The question for us is what happened in the brains of the improvisers, the group composing on the fly. First, they showed initial prefrontal dissociation—reduced attention and less executive, higher-order control. In other words, more chaos, more irrationality. Second, in the improvisers there was more—not less—left-brain language-centered activity. This goes back to what I said earlier. The rappers were working with words, making them up out of nowhere. You can't do that by being "right-brained." You need the left side's word factory. Third, for improvisers there was heightened activity in the brain's amygdala. This points to emotional investment. That is the amygdala's job; it's the brain's emotion center. A final finding is especially intriguing. The right hemisphere kicked in at the *end* of the process, around the sixth, seventh, and eighth bars. This is speculation, but perhaps the right hemisphere's job is more to *evaluate* aesthetic productions after the fact, to judge their effectiveness, their basic beauty. But what got the creativity party started, so to speak, was cognitive disinhibition—reduced prefrontal involvement—and word-finding. Spontaneous creativity, it seems, is *deactivation* of logic centers, not right-brain *activation*. It's as if the rappers locked Spock out of the room.

Shaping the Chaos

Here we depart from the field of psychology. It's odd to say this, but we know a lot about the chaos—its personality prerequisites, the forms it takes, the elements making it up, its usefulness. But when it comes to the rainbow—the shaping, the crafting—psychological science is silent. There's no research to draw on. We are talking, now, about mental atmospheres, microscopic aesthetic judgments, almost all of them made unconsciously. We're talking about beauty, and what makes art good, what makes it work, and how the artist *decides*. Diane Arbus' therapist had a theory she told me about. It revolved around what she called "taste." Taste, she said, was part of personality. Every person had taste, or built in aesthetic preferences. Taste told you what you liked, what you sought, what looked beautiful to you, what struck a chord. It was perceptual, emotional, attitudinal, and automatic. How did you get it? She wasn't sure. But it was there always, silently scouting. Did it change over time? Probably, yes. It had to. It was self-refining. In some undefinably nuanced fashion, it evolved.

I've been talking about all of this as if it were a clear-cut, two-step process: chaos followed by shaping, an ordering of disorder. Chaos, that condition of receptivity and mental readiness, throws up contents that get transformed, made into something—a song, a poem, a painting. For the most part, this formula works. But there's a minor qualification. The chaos does not do its bit and stop or depart. It's omnipresent, circling in and out of every moment of the art-making process. I think the soundtrack metaphor is a good one. It can be loud, it can be barely audible, but it's there, setting a tone, a mood.

All along we've been checking in with real artist lives and experiences. Here, that's all we've got: what artists say about how they do it. Of course, they don't always know. Magicians can tell you how the trick works. Artists can't, not exactly; if they could, we'd all be artists. But what we can do is scratch along, reverse-engineer the beauty path.

Someone asked the late Philip Roth what a writer did all day: "I turn sentences around. That's my life. I write a sentence and then I turn it around. Then I look at it and I turn it around again. Then I have lunch. Then I come back and write another sentence. Then I have tea and turn the new sentence around. Then I read the two sentences over and turn them both around. Then I lie down on my sofa and think. Then I get up and throw them out and start from the beginning. And if I knock off from this routine for as long as a day, I'm frantic with boredom and a sense of waste."

It's easy to talk about turning sentences around. The difficult part is *how*, because every how requires judgment, every how is a decision, and *the decision is where the art is*. It's like when Jobs talked about combining things. Not every combination works. Most of the mess you discard. You need to know where the best mess is. Is that an instinct some people just have? Can you learn it?

How do you know when you are done turning sentences around?

Models

It starts here. Van Gogh had Gauguin. For Arbus, it was Weegee and Lisette Model. For Lennon, it was Chuck Berry and Bob Dylan. Your models are the prehistory of your art. They train your judgments. They are your apprenticeship.

You begin by copying, borrowing, or stealing, an overlooked but common and essential first step. You look to the artists you want to be like, the artists whose work you admire, and you set them up as touchstones, peaks you try reaching. It may seem as if this is the sort of thing only noncreative people do. It's not. Creative people do it too. You get better by trying to be good in the ways your heroes are good. In fact, for periods of time, early on, you don't just want to be *like* someone else, you want, almost literally, to *be* that person. You mimic. You role-play.

I started out as a fiction writer. First I wanted to be Thomas Wolfe. Then Fitzgerald. Then Hemingway. Then Kerouac. Then Raymond Carver. Then Kafka. Then Flannery O'Connor. Musicians begin the same way. You play like the people you admire. You learn solos. You duplicate them, note for note. There's something naive and infantile about it, like boys who want to be their dad or girls their mom. It's worshipful, and the worship is productive.

Singers take years to find their voice. It's a slow, day-by-day reveal. Take musician Elliott Smith. He didn't come into the world a singer. Singing was the last thing he wanted to do. It was hard for him to stay in key even. In his first high school bands, he tried sounding like Joe Strummer or Elvis Costello. Only years later did he become, vocally, Elliott Smith. He went from derivative bark to signature whisper.

Scores of articles have been written about the impact, on modern painters, of Matisse. It's the colors, the shapes, the disinterested brushwork. Some artists repaint paintings they love. Actors mimic other actors, poets other poets. Starting out, you do not know how you want to be as an artist, or *how to know how you want to be*, so you look to others who got there before you. Lennon was stuck in brainless, generic teenybopper formulas—"She Loves You" and "I Wanna Hold Your Hand." Then Dylan showed a way out. Dylan himself is another example. He's the great appropriator. In his folk years, he wanted to be Woody Guthrie. It was an all-consuming impersonation. He dressed like Guthrie, talked like Guthrie, smoked like Guthrie, sang like Guthrie, even claimed he was an "Okie."

To copy is to merge with another person. It's a form of pretend. You absorb an influence. You loosen boundaries between self and other. But it goes beyond this. You also immerse yourself in the person's work, you study it and learn it, you analyze it, you figure out how it got done, the creative moves behind it. Maybe you listen to the same song over and over again—a chord change or chord sequence, an eight-bar bridge, a particular drum sound. Examples of shaping by others inform and sensitize the shaping you do yourself. It's like adding color to your palette or lenses to your camera. Starting out, you just don't know, you can't know, how you are going to say what you want to say, how to make anything work. Models represent completed possible successes.

Being Okay With Not Knowing

Eventually, you exhaust the copying. You have to. You (1) get bored with it and (2) notice you've gotten bored. You've used all you can of it. When the copying starts to feel like copying you know, at that point, it's time to move on. Now you don't want to be someone else; you feel you no longer have to. You want to be you. Openness means boredom susceptibility, a desire for newness. Copying gets stale. It starts to feel tacky.

The filmmaking (and acting) Duplass brothers, Jay and Mark, describe exactly this process (Jay plays Josh in the Amazon series *Transparent*). As kids, they were obsessed with film, shooting literal remakes of movies like "The Blob" and "The Invisible Man" in their living room. They didn't make their first small feature, "Vince Del Rio," until their early 20s. But they came to realize—painfully and despondently—that what they'd done was no good. Mark says, "we were very experienced in the delicate art of making terrible movies." They saw they were trying to be the Coen brothers or Quentin Tarantino. They were stuck in copy mode. They lacked the tiny voice inside that knew the difference between what was good—uniquely theirs—and what was flatly fraudulent. The shift came by accident. One day they told themselves, "OK, we're going to make a movie." They had no 16-mm camera, no lights, nothing, so they used their parents' video device. Jay left to buy a tape, Mark came up with ideas. In one 20-minute take, they shot "This Is John," about a guy recording an answering machine message. Jay says, "I won't say that we knew we had it, but I will say when we were done shooting it, we knew that something had happened that had never happened before." "It was that feeling," Mark says, "of this movie feels like us." The film got into Sundance. Their careers took off.

Moving past copying isn't knowing what you are doing. That comes later, if it comes at all. First, it's more to do with giving yourself permission to deviate. It's a capacity for being determined but unsure. This doesn't only go for novices. Here, again, is Philip Roth: "I don't know anything in the beginning, which makes it great fun to write, you know? You don't know anything. You don't even know how to write. So you begin every book as an amateur and as a dummy. And in the writing, you discover the book. Of course, you're in charge. But gradually by writing sentence after sentence, the book, as it were, reveals itself through you to your language—through your language, rather. So each sentence is a revelation. I'm not exaggerating. Each and every sentence is a revelation. And what you're trying to do is hook one sentence to the sentence before and the next one to that sentence. And as you do, you're building a house, you know? And the architect and the contractor, they know what the house will look like when it's done. And that's the big difference. I don't have any idea what it will look like when it's done. I don't have any idea whether it will even be done because you don't know what you're doing when you're at work."

Notice how Roth calls it great fun not to know. With each new book he's a dummy, and it's the writing itself, the process, that tells him what he needs to do. He can't say where it will lead, he can't say when he'll be done. What you have to do is surrender. You do it on faith, but you also know, or fear, that it might go nowhere. You have to be okay with it going nowhere. That's the creative bargain. Uncertainty. Self-doubt. It comes with the territory. There were times, Roth says, when he got to 200 pages and realized what he had sucked. He dumped it and started again. Then, when he started again, he still didn't know.

It's essential to get comfortable with not knowing. Needing to know is equal to never starting. The uphill climbing doesn't end. It doesn't get easier. In this way art is different from other things we do. You're like a seasoned auto mechanic for whom every car is her first. This capacity for uncertainty—a talent, a skill—comes with high openness. You like the unpredictable. You prefer it. Low O people are the architects or contractors. They start when they know the ending, and if they don't know the ending, they don't start.

Finding Your Voice

Talking about voice is perilous because no one has the vaguest clue how it is acquired, and it's also conjoined with similar but misleading terms such as style, tone, and these days, brand, each of which, excepting brand, is itself opaque. Also, you find your voice—or better yet, *a* voice—amidst the chaos described before. Maybe, as Roth said, it's a sentence-by-sentence revelation. Maybe you fall into it. You can locate exceptions—*True Grit's* 14-year-old Mattie Ross, *Catcher in the Rye's* Holden Caulfield—but writers don't sit down and say to themselves, "I am going to write in voice A" this time. You tiptoe your way in. You make false starts. Finally, you get to something that feels right, that feels effortless, that feels like you, or the "you" you need at the time, at the moment. Then it's smoother sailing. The right voice makes everything easier. It's a good groove.

Capote said style is personality—you can't adopt it any more than the color of your eyes. I agree. Your style, your voice, is the tip of the temperament iceberg. It encompasses, or constellates, everything you are. It's an attitude, a mood, an atmosphere. With some artists, you notice a sameness. Kerouac is one example. He repeated characters, he focused on the same 1950's milieu. Arbus made freaks of everyone she shot. Her sitters would say they'd been "Arbused"—absorbed into Arbus' voice, seen through Arbus' eyes. But artists, most of them, have different voices. Capote's work seems to contradict what I quoted him saying because he wrote everything from tender, lyrical, autobiographical fiction to gritty, fact-based true crime. Or take Bowie, the chameleon. Or Madonna, who reinvented with every record. Voice is consistently inconsistent. Something about it remains invariant, but there is orbiting too, moving off from a base. Just like you try on different identities, you try on different voices, but in the difference there's an essence that endures.

For obvious reasons, voice relates to motive and audience too—why you are making the art and who it is intended for. Your basic, most natural-feeling voice may not work in every setting. This is why range is important. You have to be flexible. If you're a commercial photographer, you need to please your clients. If you write a symphony for a King, you please the King. It's an iterative process. It's trial and error. Slowly the voice takes shape and you fall into it. It fits the subject matter, the intended audience. Likewise, if your motive is contrition, revenge, instruction, provocation, mourning, self-discovery—the voice absorbs the mood. Even when you don't know your mood all that clearly, mood leaks in, with positive or negative consequences. It's good, then, to track the whys. Why am I making this? Why do I need to say what I am saying? What's driving me?

In the end, the thing about voice is that it's variant and invariant. Part of it you can't do anything about. It's your stamp, your signature, your tone, your taste. It's that soundtrack. You can't escape it or muffle it, but you can pivot around it, dip in and out of it as the situation demands. You're you, you're always going to be you, but you contain multitudes.

Kneading

To knead is to pummel, stretch, pound, shape. This is what Roth meant when he talked about moving sentences around; it's also what Aimee Mann meant when she emphasized how hard it was to learn your craft and make good songs. You could describe it less physically with terms like coax, cajole, elicit, conjure, and revise. But these don't work. They are too delicate. They fail to capture the delightful agony of working with raw materials, bending them to your will.

This agony—the pain of things not seeming to work, the pleasure of improving them—has lots of components, but one is the uncertainty so many artists point to. Don't think of the uncertainty as bad. It feels bad in the moment. But it's productive, it keeps you moving forward. The last thing you want is premature certainty. Discontent is your friend. Once I had my portrait painted. The artist could not stop making my face look like his brother's. So he junked the painting and started over. A different painter I know burned one of her works, a novelist friend tanked a book, a songwriter friend worked for years on a song she called "The Math Problem" before finally abandoning it. You knead and knead and knead, and sometimes, the dough just won't get shaped. That's OK. You learned, you move on. Art is a gamble. It's a little like cooking. You don't know how the dish will taste, and it tastes different every time you make it. Embrace the fun of uncertainty. Take it on joyously. It's unavoidable anyway. It's a fact you must accept.

The kneading proceeds microscopically according to your taste, so it enfolds all the elements described before, from models to voice to motive to audience. I know someone who owns a bagel business. There are lots of bagels out there. What she does is stamp her bagels with her voice. Her voice comes from eating other bagels. It also comes from a study of ingredients. And part of it, inevitably, arises out of considerations relating to what her buyers enjoy. She's a creative bagel baker. She bakes bagels that don't work out, she bakes bagels that do. Many times she has no idea why. Either way, there is no such thing as wasted effort. You are an apprentice to your own process. You learn how to make things good by making things bad. It's as much about subtraction as addition. It's as much about knowing what to leave out.

***

There's a naturally occurring process everyone experiences every day, no matter what. It confirms both the universality and the uniqueness of creativity. It also matches the process we've been working through. I'm talking about dreams.

Dreaming begins with an activation in older brain centers. You are flooded with perceptions, thoughts, memories, experiences, and feelings. It's disorganized, uninhibited, irrational. There's no deliberate selection, no logic. It's free and loose. Nothing gets excluded. Nothing is irrelevant. Raw unprocessed material floods the mind.

Everyone dreams, but no one dreams the same. Dreams are your voice, your raw material. The physiology is the same, but the results of the physiology differ.

What happens next is the kneading. Random activations trigger higher brain centers, and higher brain centers synthesize; they form the chaos. You end up with a story, a creative product that selects and connects. It's an activation/synthesis process.

Dreams are automatic; art-making is guided. So what creativity resembles most is something called lucid dreaming. This strange phenomenon was first observed by Stephen Laberge at Stanford. What some people do, a minority of us, is achieve consciousness while continuing to dream. Most of the time they wake up, say to themselves, "I am dreaming," then witness the content that pours forth, as if they wandered into a mind-movie. When this happens, it's called dream witnessing. But other people wake up and control dream contents. It's rarer but it does occur. Usually, the control isn't total. It's more a matter of moving materials around, directing plot, introducing characters, imposing outcomes. Dreams always include synthesis, even the nonlucid variety. In lucid dreams, the synthesis is deliberate. It's accompanied by the same level of awareness occurring in waking life.

Awake dreaming is a useful model for creative process, a natural equivalent. First, material erupts chaotically. It's not controllable initially. It's not chosen. Then, the self-aware, narrative mind works with it, tries doing something with it, sifts and focuses and rearranges. When people like Jobs, Dylan, Kerouac, and Joni Mitchell describe how they work, they see it in these terms. Plus, all those openness-driven effusions, from cognitive disinhibition to schizotypy, duplicate dream language—the weird perceptions, the magical thinking, the disconnected imagery. We can add to this analogy one more detail: fully 80% of the time, dreams work with negative emotion, most often fear or apprehension. This fact seems to take us away from creativity. Art isn't fear-based. If anything, fear has to be overcome. But art can be, and frequently is, rooted in trauma. It repeats and symbolizes trauma. It replies to trauma creatively. Not all the artists we've looked at have trauma histories, but many do, and when they do, they take the trauma on as a problem, it occupies the mind, and it feeds the art. The trauma is another activation, and like other activations, it's synthesized. It becomes the art's focus.

Recall those three levels we talked about: traits, characteristic adaptations, and stories. Dreams are stories. The awake dreaming of art is a story. It all comes together—personality, process, and narrative. To this point I've referenced individual creators to illustrate individual concepts. In Chapter 5, we can take a more inclusive approach. David Bowie and Frida Kahlo are two very different artists of different ethnicities working in different mediums. But let's apply this system we've got—from openness-driven chaos to synthesis—and see how the differences dissolve into sameness.

5
Two Prototypical Creators
David Bowie and Frida Kahlo

We've been working out the details of a theory of creativity based in personality first and foremost—*who you are*—and creative process—*how you work with information*—and then, *how you shape* that information, give it form that achieves beauty, sometimes by making up stories about it. No model fits any one person perfectly. That's not a flaw of models. Models are approximations that work in most cases, most of the time. They capture family resemblances within groups. The members of the group, in this instance artists, *look alike*. Models help because they allow us to predict. But they also, more commonly, allow us to understand, and when we understand, we not only make sense of another person we are interested in, we also, in addition to that, make sense of ourselves. We put ourselves in that other person's shoes. We imagine our way into his or her life.

So far, I've talked about artists in order to illustrate isolated findings. Now I take a more Big Picture view, by focusing on David Bowie and Frida Kahlo.

David Bowie

Fear of Madness

What's striking about Bowie is how happy he always seemed to be, how bouyant, how composed. His personality was winning, his mood upbeat. He was the picture of high hedonic capacity—pleasure simply found him or vice versa. He also never seemed fragile or out of sorts. He didn't experience, early on, shattering losses. His relationship with his parents wasn't toxic (though he says, about his mother, "we were

The Mind of the Artist. William Todd Schultz, Oxford University Press. © Oxford University Press 2022.
DOI: 10.1093/oso/9780197611098.003.0006

never close"; then more vaguely, "we have an understanding"). Even in lengthy and sometimes difficult filmed interviews, where personality and inner life manifest most visually, from at least around 1980 on he was funny, quick to laugh, obviously very smart, witty, erudite, and rarely discomfited or visibly nervous or sad.

The early 1970s were a different story. By that time, Bowie had put out several records. He'd been (and suddenly stopping being) "Ziggy Stardust"—the flame-haired, left-handed rock god destroyed by fans. He'd moved on to other personae—the tellingly named Alladin Sane—and in 1974 he'd found, mostly because it was impossible not to find it, cocaine. He'd be awake for days on end. His hours got reversed. He lost weight, once, according to a brilliant David Buckley biography of Bowie titled *Strange Fascination*, dropping to "well under seven stone" (or, less than 100 pounds). By mid-1975, Bowie's coke consumption was, says Buckley, "astronomical." He sat for hours in his LA bedroom, curtains drawn, black candles burning. He lived on a diet of milk and peppers he kept in a fridge. "When I wasn't hallucinating," Bowie recalls, "I was sitting on the floor in the dark, lit by the little light inside the door, cutting up peppers with my knife and cramming them into my mouth. . . . Meal times were between 4AM and 5AM. . . . I got into a lot of emotional and spiritual trouble in LA." At times his personal assistant Coco held a mirror to his sleeping face to make sure he was still breathing. By the end of a week of staying awake, "my whole life," Bowie said, "would be transformed into this bizarre nihilistic fantasy world of oncoming doom, mythological characters, and imminent totalitarianism. . . . I demonized myself and created many psychic wounds that took many years to heal."

In interviews he was clear about the fact that, as he said once, "I was a drug addict." He also began to feel, up to about 1980, that he could not create without using. Cocaine seemed necessary for artistry (an idea he later rejected).

It was during this time that Bowie appeared on the Dick Cavett Show. He sniffed and rubbed his nose. He wore suspenders and a thick plaid tie. He looked emaciated. But most notably, with him he carried a cane he never stopped fondling or visually measuring or tapping or even tracing patterns with on the studio floor as Cavett raised the usual unexciting questions. At one point, Cavett asked if Bowie felt rock stars had "premonitions of doom," why doom "seems to be a theme in their work and in their life?" He did not dismiss the idea. He said, "because they have to be pretty nutty to be doing it in the first place. Very tangled minds. Very messed up people."

On tour in the same period, Bowie performed "Rock and Roll Suicide" as images of Jimi Hendrix, Janis Joplin, and Brian Jones projected, with years and causes of death. "I have a strange death wish thing," he told an interviewer, "but that's because I was so lost in Ziggy [the persona] and the schizophrenia." He's asked if his personae ever became consuming. "I didn't know," Bowie says. "When you are that mixed up, and I've been mixed up man, I mean really, one doesn't know. One half of me is putting a concept forward, and the other half is trying to sort out my own emotions. A lot of my space creations are in fact facets of me, I have now since discovered. I wouldn't even admit that to myself at the time. I would make everything a little up-front personification of how I felt about things. Ziggy, Major Tom, Aladdin Sane, they are all facets of me." He says he got lost in it, not sure if he was writing the characters or the characters were writing him or, finally, "if they were one and the same." It's a minor point, but Bowie had no understanding of these processes in the moment. He wasn't intending to construct self-facets. Insight was retrospective.

Bowie's mention of schizophrenia comes with thick personal history. It's not a casual choice of words. A shocking number of relatives on his mother's side went flagrantly mad. Aunt Una was diagnosed schizophrenic, got shock treatments, and died in her late 30s after stays in mental hospitals. Aunt Vivienne had schizophrenic episodes. Aunt Nora had been lobotomized. His grandmother liked to refer to herself as a "mad-woman." In childhood, Bowie shared a bedroom with older half-brother Terry, with whom he grew close. Among other things, Terry turned Bowie on to music he likely wouldn't have discovered otherwise. But Terry, similar to Bowie's aunts, had mental health challenges. He was gloomy and depressive. Then, after attending a Cream show, he began hallucinating. Buckley describes how Terry "fell to his knees pawing the road; he could see cracks in the tarmac and flames rising up, as if from the underworld." This break with reality led to repeated psychotic experiences, until finally Terry was hospitalized, spending months in confined institutionalization.

Bowie didn't discuss his fear of insanity, a constant during the 1970s, until about 1993. "One puts oneself through such psychological damage in trying to avoid the threat of insanity. You start to approach the very thing that you're scared of. It had tragically afflicted particularly my mother's side of the family. There seemed to be any number of people who had various mental problems and varying states of sanity. There were far too many suicides for my liking—and that was something I was terribly fearful of. I think it really made itself some kind of weight I felt I was carrying. And I felt that I was the lucky one because I was an artist and it would never happen to me. As long as I could put those psychological excesses into my music and into my work, I could always be throwing it off."

Bowie never did go mad. He was spared that fate. But he had his moments, and some moments went on for years. When addicted to coke, he was paranoid, a virtually guaranteed side effect. Obsessed then with ufology, he scanned the skies "for signs of extraterrestrial life," says Buckley, "each flashing, moving object" suggestive of alien invasion. The drug's euphoria got replaced by what Buckley calls "blank pain" and "emotional emptiness." He was unable to feel, "to enter into normal relationships." His characters, too, messed with his mind, as he understood all too clearly. Audiences made little distinction between, say, Ziggy and Bowie, and in time, nor did Bowie himself. His ability to know where he began and where his characters did was tenuous and made more so by the fact that he kept on "playing" the characters offstage. It's not as if Bowie's fear of madness was theoretical. He had his own experiences of unreality and dissociation, some drug-created, some self-created. States of unreality, particularly the dream state, were central to his art.

Madness was Bowie's trauma—or, one of them. It scared him "shitless" when Terry hallucinated; it freaked him out to be part of a family with obvious genetic "taints." So, his fear was both empirically based (he'd seen Terry go psychotic) and future-directed (will I meet the same fate?). It's common to think of trauma as something that happened in the past, some event (thus, "post-traumatic"). But it can involve imagined destinies, too. It's traumatizing to *make the prediction*. (For

Bowie, "One day I shall go mad.") In fact, a staple of anxiety theory/therapy is anxiety's futurity; it lacks immediate aboutness; the feeling is anticipatory—linked to whatever dreadful thing the person *thinks will* happen at some later date, not what *is* happening in the now.

As for Bowie intentionally playing with the thing he feared, the best example is not so much Ziggy, but Aladdin Sane, Ziggy's act two. Bowie was ambitious, he wanted to be a rock star. What he did was invent a rock star character, Ziggy, who, a little miraculously, actually made him famous. The fiction became the reality. Yet day by day, Bowie felt more lost. "I fell for Ziggy too," he says. "It was quite easy to become obsessed day and night with the character. I became Ziggy Stardust, and David Bowie went totally out the window." It was a "real problem," he says. He found it easy to "live within the character," to "blur the lines between reality and the blessed creature I'd created—my doppelganger." He "wasn't getting rid of him." He was "joining forces with him," and starting "on this trail of psychological destruction." Feeling adrift, more fictional than real, as well as simply bored with the alter ego that brought him the fame he craved, Bowie decided, very suddenly, and at the end of a live performance, to kill Ziggy off, to announce Ziggy was over, along with Ziggy's band, The Spiders From Mars.

Yet instead of replacing Ziggy with real David, Bowie veered. He went in the crazy direction. The "Aladdin Sane" record, released in 1973, was a "Ziggy Goes to America" companion piece. Bowie explains: "I kind of knew I had said all that I could say about Ziggy, and what I'd end up doing would be Ziggy Part 2. I thought, well, you know, I'm very tempted to go further with this Ziggy thing only because it's so popular, but actually it's not really what I want to do." Aladdin Sane, then, as record and character, was an "interim measure"—partly more Ziggy, but partly a new, musically "schizoid amalgamation," as David Buckley says. Bowie fixed on how Ziggy made him feel—fragmented—then sculpted a new persona: Ziggy schizophrenic. Ziggy insane.

The cover split Bowie's face in half, painted thunderbolt running diagonally from forehead to eye and cheek. The title track, Bowie said, was inspired by Terry, the original insane lad. Lyrics feature Bowie watching Terry dash away, swinging a dead bouquet. He speaks of the "strange divine," of "saddening glissando strings," of "clutches of sad remains," with a repeated question interspersed: "Who will love Aladdin Sane?" On tour the songs, as *Rolling Stone* described them, dealt with Bowie's "frankly paranoid themes of rock star death, impending planetary doom and up and coming suicide." They were performed as "little theater pieces, playlets acted and recited rather than sung." Costumes changed constantly, as in Kabuki theater, where a "change of kimono meant a change of personality."

Bowie was never comfortable performing. He didn't consider himself a talented singer. And so, as he explained many times, it was easier to be a concept. Ziggy and Aladdin Sane and "Hunger City" characters from a different tour—little Johnny Rottens and Sid Viciouses—freed him up emotionally, allowed him to fashion what he'd always envisioned: an aesthetic beyond conventional rock and roll, a *different kind* of rock and roll, with pantomime, theater, set pieces, costuming. For one tour, the band sat in an orchestra pit; they weren't seen on stage. It was only Bowie, in character.

Bowie did lose himself in these characters. He did cop to feeling unreal and fragmented. So, what about his claim that art spared him his family's fate, that he could "throw off" insanity? It's hard to say. The characters made him *feel* insane. He did not totally lose it, but he was far from stable.

Need for Isolation

Bowie didn't experience major loss, but he was surrounded by madness, worried he might go mad, and traumatized by what he'd seen happen to Terry. There was a more important factor at work, however, one recalling earlier ideas about solitude and loneliness. It's *isolation*—an atmosphere Bowie required to create. It fed him, inspired him, drove him.

Most people avoid the state. It doesn't feel good, it's unnerving. But Bowie needed it. He sought it. "Thematically," he says, "I've always dealt with isolation, in everything I've written, so it's something that triggers me off and always makes me interested in a new project if it has anything to do with alienation or isolation." He wasn't naturally isolated; isolation wasn't a feeling he felt especially prone to. So what he did, he says, was put himself in situations "where I feel isolated just so I can write about it."

People in isolation, Bowie says, "don't receive the world as their own but create a micro-world inside themselves." To him, "it's that peculiar part of the human mind that fascinates me, those small universes that can be created inside the mind, some of them fairly schizophrenic and quite off the wall." He's getting at two things here: madness again, but also fantasy, the creation of inner worlds when outer worlds don't seem to belong to you.

Bowie even "shelters" himself from love "incredibly"—it's the opposite of isolating. It takes time better spent creating. He took himself to LA specifically, "a city I detest," with "people I didn't like very much," in order "to see what happened to my writing." On what first drew him to Berlin, where he recorded two albums, he said: "I like the friction. That's what I look for in any city. West Berlin has the right kind of push. I can't write in a peaceful atmosphere at all. I've nothing to bounce off of. I need the terror."

These thoughts come from an interview Bowie sat for in 1979. But they aren't just time- or situation-specific. Twenty-three years later, he said, "As I get older my questions are fewer, but I ask them, I bark them, more. I've consistently written about the same subjects, nearly 35, nearly 40 years. There's really been no change with me. It's all despondency, despair, fear, isolation."

Feeling isolated is feeling cut off, untethered, out of place, apart. No wonder Bowie imagined star men and space oddities, high above the world, circuits dead. They matched his inner experience. The first song Bowie recorded under his own name, a 1965 tune called "Can't Help Thinking About Me," is isolation lite, a solipsism manifesto. The feelings in the lyrics are shame, guilt, and terror. He's "blackened the family name." His mother "can't stand the neighbors talking." He thinks back on his friends—"always been found and I can't." He wishes he were "secure again." The line "can't help thinking about me" refers to a need, sometimes, to be selfish, to act in your own interests. He decides he will leave them all—friends and family—"in the never never land." He has a ticket in his hand. "Oh, I'm on my own," he realizes. "I've got a long way to go. I hope I make it on my own." He rejects the familiar, he wishes he were sorry (he's not), and he chooses aloneness and isolation over qualified belongingness.

Two things ignited Bowie: fear of madness and alienation. The latter involved fear too, as Bowie sought out living environments that were frightening and difficult to cope with. He may not have *seemed* tortured, but he *tortured himself*, he needed torturous atmospheres. Isolation may have been, for Bowie, a psychological repetition. Buckley refers to the "sub-zero emotional climate" of the household he grew up in, the "austere, non-physical nature of his relationship with his parents," his father's "quizzical, melancholic withdrawal," suggesting that all this "may have left Bowie scarred." In this sense, apartness duplicated childhood experience. What it did was recreate the source of Bowie's first anxieties.

Suffering was at the core of Bowie's artistic endeavors. If he wasn't feeling it, he sought it. No one wants to suffer. Suffering is bad. But Bowie used it. He took it on as a creative problem. He made the suffering beautiful.

Openness

Searching for signs of openness in Bowie is like searching for signs of water in the sea. He had a motto he tossed out now and then: "Do the contrary thing." This itself illustrates the trait—he rarely stood pat, he was a convention-breaker. Even fame bored him. He made it with Ziggy, then "retired" him, out of what one biographer calls "a hunger for musical experimentation" and "a low boredom threshold." Bowie moved; he never stayed put artistically.

Sifting through what biographers, friends, bandmates, and producers/engineers say about Bowie suggests a basic sameness of opinion (or, high interrater reliability). Here's a sampling of characteristic descriptions:

- "supreme mental acquisitiveness"
- "vivid, unusual, imaginative flair for composition" at a young age
- "innate love of the bizarre"
- "stylishly rebellious dresser"
- "a unique, enigmatic, imaginative person"
- "an aesthete, a cerebral outsider"

- "the most talented, magical person"
- "bursting with creativity"
- "on a higher plane, really. He wouldn't be talking about the weather or the latest Who single; he was simply off in his own world"
- "someone who really is an individual talent—who follows his own ideas, takes creative risks"

Bowie understood how drawn he was to rule-breaking. In 1992 he said, "From an early age I was always fascinated by those who transgressed the norm, who defied convention, whether in painting or in music or anything. Those were my heroes—the artists Marcel Duchamp and Salvador Dali and, in rock, Little Richard. . . . It was usually Dada. Yeah, applying Dada, creating these absolutely frightening, extraordinary monsters of rock that nobody could possibly love. . . . I would like to believe that I and a number of others in the early 70s changed the fabric of pop, made it a wider receiver; one that could incorporate ideas from other arts."

He played ukulele, sax, harmonica, guitar, piano; he sang, he wrote, he painted (gallery owners offered exhibitions), he acted; he studied mime and Kabuki theater. He was not much interested in technique. It's not that he undervalued it or thought it unimpressive. It's more that he preferred, in his Dada fashion, the "inharmonious, the right combination of wrong elements." He said, "It's like playing around with colors when you are doing a painting. You're trying to put this pastiche of things together, this juxtaposition."

This tendency—toward cacophony, incongruity—was one Bowie had to curb. It was openness run amok. His first record, *David Bowie*, released in 1967 (on the same day as *Sgt. Pepper's Lonely Hearts Club Band*), was a failure. Reviewers called it "shocking" or, at best, "simply quaint." Biographer Buckley goes further: "the most bizarre record of [Bowie's] entire career," "an all-out attack of the barking mad," "the vinyl equivalent of the madwoman in the attic." Bowie said, "it seemed to have its roots all over the place, in rock and vaudeville and music hall. I didn't know if I was Max Miller [a British comedian] or Elvis Presley." One song in particular, "Please Mr. Gravedigger," constellates the lunacy. In it, Bowie sings/narrates the story of a child-murderer watching a small, fag-puffing gravedigger. He's killed a 10-year-old girl.

He figures the gravedigger knows this, so he contemplates killing the gravedigger too. There is no instrumentation, but bells toll, rain falls, thunder rolls, and twice Bowie sneezes. It's the record's "looniest moment," says Buckley, on "a new plane of daftness."

The next album, from 1969, included the spectacular "Space Oddity," but critics called it "all jumbled up" and "vastly incongruous"—folky, but with ballads and prog rock numbers wedged in, a badly tossed salad. Buckley maintains, probably correctly, that Bowie had "more false starts than any other superstar in pop." This makes sense. He was un–self-limiting. He went in every direction. In fact, between these two records Bowie decided to junk it all and become a dancer. He studied pantomime and danced and sang in shows, dressed "in a huge pink shirt with maroon spots on it, a big maroon and pink ruff and little knee britches in grey with red velvet stripes." There followed multimedia extravaganzas with a trio called Turquoise. This, too, was monumentally weird. Weird, but not uncharacteristic. Bowie took creative risks. He was artistically restless. He pivoted.

It's easy to see Bowie's iterations, his shape-shifting, as rooted in personality, in openness. He was Ziggy, he was Aladdin Sane; he was an avatar of apocalypse for *Diamond Dogs*, a spokesman for "plastic soul" in *Young Americans*, the Thin White Duke, the cool dysthymic for the Berlin Trilogy (the records *Low*, *Heroes*, and *Lodger*); he was even, in some fashion, David Bowie when he desired mainstream pop success on *Let's Dance* in 1983. Those who are high in openness (high O) reinvent, start fresh, throw off the past. Bowie was like Coltrane. As soon as he mastered a style, it stopped interesting him. He wanted fame badly, especially early on; he was hotly ambitious. But it was not the end-all, be-all. He'd set it aside if stirred by new sounds or interests or styles or personifications.

Those who are high O are drawn to the mystical, the strange, the exotic. They believe in astrology and past lives. Bowie was a UFO spotter. He took part in meditation sessions during which, as a friend said, "we hoped the flying saucers would come and take us away." He believed in communicating with other worlds. He insisted one of his houses was haunted.

Then there was the subject, and the lived reality, of sex. Early on, Bowie was described as voraciously heterosexual. Yet he was also a "mod boy" who liked to experiment: "We all suddenly thought, 'Nobody cares! Anything goes!' Those were incredible times." In January 1972, Bowie told *Melody Maker*, "I'm gay and I always have been, even when I was David Jones." Some say he made this statement strategically; that it wasn't entirely true, nor entirely false, since by 1972 Bowie had been with men, though not exclusively. In any case, he also declared "I knew I was bisexual," and the subject seemed closed. At times interviewers revisited this question, asking Bowie if he liked boys or girls. It's one of the few topics that rankled him. He could get testy. It's not clear why. Either he found the line of inquiry intrusive or boring, or he knew, at some level, that his statements about his sexuality were calculated.

It was in 1970—*before* declaring he was gay—that Bowie married his first wife Angie. She's a nerve center in the Bowie story. Bowie called her an "intellectual." Buckley describes her as utterly "out there," into "outrage and bisexuality," her hair shorter and spikier and "punkier" than her husband's. Others in Bowie's circle did not "get" or like her. Gus Dudgeon, Bowie engineer/producer, says, "I thought she was just a typical groupie. I just thought she was really loud and full of crap."

The two were massively promiscuous, their relationship "open." They lived in a Victorian home they christened Haddon Hall, a "sex-and-style laboratory." The "sexcapades" were endless. Ultimately, in a nifty turn of phrase, Bowie came to regard himself as "try-sexual," meaning he'd "have a go at anything." This was a limitlessly experimental pansexuality. Part of it had to do with the "erotic appeal of transgression," Bowie's "sexual tourism," which called out sanctimonies. Sex, then, expressed desires for disorientation more than biological or psychological needs. Its roots were adventurousness, a need for experience, an attraction to the bizarre, a devotion to nonconformity—all elements of the openness dimension. Biographer Buckley offers this summary, a testimonial to Bowie's high O tendencies: "He was a pop art provocateur. What really fired him was the desire to be different, radically different, to challenge and overturn both the dominant musical conventions and the moral and sexual codes of his day."

Creative Process

Bowie was committed to the irrational, nonlinear, nonliteral, and unconscious. He believed in the usefulness, the *necessity* of system 1 thinking.

He had confidence in his ability ("I was absolutely convinced that I could write anything as good as anybody else"), he was the opposite of lazy ("I work, all the time")—but to come up with something new and fresh in the moment of creating, he cultivated surrender, he found ways of opening up the strange and unexpected.

One of these ways had to do with simulated surprise. "I understand that very well," Bowie said. "And it is terribly important for me. . . . It's absolutely essential that I get surprised and excited by what I'm doing, even if it's just me. To allow the accidental to take place is often very good. So I trick myself into things like that." He gave an example of beginning with five or six chords, then disciplining himself to write a song with no others. It's a sort of "dogma," he says, that subtracts his "sense of emotional self." Out of the blue, an F-sharp emerges. It breaks through "accidentally." So first, Bowie said, "define the rules, but then take [things] as far as you can with that little rule, then break it."

Bowie admired the writer William Burroughs, whom he knew personally. He borrowed from Burroughs the "cut-up" technique: taking sets of words and plucking them out of context, then combining them more or less randomly. In the BBC film *Cracked Actor*—a bizarre masterpiece of an intro to Bowie, roughly 1 hour long and available to watch on YouTube.com—Bowie shows how he does it. On a table in front of him lie a number of printed-out lines of words forming coherent sentences. With scissors, Bowie snips them into fragments, then reassembles them, rearranges them. He calls the technique a "Western Tarot." He says he used cut-up with his diaries and it told him quite a bit about the future and the past. In most instances, he says, he found it "ignited" his imagination, taking his mind to places he hadn't expected. By 1994, scissors got replaced by the computer. Bowie had a program devised "so that I could specifically . . . hit the cut-up button and slice it up." Most of the lyric content of the *Outside* album (2003) actually "came out of that program," said Bowie. "There are a lot of poets who still work in that method, so I'm not alone."

Bowie also tried accessing dreams, or what he called "the dream-state," a generator of imagery. "I try to work my way into those crevices of the mind that are generally blocked by rationality, by figurative or linear thought. . . . It's about breaking that down." His belief was that our "system of living" had become so fragmented that it's "only by mirroring that fragmentation that we can get a sense of what's really going on, even if it's an unconscious understanding." In fact, so much of our understanding, Bowie says, proceeds "at an unconscious level." "I think, pretty assuredly, that's what our dreams throw up at us: a sort of metaphysical mirroring of these daily events through strange, surreal images."

He said he was very seriously affected by his dreams. He found the dream state "potent." He saw similarly powerful juxtapositions in art, too—Dali, he says, and De Chirico. "That's how I want to write," he decided. "How do you work like that?" Cut-ups were part of this evolution, but originally it was the dream-state Bowie saw as most "magnetic." "It just captured everything for me."

Two particular Bowie songs erupted out of surreally generated experience. One was "Space Oddity," his first hit. It arrived spontaneously. He had gone "stoned out of my mind" to see the film *Space Odyssey*, feeling entirely "freaked out." From this the song came—a finished entity. A bandmate said, "Most musicians make songs with a structure that has been used before. His songs have a structure that he dreams up for himself." In this case it's true: "Space Oddity" lacks a chorus, it lacks a middle eight. It wasn't even songlike. It floated, just like Major Tom.

A second example is the 1971 "Oh! You Pretty Things." The song had lodged itself in Bowie's mind. Again, it appeared fully formed. He said, "I woke up at 4 AM, had this song going in my head, and I had to get it out of my head, work it out on the piano and get it out of my head." His writing was becoming more inspired, less planned. He had bypassed the critical part of his consciousness.

This bypassing also directed Bowie's work with collaborators. He was drawn to people with similar mindsets, for instance Brian Eno, who discovered ambient music in a way Bowie would have applauded: accidentally. Eno was laid up in bed after being hit by a car. Music played on a malfunctioning speaker, the sound muffled and almost inaudible. Eno resisted getting up. He decided not to fix the system, then realized "this peripheral music was providing a background ambience and mood that he liked very much." In a moment, a musical language was born, sound as noise, disconnected from any maker of it.

Eno produced three albums with Bowie, *Low*, *Heroes*, and *Lodger*, the so-called "Berlin Trilogy" (though the last record was recorded in Switzerland). Personally, Bowie and Eno were opposites. As Buckley explains, Eno aimed to "eliminate himself from his work," to disappear as author, to "minimize his degree of participation" and to "cleanse his art of the idea of the individual artist." The music was to "play itself."

Eno organized Bowie's process by way of "oblique strategic cards." Every card voiced a directive geared toward eliminating blocks: "Listen to the quiet voice," "Use an unacceptable color," "Emphasize the flaws," "Honor thy error as hidden intention." Bowie says Eno got him off narration, with which he had grown "intolerably bored." In its place, the two planned accidents and reacted. Mistakes, chance, juxtaposition, and randomness were woven into the enterprise.

There are several examples of how this worked in practice. Bowie would write songs in first and third person, then "randomize the perspective." At one point, the last of the three records, *Lodger*, was set to be titled *Planned Accidents*. Guitarist Adrian Belew, who took his time getting used to the card conceit, said, "What they wanted to do was elicit accidental responses from me. They said to me, 'We're not going to let you hear the songs first. You won't have any idea of what the chords are, or what the tempo is, or anything. You're just going to hear the count-off in your headphones and then you start playing something.'" By the third go-round, he said, he'd begin to find some focus. The best bits of what he came up with would be edited together. One tune, "Boys Keep Swinging," came across as excessively polished. It didn't sound like what Bowie had in mind: "young kids in the basement just discovering their instruments." Eno pulled a card that said, "Change instrument roles," so that's what they did. As another example, the song "Broken Glass," a short, unfinished fragment, seemed in need of editing. Eno said no: "Leave it abnormal, leave it strange, don't normalize it. . . . Why fix it? It's not broken."

I'm not saying art is all system 1. We've already talked about wrongheaded "right brain" fixations. There's always revision and shaping, careful, system 2 arranging of elements, or Roth's moving sentences around. In Bowie's case, there was constant involvement of band members, too, who in several instances took a riff and transformed it. But with accident, surprise, cut-ups, dreams, and "oblique strategies," Bowie manipulated *inception*, the discovery phase of creativity. For him, things worked best when rationality exited. He devised ways of scripting chaos, of breaking into a boundarylessness that threw out content more found than made. At the origin, it's more about losing control, or relinquishing, finding ways to listen that are goalless and directionless, unattached to outcome. You take what you put yourself in position to find, then you go with it. It's not "sitting down and deciding to write a song." It's about being seized, being struck, randomly or unexpectedly, then following impulses that start out formless, as with "Space Oddity."

Frida Kahlo

An Originating Trauma

What the Mexican painter Frida Kahlo understood more than most people alive or dead was suffering. Her life was pain, both physical and psychological. Her work, her art, depicted those states—the anguish there for all to see. She was alive by chance, and her body never let her forget it. In Mexico she's known as "la heroina del dolor"—the heroine of pain.

From her early teenage years, before she'd had too much of it, Kahlo adored suffering. This love affair began with a diagnosis of polio at age 6 or 7. Her peers called her "peg leg." Looking back on those days, Kahlo said, "My mama and papa began to spoil me a lot and love me more," on account of her infirmity. For the rest of her life, some contend, she "would associate pain with love." She elevated misery. She made it part of her, a central part, and perhaps "used illness to extract from others the attention she so desperately craved," according to *Vanity Fair's* Amy Fine Collins. In love with a boy named Alejandro who was several classes ahead of her in school—a mentor and a boyfriend—and beset with what her gifted biographer Hayden Herrera calls a "compulsion to tell about her feelings," Kahlo wrote letter after letter (still, amazingly, in Alejandro's possession). If these letters have any theme—apart from an obvious neediness and fear of love loss, combined with candor and bluntness—it's suffering. Suffering is what Kahlo wants to get across. "We came into the world to suffer," she writes. "I have felt in my soul this pain," she says. "How much I would like to explain my suffering to you," she declares. Then: "No one can ever imagine how much I have suffered." The nature of the suffering is not laid out in the letters her biographer reproduces. It's also not clear if she's dramatizing for effect. Still, the focus is undeniable. Kahlo's sense of self was entwined with an inner experience of pain.

Then came a catastrophic outer confirmation. When Kahlo was 17 (the date was September 17, 1925), a bus she was on collided with a streetcar. On impact, in Kahlo's words, "a handrail pierced me the way a sword pierces a bull." The steel pole entered her body at the abdomen and exited through her vagina. Kahlo said, "I lost my virginity." As the vehicles came to rest, Kahlo was nude—it's not clear why. A painter on the bus carried with him a packet of powdered gold, and Kahlo was covered with it: sparkling and bloody. The list of injuries whose effects would linger to the day Kahlo died is long. Spinal column broken in three places. Collarbone broken. Two ribs broken. Eleven fractures in the right leg. Right foot crushed. Pelvis broken in three places.

During a very long hospital recovery Kahlo saw death "dancing around my bed." The realization of the necessity of suffering returned: "I am beginning to grow accustomed to suffering. One has to put up with it." To "suffer a little," she decided, "always serves a purpose."

The effort to paint, which Kahlo says she made "without paying much attention" at all, was listless. She felt no burning desire to do it. But "ever since I was a little girl," Kahlo recalls, "I had been casting an eye in the direction of the box of colors. I could not explain why." After the accident she was bored, bedridden in a plaster cast. So, she pilfered oil paints from her father. Her intention, as she explained it at the time, was that "this misfortune did not take on the character of a tragedy." She chose life (she could have done otherwise), and slowly and lazily she chose art, too, as a way to both show and "hide the disquiet within."

Her first of dozens of self-portraits was made in 1926. She was dangerously ill at the time, out of hospital but confined to home. Alejandro was trying to break things off. As a "visual entreaty," a plea not to leave her, Kahlo made him a painting that Herrera calls an "alternate self." It's a minor moment in the history of her art, but telling: an effort to avert loss. It was not done for its own sake. Its aims were instrumental.

Apart from herself, always her art's number one focus, Kahlo was drawn to the idea of painting her accident, assembling a visual record. She couldn't bring it off. It was a subject too "complicated" and too "important," maybe also too literal, too real. She finally managed one undated, rough drawing, but that's it. Still, she committed to "making painful feelings known" as a form of "psychological surgery." She didn't paint the accident itself, but its aftermath, its residues. "The accident changed my path," Kahlo said. "So nothing seemed more normal than to paint what had not been fulfilled"—a life and body arrested, an existence filled with nonstop pain. As her husband, Diego Rivera, remarked, "Never before had a woman put such agonized poetry on canvas."

More "bloody and terrifying" self-portraits followed, as Kahlo sought to "tease and laugh at death so that it won't get the better of me." She experimented with technique—painting on tin, trying out frescoes. Biographer Zamora sees a change in content, too: Now more than ever, "her work was beginning to emphasize terror, suffering, wounds, and pain."

In 1932 her mother died, so she painted "My Birth," in which an infant Frida emerges large-headed from her mother's legs—which form a perfect letter "M"—blood pooling on the sheets. *Vanity Fair* called the work "painfully obstetric"—according to Lucienne Bloch, Kahlo's close friend, "she loved her father very much but she did not have the same feelings for her mother." Kahlo said the painting was a self-birth. In fact, it looks like murder—Kahlo kills her mother in the act of coming to life.

On July 4, 1932, Kahlo had a miscarriage and she lost enormous clots of blood. She was with Rivera in Detroit (where he had commissions to paint frescoes), so friends rushed her to Henry Ford Hospital, "bleeding and weeping." Kahlo was hospitalized for 13 days. She begged her doctor for medical books, insisted on drawing her lost infant, seeing him as he would have appeared. Rivera told the physician, "You aren't dealing with an average person. Frida will do something with it. She will do an artwork." First she tried a pencil study of a male fetus. This led to the painting "Henry Ford Hospital (The Flying Bed)." In it, Kahlo lies naked on white sheets, in a pool of flowering blood, a single tear at her cheek. Six red threads Kahlo holds in her left hand are tied loosely to six hovering objects, one a fetus as large as Kahlo herself. Factories of the industrial city frame the horizon. The words "Henry Ford Hospital" are inscribed along the bedframe.

The painting makes use of symbols. But, as Kahlo's biographer insists, "when Frida paints a stabbed naked woman, or her own stabbed flesh [or in this instance, her bleeding naked body exposed on white sheets], it is not an anonymous image of pain, nor a Freudian symbol. . . . It is not make-believe; she is reporting on her own physical condition. . . . It was a way," Herrera argues, "of coming to terms with reality, not of passing beyond reality." Kahlo seems to agree: "I do not believe in illusion, the great vacillator. . . . My painting carries within it the message of pain."

"A Few Small Nips" is another example. This 1935 painting has twin origins. Kahlo read a news account of a woman stabbed by her drunken lover. He cut her 20 times, then explained to the court, "But I only gave her a few small nips." In the moment, Kahlo's sympathy for the victim would have been strong. She felt "murdered by life." She meant this generally, but there were specifics, too—Rivera had begun an affair with Kahlo's sister, Cristina. Critics see the painting as suffering projected. She transferred her agony onto the woman in the story.

The work is a bloodbath, a female figure naked on a bed, a man standing above, knife in hand, his shirt stained red. He cuts without emotion. There is no struggle; what's shown is the aftermath. The woman's eyes are closed. She wears one shoe and leans to her right. Blood drips from her body onto the floor. Above the scene a banner records what the man said to the court—"A few small nips." (Preliminary sketches feature a different inscription, "My sweetie doesn't love me anymore," a reference to Rivera.) As Kahlo painted, she continuously added blood. She made the frame blood red too, painting on it blood-colored smudges like handprints or fingerprints. Photos of the work in Kahlo's studio show that she hung a bird cage to the left of the composition, its door ajar. A real knife is stabbed into the middle top of the frame.

What Kahlo did was seize on a story that captured the feeling of being cheated on. It wasn't, this time, a repetition of something that happened to her, as with "Henry Ford Hospital" or the 1944 "The Broken Column"—painted after spinal surgery, and showing a vertical metal bar splitting her peeled torso. Instead, she finds an event mirroring the intensity of her suffering and paints it as autobiography. Rivera took many lovers; he was massively promiscuous. Kahlo did, too, to even the scales, or else, as Bowie did, to express sexual amorality. In this case, the betrayal was squared—the girl was Frida's sister. Kahlo responded by moving out, renting an apartment in Mexico City, taking off for New York with friends, cutting her hair, and wearing American clothes, all "a reaction to Diego's affair with Cristina," according to photographer friend Lucienne Bloch. Eventually she returned to Mexico, forgave her sister, and reconciled with Rivera, concluding, on the subject of his infidelities, "I cannot love him for what he is not."

Another example of Kahlo making use of real-world events is the bizarre and weirdly provenanced "The Suicide of Dorothy Hale." Hale was a Ziegfeld girl of extraordinary beauty but, according to friend Clare Boothe Luce, "very little talent and no luck." Like Kahlo, she had numerous affairs; she was also dependent on men, whose largesse she profited from. Her husband died when his car went over a cliff. She tried finding work as an actress, but her screen tests were failures (confirming Luce's judgment). Adrift and hopeless, Hale staged a "farewell party," telling friends she planned "a long trip." Around 1:15 AM she exited the festivities, returned to her apartment, typed out goodbye notes, then threw herself out the window in a black velvet dress. Kahlo's link to the event was through Luce, whose idea it was to memorialize Hale with a stately, sanitized portrait. Kahlo took the commission. At the time, she was contemplating suicide, too—it was 1938, and she'd separated from Rivera (in 1939, he would ask for a divorce).

The painting shows three stages of the dying: Hale leaping, falling, and lying lifeless below dove-like clouds extending into the frame. Hale is splayed on her side at the bottom of the picture, her eyes open, blood spreading from her head and soaking into the bottom third of the frame, which is painted red. An inscription records the details of what occurred, concluding with, "this retablo was executed by Frida

Kahlo." Also included was the statement, "Mrs. Clare Boothe Luce commissioned."

When Luce received the work she was mortified. It's worth quoting her response. "Among Dorothy's many ardent admirers were Constantin Alajalov, a well-known *New Yorker* cover artist, and Isamu Noguchi, the sculptor. I don't remember which one I telephoned, asking him to come to see me on an urgent matter about Dorothy. In any event, I told whichever one arrived that I was going to destroy the painting with a pair of library scissors, and I wanted a witness to this act. In the end, however, I agreed not to destroy the painting, if the banner proclaiming I had commissioned it could be scrubbed off, and painted over. So Dorothy's admirer took the painting away and wiped out the offensive legend."

Some say the painting reflects Kahlo's "compassion for women who are driven to despair by male desertion." Herrera connects the work to "A Few Small Nips." Both "besmirch the painting's frame" with illusionistically painted blood. Also, "in her two most terrifying images of women's violent deaths—both of them, significantly, painted during periods when Diego was causing her great pain—Frida felt compelled to extend the painting's space out into the real space of the spectator, bringing the horror of the subject home." To Herrera, the subject of the work is loneliness or despair. The space in which Hale lies lifeless is "bleak," "unreal," and "anonymous"—not a city street, nor the sidewalk in front of Hale's residence.

In a short 1999 essay that's mainly descriptive and distressingly light on argument, psychotherapist Gail Carr Feldman tries making sense of Kahlo's art psychologically. It's Feldman's belief that "when Kahlo painted . . . she dissociated from her pain and from the limitations her wounds imposed." The opposite seems more likely. Kahlo lived suffering. She painted of pain while in pain. She reworked stories that described it. Her art wasn't some sort of escape, it wasn't a blindfold. She didn't do it to know less about what was inside her. It was immersion, a visual record of experience.

Others see Kahlo as a symbolist, intent on subverting or distorting reality. That also seems off the mark. She says she painted whatever was in her head, without thought or consideration. Reality is what she was wanted to come to terms with. Taking the paintings at their word, this reality was bloody, injury-obsessed, beset by uncertainties about who she was and how she appeared to the world. These were her subjects, and as she explained, "my work consisted of eliminating everything that did not come from the internal lyrical motives that impelled me to paint." Each painting, she said, "is treated as a separate self-confrontation."

Openness

To start with the obvious, Kahlo was creative, her creative accomplishments numerous. It's good to remember, now and then, where we started. Openness is the artist type, and it predicts, in every single scientific study I know of, creativity and creative achievement.

Kahlo also had wide sets of feelings, another O facet. She didn't suppress emotion. Typically, she was droll, sarcastic, saucy, a jokester and a prankster, but she could also be sad, angry, fearful, vain, needy, and—especially toward the end of her life when the pain and the surgeries left her demoralized—suicidal. One crisis followed the amputation of her leg, which Herrera calls "a terrible offense to Frida's aesthetic sensibility, her sense of integrity, and her self-esteem." After surgery she was depressed. Rivera notes, strangely, "She no longer even wanted to hear me tell her of my love affairs." A doctor said friends should force her to paint. Later, a psychiatrist advised, "Don't force her to do anything. She doesn't want to live. We are forcing her to live." Openness correlates with depression. It predicts more positive (joy) and negative (sadness) states.

Kahlo was easily bored, too, with a quick unconventional mind and a "dramatic urge to discover life." Her need for experience was intense. One way this expressed itself was sexually. A friend says, "there is no question that she had strong sexual needs." Her motto, according to the same friend, was "make love, take a bath, make love again." Especially telling is the fact that she had no shame. There was no repression (another O correlate). She philandered, as did Rivera; she seemed to have been "try-sexual"—just like Bowie. Her affairs, which she made little effort to conceal, are legendary. Rivera brought Marxist Leon Trotsky to Mexico in 1937—Kahlo had sex with him, then seduced his female secretary. She met surrealist André Breton, then had sex with his wife. Other partners included photographer Nickolas Murray, sculptor Isamu Noguchi, and (some say) Georgia O'Keefe. Herrera sees Kahlo's "powerful sexual appetite" radiating "from the surfaces of all her paintings," and finds a "self-fascinated autoeroticism" even in "her display of wounds." That may be. The fact is that Kahlo was sexually adventurous and unapologetic about it. Sex was another way, maybe the best way, to gather experience. There were no limits on it. She took lovers when she wanted to.

Kahlo's imagination was set high early on. The polio confined her to her room for 9 months. Her response was to invent an "intense" imaginary friend. With a finger she drew a door in her room and "went out in my imagination . . . into the interior of the earth where my imaginary friend was always waiting for me." She told the "friend" her secret problems as the girl danced. Looking back after 34 years, Kahlo says the "magic friendship" revived and became "larger and larger inside of my world." By age 14 she was rarely without her trademark knapsack, a "little world" on her back filled with texts, notebooks, drawings, butterflies, dried flowers, and "books in Gothic script."

As an adult, Kahlo's dress was a "ceremonial affair," says Zamora. It was always changing, always meticulously planned out, from clothing to hair to jewelry. Her goal was to compose herself in a way that "ridiculed conventionality." She adored dime stores where, a friend says, "she'd find cheap costume jewelry and make it look fantastic."

Kahlo had a great difficulty doing things regularly, friends observed. She was devilish, mischievous, irreverent. She "worshipped nonsense." Anything pompous or average or hifalutin she detested and mocked. As a child she petitioned directors to fire teachers she felt to be mediocre or uninspiring. She hated official organized talks and "found abstract political theory wearisome"—though, like those who are high O, her political beliefs were radical. "Artistes" she found revolting. She saw them "wasting their time on stupid gossip and intellectual discussions. . . . There is something so false and unreal about them." It's not that Kahlo had no interest in ideas—she did. What annoyed her was the habit of wasting time talking abstractly and getting nothing done.

Critic Nicolas Calas saw Kahlo as "the surrealist ideal of woman. She had a great theatrical quality, a high eccentricity. . . . Her exoticism immediately attracted attention." Art dealer Julien Levy called her "a mythical creature, not of this world."

So, whether because of her need for experience, her sexual adventurousness, her lack of repression, her imaginativeness, her radical beliefs, her unconventionality, her range of feeling, her high boredom susceptibility, her sensation-seeking—Kahlo fits the definition of an open personality. These tendencies enhanced her art and complicated her life. Her personality is a perplexing combination of startling strength and pathetic weakness. Her "worshipful hordes" of "idol seekers"—as *Vanity Fair* describes them—tend to focus on the former and deny the latter.

Creative Process

On this subject Kahlo was less specific than Bowie, and less deliberate about creating auspicious conditions. She was lazy, too, as she said many times, whereas Bowie was ambitious and creatively tireless. She didn't think as a careerist would; she never pushed for exhibitions. Herrera says she pretended she merely "played at" art, quietly "making tiny private paintings."

Her words on the occasion of one of her first shows in 1938 are revealing: "I have painted about 12 paintings, all small and unimportant, with the same personal subjects that only appeal to myself . . . 4 or 5 people told me they were swell, the rest think they are too crazy. . . . I am lazy and I paint very little."

There's no trace of self-importance; there's the sense that the work is so personal that few could hope to appreciate or understand it. At this point she regarded herself as a hobbyist—especially compared to the far more lionized Rivera—the work a trifling indulgence.

The surrealists adored Kahlo. They set about absorbing her as one of their own. But as with any attempt at categorization, she was ambivalent, the opposite of a joiner. When André Breton discovered her in Mexico in 1938, her called the work "pure surreality," a "spontaneous outpouring," following "irrational laws" and "subjective signals." He compared it to a "ribbon around a bomb." Kahlo was unimpressed. She found Breton insufferable. "I never knew I was a surrealist until

Breton came to Mexico and told me. . . . I myself don't know what I am. . . . The only thing I know is that I paint because I need to." She added, "I'd rather sit on the floor in the market of Toluca and sell tortillas, than to have anything to do with those 'artistic' bitches of Paris. . . . None of them work and they live as parasites of the bunch of rich bitches who admire their 'genius.' . . Shit and only shit is what they are."

Her sense of what she was really up to was simple. She said she adored "surprise and the unexpected." "I like to go beyond realism. For this reason, I would like to see lions come out of a bookshelf and not books. My paintings naturally reflect these predilections and also my state of mind." In a Guggenheim application from 1940, she says she works with "the spontaneous impulse of my feeling. I have never followed any school or anyone's influence."

What compelled Kahlo were those "internal lyrical motives." Anything unconnected to them she pushed aside. The art expressed feelings that passed through her head. There were no additional considerations, nothing unnecessary added. Bowie invented techniques to release the uncanny, or mined his dreams, or put himself in situations he hoped would force creative responses. Kahlo was less calculating, less intentional. Whether her mind was organized in such a way that manipulations like Bowie's were needless, or whether she simply thought about her process less, is hard to say. But the two of them valued the same things: spontaneity, surprise, inner vision, bizarreness, and the unexpected. Neither were followers of schools or styles. As Kahlo wrote in the same Guggenheim letter, "I have been able to find, without being forced by any prejudice, a personal expression in painting. . . . My subjects have always been my sensations, my states of mind, and the profound reactions that life has been producing in me." She "objectified" all this in "figures of herself." To her, this seemed to be "the most sincere and real thing that I could do in order to express what I felt inside." It's striking how simple and plain Kahlo's sense of her work is. To the end, she side-stepped bullshit. Herrera calls her application a "model of modesty." She suggests Kahlo might have done better to "sound more complex and self-important" (she did not get the fellowship). But if Kahlo had done so, she wouldn't have been Kahlo. It would have been a lie.

Taking Stock

First is the matter of unconventionality. Bowie and Kahlo were rule-breakers. They defied norms. They had a distaste for categories. What they followed, if they followed anything, were inner stirrings, inner aesthetic instincts. On one hand, this is simply more openness—being "anti," risky, untethered. It's also low conscientiousness, another creativity correlate. High C people need rules, they need structure. Uncertainty, no clear plan, no boundaries—all these make them uneasy.

We've talked about an antisocial posture in artists, the need for solitude, for aloneness. Bowie knew he needed this, he knew it triggered him. He isolated himself on purpose. He liked the feeling. The feeling inspired him. With Kahlo, isolation was forced, first because of her polio, then because of her injuries and surgeries. She was alone a lot, and it was the aloneness that got her going.

Both also twisted art out of pain, made stories of it, not by avoiding the pain, or disguising it, but by going straight into it, playing with it, reimagining it, riding the wave of it. For Bowie it was madness, for Kahlo it was injury, the fact of suffering. There is a sense in which openness is required for artists but trauma isn't. You work from experience, especially strong, forceful, jarring experience, experience that leaves impressions, and if trauma is there, and if it's potent, it rises to the top as something to be narrated, storied-up, kneaded. It's a mistake to think of art as automatically therapeutic (for the artist making it). I don't believe in that idea. And as I said before, most artists I've talked to don't believe in it either. One person who's weighed in directly on this question is the writer Alice Sebold, whose books include *The Lovely Bones* and *Lucky*. As a young woman she suffered a brutal rape and beating. *Fresh Air's* Terry Gross asked her if writing "helped the pain of trauma recede." Sebold says: "My feeling—and it's pretty rigorous—is that therapy is for therapy and that writing can be therapeutic, but therapeutic writing should not be published. My job as a writer is to go through the therapy myself. . . . But I don't write novels and seek to have them published so that I can get therapy from having written them. That's really the responsibility of an individual to do outside the context of the published work."

It's not necessary, and usually not accurate, to think of art as an escape or unintended cure. It's repetition, in thin or thick symbolic terms, of uniquely important experiences. Oscar Wilde said there is no moral or immoral art. Art is good or bad, that's all. It's a solid motto. Bowie and Kahlo didn't make art to get over something. In fact, for Bowie, all the playing around with madness got him into psychological trouble. They did it to express what was in them. They did it because they had the power to do it.

We took a deep dive and fit the model to these two cases. No theory's perfect, but the match was a good one, from personality, to process, to shaping and forming. To this point the inside has been our focus, the mind and its products. There's an outside factor too, also supported by science, one the artist does not control. It's reacted to, but it's not brought into being. That's our topic in Chapter 6: a chance element that mobilizes creative replies.

6
The Unhappiness Muse

Edvard Munch. Salvador Dali. Elvis Presley. Vincent Van Gogh. Jack Kerouac. Sylvia Plath. Roald Dahl. William Styron. John Lennon. Paul McCartney. "Peter Pan" author J. M. Barrie. Barbra Streisand.

All these people I discuss in a class I teach on the mind of the artist. The list looks like a random assortment of eminences from a range of media (that, or a hugely entertaining fantasy cocktail party). Streisand and Dali? Plath and Dahl?

The fact is, something agonizing joins them all together, a red thread with, in some cases, bizarre permutations. All experienced early loss, a death in the family. Munch's mother and sister both died by the time he turned 13. Dali was the second Salvador Dali—a brother of the same name died when he was 3. Elvis lost a twin, who was to be called Jesse. Van Gogh's brother, also named Vincent, died *exactly 1 year* before the artist's birth; Kerouac's brother, Gerard, when Jack was 4. Plath lost her father Otto when she was 8, Dahl a father and sister, Styron his mother at 12, Lennon his mother at 16, McCartney his mother to cancer, and Barrie a brother named David. Streisand's father died suddenly when she was 15 months old. And "who knows," she wonders, "if that didn't make me extra sensitive to what I need as an actress or a singer or a director."

It's a very small sample, but these life history similarities get one thinking. Are they random? Startling but meaningless? Or, are they possibly significant emotionally and psychologically and, most to the point, *creatively*?

Elvis was told by his mother Gladys that he was living two lives, a twinless twin. Kerouac's brother Gerard was regarded as saintly—nuns sat by his death bed to scribble down last words. Dali was ushered to his brother's grave and informed he was a reincarnation. Van Gogh was also a sort of double—a reality made all the more stunning by the fact of his birth, a death anniversary. When Barrie's brother David died, his

The Mind of the Artist. William Todd Schultz, Oxford University Press. © Oxford University Press 2022.
DOI: 10.1093/oso/9780197611098.003.0007

mother went into a tailspin. Barrie did what he could to derail her grief, but there were times he entered her gloomy room only to be asked, "Is that you, David?"

These five artists lived in terminal shadow. Their lives were death-haunted. Dali went on to paint his brother, directly and obliquely. Kerouac wrote a book about Gerard, and features him in several novels. Some say Peter Pan was a David-driven character—ageless (as those who die young are), appearing at windows like an angel. Beyond these examples, Lennon, of course, wrote "Julia" about his mother of the same name, as well as the very dark dirge "My Mummy's Dead." As for Plath, there was the poem "Daddy," along with others zeroing in on her father's death, including that group of poems referred to as the "Bee Sequence."

Loss has been noted in the lives of artists for decades. It comes in the form of death; it comes in other ways, too. Certain artists, like Styron and Kerouac (also Virginia Woolf, who lost her mother when she was 13), see it as key to their creativity. Others are only vaguely aware of the effects it has. They don't discuss it, they don't link it up with their fictions, or like Styron, they connect the dots years later.

Frequency of *parental death*, especially, in the lives of eminent persons is accepted scientific fact. The classic study was by Eisenstadt in 1978. He combed through 1963 *Encyclopedia Britannica* listings, defining eminence as a function of text allotted to persons described: one-half page or more equaled eminence, in Eisenstadt's formulation. This yielded 699 individuals (mostly men), from Homer to JFK. Close to half the sample were writers. What Eisenstadt found was this: by age 10, 25% had one parent dead; by age 15, 35%; by age 25, 52%. These figures double loss rates found at comparable ages in the general population. In simple terms, *if you achieve at an exceptionally high level, you are twice as likely to have experienced parental loss.*

Other studies narrowed eminence to look more closely at types of achievement. One focused on distinguished writers, a whopping 55% of whom lost a parent before the age of 15.

So, the question isn't about loss frequency—that's been established. More interesting is the matter of *why*. What is it about loss that mobilizes creativity? What's the nature of the correlation? Does loss propel art?

To be clear, not every artist experiences loss. It's common, but hardly universal. Also, loss comes in different shadings. Death of a parent may be especially traumatic, but there's sibling loss too (as with Van Gogh, Munch, Kerouac, Elvis, and Dali), loss via abandonment (Capote), and loss of physical well-being (Borges). On one end of the spectrum lies the loss of a brother of the same name, precisely 1 year before your birth; on the other, loss of a grandmother you barely knew. Loss suggests trauma, but that's not guaranteed.

Loss and Writer William Styron

Styron wrote what may be the most powerful memoir ever on the subject of depression, *Darkness Visible*. He describes his descent into madness with painful specificity—the "dank joylessness" of it, the "torpid indifference," "palpable qualities of ominousness," the feeling of thought processes "engulfed by a toxic and unnameable tide." Along the way he begins thinking-through potential causes. Was it chemical, just bad luck? Was it genetic? He mulls over alternatives, and settles on a prospect more external, more significant, and more central to his art: "incomplete mourning" of his mother's death. "This disorder and early sorrow," Styron explains, "the death or disappearance of a parent, especially a mother, before or during puberty, appears repeatedly in the literature on depression as a trauma likely to create nearly irreparable emotional havoc." He says that, before his illness, he never gave much thought to the role of the "subconscious," leaving the subject to "literary detectives." But he came to see how loss and depression "had clung close to the outer edges of my life for many years." He reread sections of novels, his heroines lurching down pathways of doom. "I was stunned to perceive how accurately I had created the landscape of depression in the minds of these young women, describing with what could only be instinct, out of a subconscious already roiled . . . the psychic imbalance that led them to destruction."

Literary detectives agreed. An obsession with lost or unobtainable women ran through Styron's corpus, they said, from *Lie Down in Darkness* to *Sophie's Choice*. "When art failed to ease permanently the trauma of loss, darkness fell on Styron and nearly forced him to suicide," according to Freudian psychotherapist Wanamaker. Styron reached the same conclusion. His art, he felt, was a refinding, "an imaginative reshaping of real events linked by a chain of memories." Wanamaker says loss made Styron into an artist, by which she means "someone who 'masters' his experience in such a way that it is defensively recast and projected onto some external form, whether novel or poem, painting or music."

Loss and Writer Jorge Luis Borges

A different case is the genre-spanning writer Borges. He was born with a malformation of the eyes; it caused impaired vision from birth, then deteriorated to the point where, by age 55, he could no longer read or write. These paired losses were crushing—of the capacity to write and also, to the same degree, of the ability to read. As a child Borges consumed voraciously his father's English language library. Reading was a way of life. He made this observation: "If I were asked to name the chief event of my life, I should say my father's library. In fact, I sometimes think I have never strayed outside of that library." For Borges, no longer being able to read or write would be on par with Leonardo no longer being able to paint, or Aretha Franklin no longer being able to sing. A gigantic blow to everything he felt he was. A loss of self-definition.

So how did he respond? By "writing" about not being able to write. He dictated verbally to scribes. This limited him to shorter prose poems "of a far less tightly woven structure than those of the earlier fictions, and to poetry of metrical verse as opposed to the earlier free verse," in the words of analyst Thomas Ogden.

Borges said that "every poem in time becomes an elegy," so he built loss into his aesthetic. The particular loss of vision gets its fullest treatment in the prose piece "Borges and I," composed in 1957, 2 years after blindness set in. It's written from the perspective of his former sighted self, who calls "Borges" the "one things happen to." The prior self knows of Borges—the blind one—"from the mail," and it "[sees] his name on a list of professors or in a biographical dictionary." The old sighted Borges catalogues its likes: hourglasses, maps, 18th-century typography. It concludes that blind "Borges" likes the same things, "but in a vain way that turns them into the attributes of an actor." In other words, blind Borges is a faker. He can't like those things in the same way because he can't see. What he likes is the memory of what he once experienced.

Sighted Borges notes the relationship is not hostile. It goes on living so that blind Borges "may contrive his literature," despite the fact that "those pages cannot save me, perhaps because what is good belongs to no one, not even to him." "I am destined to perish," says sighted Borges, "definitively, and only some instant of myself can survive in him. . . . Thus my life is a flight and I lose everything and everything belongs to oblivion, or to him." The final line goes meta: "I do not know which of us has written this page."

At issue wasn't just Borges' loss of vision but also his father's, since "It was [my father] who would reveal the power of poetry to me—the fact that words are not only a means of communication but also magic symbols." From when Borges was a boy, "as blindness came to him [the father], it was tacitly understood that I was to fulfill the literary destiny that circumstances had denied my father. This was something that was taken for granted (such things are far more important than things that are merely said)." So Borges was like Elvis or Dali or Kerouac or Van Gogh. He lived two lives, two destinies. His art was his father's, too; he mourned what his father could never do.

Emotionally, the tone of the essay is distant. There's no feeling of sadness. Instead the question seems to be: Who am I if I can't see anymore? What remains of the sighted Borges, and how is the blind Borges related to the Borges who came before?

Loss and Writer Jack Kerouac

A stellar example of a loss-driven writer is one who wouldn't, for most people, spring instantly to mind: Jack Kerouac. Kerouac lived and breathed gloom. He never got over the death of his brother Gerard. The nuns may have labeled Gerard a saint; but to Kerouac, he was a haunter, a mostly friendly ghost to whom and for whom Kerouac wrote.

Jack was 4 when Gerard—age 9—died, of complications from rheumatic fever. Kerouac spends a lot of time thinking and writing about who Gerard was and what he meant to him, hoping for "healing virtues" but fearing he's "lost all my molecules of then," the "bridge" of memory broken. Memory is a complex subject in Kerouac's work. He makes no distinction between facts and what he calls, in his book titles, "visions." What he thinks he remembers is what happened. The world is a "crystal ball of mind," he says, "it's neither what you think it is, nor what you think it isn't. . . . None of it is even there, it's a mind movie." Along the way, in letters and journals and fiction, we hear about Gerard's dreams, Jack's dreams, Jack's first memory, Gerard's visions of heaven, Jack's thoughts while in his baby crib—in other words, things that may have happened, things that did happen, and things that must be totally invented, all on equal terms vis-à-vis reality.

In one set of visions, Gerard is Christ. Birds feed from his hand. He nurses wounded mice. Jack remembers Gerard lying in the backyard grass with a hand cupped over his eyes. What are you doing? his mother asks. "Watching heaven," Gerard replies. In moments, all the "Christ-likeness" sounds like a protest. Kerouac writes to *On the Road* hero Neal Cassady: "It's as though Jesus was my brother and I was his flesh-and-blood Judas. . . . I betrayed him merely by living when he died. He was an angel, I was a mortal; what he could have brought to the world, I destroyed by my mere presence; because if I had not lived, Gerard would have lived."

This is heavy stuff. And it gets more convoluted. Jack isn't just Jack. He is Gerard too. "I am made of loss," he intones. "I have not been the same since my brother Gerard died." He goes on: "My brother is my true self" and "while he lived I was not [Jack], I was Gerard, the world was his face, the flower of his face. . . . The first four years of my life are permeant and grey with the memory of a kindly serious face bending over me and being me and blessing me." In a long letter to Cassady that Kerouac intended as a full confession of his life, he describes a "witching hour" memory (or vision, or dream, or fantasy). "I woke up . . . and saw a tall, lank figure standing above my crib in stiff watchfulness of me." The figure had "wild unruly hair and seemed intent on me with hate." Jack drives it out of his mind that it was Gerard, "risen like a ghost from his bed of miseries." And yet, "it *was* Gerard and no one else. . . . I stared back with rue at my haunter. Stiff, stiff, he never moved, never said a word, never barely breathed, and so persistent in his sullen, lidded look into my babycrib soul. . . . These are the beginnings of my mysteries. Was it my brother? Of course it was my brother. Who was my brother?" Skeletons dance in his dreams "because my brother Gerard haunted them." He longs for a way to move past hate and shame. Once writer William Burroughs performed an "amateur psychoanalysis" on Kerouac (focused, logically, on Gerard), so Jack wonders if a Freudian approach might "make me remember the kind things Gerard did to me, and the kind feelings I had for him—which would thus balance against the terrible guilt complex and restore normalcy to my personality."

It's not just his dreams Gerard haunts, but his art, which Kerouac saw as a form of dream anyway. It's as if Jack lived to tell the story of his brother, to compose a gospel. He recognized this and proclaimed it ecstatically. "The whole reason I ever wrote at all," he declares, "and drew breath to bite in vain with pen of ink . . . because of Gerard, the idealism, Gerard the religious hero—'Write in honor of his death' (Ecrivez pour l'amour de son mort) (as one would say, write for the love of God)." No wonder he called his little, illustrated book about Gerard, *Visions of Gerard*, his "most true."

There's much to say about what was going on in Kerouac psychologically, but the key point is this: He was made of loss, and he wrote to address it somehow. Kerouac was a word-machine. He couldn't *not* write. Poet Allen Ginsberg called him "the Great Rememberer." He suffered—or, better yet, *profited from*—a nostalgia fetish, a constant feeling of "tender brooding compassion," as Ginsberg put it. And it all revolved around a dead brother. Like Borges, Kerouac needed to make something equal to Colossus Gerard. Like Elvis, Dali, and Van Gogh, he dealt with survivor guilt. That Gerard died while Jack lived haunted Kerouac. He had stolen Gerard's life. So, he performed symbolic CPR. He conjured Gerard with words, and he put him everywhere.

***

What is it about the loss experience that's so fixating for artists? What's the mystery link between loss and creativity?

Eisenstadt tries working out the details, but what he comes up with isn't all that illuminating, much of it couched in Freudian terminology such as, "the child will become his own parent surrogate. . . . An ego ideal may be developed that leads to outstanding accomplishment." What's this mean? The dead parent is a motivator, a task master, and creativity an attempt to "prove to the world the individual's essential goodness." It's as if the child says to the parent, "See? My life was worth it. I made something of value. I lived up to the moral charge you left inside me."

To me, there is more to figure out. The roots of the loss–art connection run deeper, the linkages more mysterious than a need to prove self-worth.

Kerouac's case is messy, and therefore especially useful. He knew the family wisdom that Gerard was a saint, yet he felt him as a hater, a haunter, at least in part. There was incongruity. He tried getting Gerard more right, less one-dimensional, but this made him feel guilty, since his picture of Gerard was at odds with the saintly one offered up when Jack was a child. His writing did violence against Gerard's image, in other words. Kerouac realized this strategy got him nowhere; he figures psychoanalysis might have solved things, yet he never acts on that belief.

What Kerouac wanted most in "visioning" Gerard was the continuation of a relationship that ended, that in some ways never existed because Jack was 4 when Gerard died. He wrote to refind Gerard, to know him more than he had in life. Like grief-racked parents who keep a dead child's bedroom as-is forever, Kerouac fixed his brother in place, and even, to go one step further, extended him in time. He projected Gerard into male heroes, each a Gerard duplicate. He imagined conversations with Gerard, who gave him adult and essentially self-serving advice. In published journals, Kerouac repeats the idea that Gerard "is my original self returning," then records what Gerard has to say about Jack and his life and ideas. "If you can't find a way of living today, you won't find it tomorrow. Stop waiting and start," says Gerard. "Work and make your life. Find a woman and marry. Have children and shut your mouth. Be a man and not a child." Gerard tells Jack to go to church. He tells him to write in French, to not de-French himself. He tells him to "slap my lady love down and make her mind." There are two particular thoughts or exchanges Kerouac includes, and both are obscure. First he says, "nothing is left in this experienced soul of mine except repetition." It's not clear what he's talking about. He seems to be describing a stuckness, an attachment to patterns and the past. He also has Gerard tell him repeatedly to "shut up." It's Gerard's main message. What he's saying is stop worrying, stop doubting, stop getting tangled up in meaningless neuroses, but also, perhaps, stop writing so much. Be quiet. End the "sick neurotic need" to put words on paper.

But that is exactly what Kerouac could not stop. The reason he wrote at all, he said, was to honor Gerard—the person telling him to "shut up"—and to "accept lostness forever." Kerouac's is a weirdly unimaginative body of work. As he says many times, he isn't all that interested in fiction. Fiction isn't his project. In a literal sense, he's not a novelist because he wants to avoid making anything up. Life isn't symbolized in his work; it's repeated. In *Visions of Cody* (a book about Neal Cassady), he includes long printed transcripts of actual conversations. All he hopes to achieve, in the end, is a "lifetime of writing about what I'd seen with my own eyes, told in my own words, according to the style I'd decided on . . . and put all together as a contemporary record for future times to see what really happened and what people really thought." He can "die happy," he says, if he can only "collect all my work and re-insert my pantheon of uniform names, [and] leave the long shelf full of books there." The books put the life between the pages. They are a second life, in word form.

There's a psychological concept that applies to Kerouac, and possibly to other loss-fueled artists. It comes out of script theory, the invention of a brilliant polymath named Silvan Tomkins, who died in 1991. It's also a formulation of what we've been talking about in terms of personality's third level—a need to narrate, a need to make stories.

Tomkins' driving idea is that "affect (i.e., emotion) is everything." Not thought, not drives, not motives, but feelings. Most things occurring in the course of an average day lack strong emotion. We make coffee. We pay bills. We walk the dog. We pick someone up at the airport. These things just occur. We forget them. They leave no trace. But affect-charged events register. They focus attention. We feel as if we have to do something about them, and what we do, Tomkins says, is sort and arrange the feelings. We bind feelings together into what he calls "scenes," or affect-laden happenings. Scenes are events. You lose at poker and angrily flip the card table over—that is a scene. Your father calls you an idiot and you recoil in disgust—that is a scene. Life includes thousands of scenes, each with at least one strong affect and one object of that affect. But scenes don't exist in isolation. The mind has a need to combine them, Tomkins says, to bundle them together so as manage and order them and interpret their meaning. These scene bundles Tomkins calls scripts. Scripts bring together families of interrelated scenes, all on similar themes, all containing similar sets of feeling. This idea is sometimes expressed colloquially. We've all heard of victim scripts, or redemption scripts, or underdog scripts. Tomkins addresses all these, with different terminology. In the course of his theorizing he described roughly 50 common scripts—addiction scripts, commitment scripts, toxicity scripts. They control affect, they allow us to predict and explain, they make meaning out of disconnected experiences, and they become, in time, self-perpetuating.

One script Tomkins privileged above all others, maybe because it was his. He called it the "nuclear script." Here is his definition: "Nuclear scripts arise from the unwillingness to renounce or mourn what has become irresistibly seductive and the inability to recover what has become lost, to purify or integrate what has become intolerably contaminated or conflicted, and to simplify or unify what has become hopelessly turbulent." This captures Kerouac's special agony. Death is the ultimate "inability to recover." The person is gone forever, the finality absolute. But if the death is jarring, or unfair, or somehow fated, or secretly wished for, or in some convoluted sense the fault of the survivor, it becomes "irresistibly seductive." One can't stop returning to it. It has to be made sense of, integrated, purified. Usually in nuclear scripts there's a surplus of confusion and ambivalence. The script generates subscripts, Tomkins says: rehearsals (a replay of the loss), avoidance or escape strategies, efforts to undo the damage or recover or repair. It's a potent mix. The script is unrelenting. In its grip the person appears haunted. He can't stop trying to recover what is unrecoverable, to repair what's irreparable.

Take John Lennon. His mother Julia abandoned him repeatedly. He loved and hated her. He visualized fantasy scenarios in which she floated down to save him. When she died, run over by an off-duty policeman, he was just beginning to reconnect with her, so he lost her twice, as a small child and as an adolescent. Lennon insisted on characterizing some of his songs as nonsense, as meaningless. But in the nonsense there is meaning, as there often is. "I Am the Walrus" replays his mother's death, though it's easy to miss the message. In a bridge, Lennon includes these seemingly random associations: "Mister City policeman sitting, pretty little policemen in a row / see how they fly like Lucy in the sky, see how they run / I'm crying." In context, the reference gets clear. There's the policeman, there's his mother as Lucy (a linkage made by psychologist Tim Kasser in his book *Lucy in the Mind of Lennon*), that female in the sky, and there's the emotional response, "I'm crying." Lennon recreates the scene unconsciously; it's there, degraded in bizarre symbolism.

Kerouac was stuck on one particular scene from his brother's life that he described over and over and also finessed more than once into fiction. He could never get control of it, it never let him alone. It concentrated a universe of feeling within a single bloated dot and it metastasized. Here's how he tells it in one of its many appearances. "Just before [Gerard] died he slapped me in the face. It was the last thing I remember before he died. It was a grey morning. . . . Gerard sat at his erector set before the most magnificent structure of his brief career; it was huge, towering, a crane of some sort, arranged and hung in strange new ways and calculated to do a thousand strange feats. . . . But I had to come along and grab at his arrangements: knock a subsidiary structure down, disturbing him so suddenly that with understandable rage he impulsively tightened inside and his hand shot out and slapped me in the face: 'Get away from here!' he cried. . . . I resented the slap in the face and wished Gerard would die, and he died a few days later."

There's much in this homely little recollection to take stock of. The first question is: Did it even happen? Again, with Kerouac, it's hard to say because he was disinclined to make those sorts of distinctions. Possibly it didn't, but it may not matter. To Kerouac it was subjectively real. If he made it up, that adds to its potency: a fiction he presented as fact, a "lie" he repeated.

The slap violated a status quo—Gerard is kind and good—and it's this violation that made it seductive. Kerouac *has* to go back to it to make sense of it. Is there rage in the saint? Is the saint flawed? In *Visions of Gerard* Jack knocks the structure over by accident, so the slap is less forgivable. In the version of the memory presented before, it's Jack's fault. He grabs at the structure. He destroys Gerard's work of art. The story makes Jack into a killer. He was slapped. He wished Gerard dead. Gerard died.

This is how loss works as a stimulant. It's packed into scenes containing scripts that grow self-defining. The scripts are recycled out of a need to know—somehow order has to be made out of disorder, sense out of senselessness.

The Persistence of Memory

Loss is a memory. So, if art responds to loss it responds to a memory that's plucked out and reshaped because it's attracting, because it's unfinished, as with Styron and Kerouac. The art confronts a problem, and the problem is a need to know more.

But we don't remember equally, according to research. Emotional events—positive or negative—get laid down more forcefully than neutral events. Memory, art's data, is emotion-driven. Beyond this fact, however, things get more interesting. *Negative emotional experiences are better retained than positive*. Consider these examples:

1. Subjects who listened either to a story of a pleasant first date or a story of a date rape showed better memory for all aspects of the date rape.
2. People recall more visual detail, with more vividness, if the question is which snake or grenade they saw rather than which gown or cake.
3. Red Sox fans elated by victory over the Yankees in the 2004 championship series showed more inconsistent recall than devastated Yankees fans.
4. Subjects pleased about the O. J. Simpson verdict endorsed more fictitious events from the trial than did those displeased by the outcome.

Across the board, negative memories are more vivid, detailed, and accurate. Part of this has to do with the fact that they arouse us more; they stimulate the brain's amygdala, which specializes in processing emotion. The results aren't limited to events in real life, either. As we saw before, 80% of dreams also feature negative feelings. So, it doesn't matter whether we happen to be asleep or awake: Negative events rise to the top of the memory stack. They come with extra detail and vividness.

Here is Truman Capote on his early life in Alabama. He said it was "ghastly." He was "very lonely." He had zero "sense of being particularly wanted by anybody": "I never felt I belonged anywhere. . . . I had the most insecure childhood I know of. . . . It was just total emotional neglect. . . . I certainly don't feel as if I had any sturdy foundation to stand on. . . . When I was five, living in Alabama, I might as well have been a deaf mute. . . ." Then finally, as a sort of summation, "Every day was a nightmare, because I was afraid they would leave me when it turned dark. I had an intense fear of being abandoned, and I remember practically all of my childhood as being lived in a state of constant tension and fear."

This is as bad as it gets. Lonely. Unwanted. Neglected. Foundationless. Nightmarish. Fearful. What caused it? Repeated separation and abandonment. Capote's mother and father simply left, a form of loss just as searing as death. Adding insult to injury, the child is judged unworthy, by others and by himself.

Capote was seduced by and fixated on three particular negative memories, scenes he embellished over and over. One we've already talked about. He's 2 years old, he's hysterical, he's locked in a room as his parents party the night away. In another, he watches his mother's black Buick kick up dust as she drives it off, leaving him behind again. "Imagine a dog," he says, "waiting and hoping to be taken away. That is the picture of me then." One last scene places 3-year-old Truman at the St. Louis Zoo. He's with a "large black woman my mother had hired to take me there." Pandemonium ensues. Lions have escaped their cages. "Two bloodthirsty beasts on the prowl," says Capote. His nurse panics. "She simply turned and ran, leaving me alone on the path. That's all I remember about it."

Capote's losses evolved, over time, into an insecure attachment style. His parents were selfish, self-involved, and nonresponsive. He expected to be left. His radar for loss grew fine-tuned. As he said once, "You know, the only way people can ever hurt me is if I let them get close to me. . . . I'm very careful about that, about who I get close to."

Capote's biographer Gerald Clarke sums the situation up nicely: "[His mother] did not hate him; if she had, he could at least have hated her in return. . . . Nor, though she continued to dump him in the laps of other people, did she really ignore him. . . . What she did was worse. . . . She regarded him with ambivalence: she loved him and she did not love him; she wanted him and she did not want him; she was proud to be his mother and she was ashamed of him." Capote was a lot like Lennon: The message he got from his parents was "you aren't important." If Lillie Mae had died, it might have been better for him emotionally. Death would not have carried the same judgments.

But what does all this have to do with art? A lot. Capote wrote books that repeated his childhood agonies. He made loss a muse. He couldn't let it go. Dark memories plagued him. As a high in openness (high O) artist, he did what made sense, what was probably inevitable: He fictionalized trauma. He became a loss hero. He turned misery into poetry.

Here's how he finessed the plot.

Capote's first novel, *Other Voices, Other Rooms*, features an orphaned boy named Joel Knox who's summoned by his long-lost father. He heads off excitedly. At last he is wanted. His father has called for him. The first half of the book is a mystery tale. Joel reaches his destination, but no one tells him who or where his father is. Everyone he asks changes the subject or replies elliptically. Joel keeps telling himself, "Dad will probably want me in a minute," but on the other hand he's not so sure; maybe he's been "played a mean trick." A cook named Zoo suggests he pray. "Let me be loved," Joel says to God.

Not until page 121 does Joel lay eyes on "Samson," his father. The sight is gutting. He's kept in an isolated room upstairs. His head is shaved. He lies "with invalid looseness on unsanitary pillows." His eyes search Joel with a kind of "dumb glitter." His needs he communicates by feebly tossing a red tennis ball down the stairs. Joel tries reading to him, he tries connecting, but Samson never listens. Prices recited from a Sears Roebuck catalog interest Samson as much as the best Wild West story.

Other Voices is Capote's father-driven replotting. Ten years later came *Breakfast at Tiffany's*, the mother side of the reconstruction. The book is a case study, its focus "fragile eyeful" Holly Golightly, whose calling card lists her occupation as "Traveling." It's true. She does not stay put. She is a wild thing who can't be trapped. The book's narrator, whom Holly calls "Fred," can't get her out of his mind. He's charmed by her. He detests her, too.

The plot reduces to Fred stalking intoxicating Holly. She can take him or leave him. She can take or leave anybody. In the end she disappears—to Brazil or Africa, no one knows—never to be seen again. "You can't really run off and leave everybody," Fred tells her, but he knows he's wrong. Holly already prepared him, in fact, in a speech full of Capote's own hard-won wisdom: "Never love a wild thing. . . . The more you do, the stronger they get. . . . You'll end up looking at the sky. . . . Such an empty place; so vague. Just a country where the thunder goes and things disappear."

In making Holly, Capote had Jodie Foster in mind (for future movie versions), though Holly is more Geisha than tough tomboy. She's a social climber, a movie star wannabe. She reads all the star magazines. She's a drinker, a nutcase prone to violent tantrums. Pointedly, she's from the South—both her parents died when she was young, so she was sent away to live with "mean people." She married at a young age, and the marriage ended disastrously. Her true name, before she transmogrified into Holly, was "Lulamae." This final detail is the clincher, but the others match up too. Each describes Capote's capricious, unreachable, unlovable mother, whose real name, in a similarity impossible to dismiss, was "Lillie Mae." Holly might be a lot of people, even Capote himself, as fictional characters always are. But most important of all, and most indisputably, she was his mother—self-obsessed and chronically unavailable.

Even Capote's masterpiece *In Cold Blood* recycles similar dynamics, this time in real life. It's a nonfiction novel, as Capote called it, centered on the brutal, pointless murder of a Kansas farm family, the Clutters.

Capote gave years of his life to the book. He traveled to Kansas. He finagled his way into countless interviews (with the help of Harper Lee, who went with him). When it came to the writing itself, much of which Capote did in Europe, the task nearly killed him. In letter after letter he describes his agony. But he knew what he had. He knew it was genius. So he kept on and somehow prevailed over what must have been a hurricane of material to shape. He saw it as an artistic exercise. No one had really made fact into a novel before. The challenge fueled Capote. He created his own personal gauntlet.

But what Capote did not expect, what he didn't see coming, were the feelings he developed for one of the murderers, Perry Smith. In some ways Capote was Smith. Both had nasty childhoods. Both were interested in art from an early age. Both had been orphaned. There were physical similarities, too. Both were small—Smith dark-skinned, Capote light, a towhead. To Capote, Smith was a doppelganger. He said they had traveled the same path in life, up to a critical point. Capote went one way, Smith another, the reason why inscrutable. Everyone who knew Capote saw what was happening to him: He'd fallen in love with a killer. Capote knew it too. He describes the relationship as "intimate" in "every conceivable way." In an eerie sense, *In Cold Blood* is a love story. It's never explicit, but it's there in subtext, where most framing feelings reside. Smith is put to death by hanging; Capote loses another love.

The Loss Muse

This is how the loss dynamic repeats itself. You plot it. You fold it into stories. It's your experience, it's left painful memories you can't set aside, so you channel it any way you want. Most experiences we have do not automatically mean anything. Meaning comes from scripting. That's your freedom, and it's a total freedom: how you choose to tell the story about what's happened to you.

Bowie called art-making "loony" and "unnecessary," the opposite of "sane" and "rational." It is a sign, he says, of "irrational man." Sex is pleasure, Bowie says. Likewise, we need to eat; food is essential to survival. What is "extra" is art, the plates of many shapes and colors we produce so that we have something to put our food on. Why do we do it? We don't need to. What's the point? He says, "it's an extraordinary thing to want to do, to express yourself, in such rarified terms."

Unrest—or what Bowie calls "volatility"—is at the core of the process because art is a going beyond to say what wasn't verbalized. It's a dissatisfaction with reality. Loss is the ultimate cosmic gut-punch. It's uncontrollable. It's untreatable. It's often perceived as unfair or undeserved. And it's heartbreakingly final. There seems to be nothing to be done about it. One can't protest loss. There's no do-over. Because of all these things, it possesses, or better yet, it is *felt* to possess, qualities of meaninglessness and randomness.

Loss, therefore, is a perfect artistic challenge. It's the most colossal, soul-shattering *why* of all. It fires creativity because it presents exactly the sort of challenge artists are always responding to anyway: a challenge of meaning-making. Why did Jesse die and not me, Elvis wondered. Kerouac wondered the same, especially in light of his brother's saintliness. Why do my parent's not love me, Capote wondered. Why did they leave me over and over? Then John Lennon—why did my mother *have to* die just when I was beginning to get close to her again? Art answers questions that are unsettled. With the nuclear script, Tomkins pointed to an inability to renounce or mourn what has been irretrievably lost. The person can't simply get on with it. He won't accept it. He's haunted, not just by the loss of love or of a particular person, but by a loss of meaningfulness. Artists are the opposite of fatalists. They don't shrug and say whatever. They protest. They do that unnecessary and irrational thing Bowie described. It's not just that they can't take it. They *won't* take it.

A question is, when you write about loss, or paint about it or sing about it, are you mastering it? In therapy, the therapist acts as a guide, an external helper. The patient uncovers, works through, and integrates trauma—all very deliberately, all in a supportive therapeutic context. The purpose of the artist is not to do this. The purpose of the artist is to make art.

I'm not arguing that no one overcomes trauma or loss. Clearly, people do sometimes. What I'm arguing is that art isn't set up to produce that outcome, mainly because the artist doesn't realize, in most cases, that loss is being repeated in the work. Capote, for instance, reread all his work and was embarrassed to discover autobiographical sources he'd been unaware of. He couldn't believe he'd missed them, but he did. Kerouac knew he was writing about Gerard, so he's in a different category from Capote. He knew the art wasn't solving anything, however. He was creating a Gerard in his head who was different and far more problematic than the Gerard everyone gushed about. What he said was that he needed psychoanalysis to figure it all out. He needed therapy, not art, to make sense of his feelings for his brother.

I'm also not arguing that there's no pleasure in the artistic recreation of trauma. Psychoanalysts talk about how "the painful element of memory is wrought into pleasure in the manifestations of art" even if the "content of the repeated is unpleasant." What they seem to mean is that making something, creating something beautiful, being gifted at what one does, feeling satisfied with what one produces, simply feels good. We take pleasure in doing anything well, whether it's writing a song about pain, a poem about pain, or a book about pain. But this is mastery in composition, aesthetic mastery. It has nothing to do with mastery of conflicts in real life. The art can feel good to make without changing anything.

Brain science reduces this loss fixation to a basic level. Relentless ruminative repetition (the three Rs) seems to be hard-wired. Most of this research centers on traumas that are extreme—rape, combat, kidnapping, abuse—but early loss of the sort I've been talking about seems capable of producing similar changes, with similar long-term effects. In any case, trauma gives rise to the following:

1. High arousal to images and thoughts related to the trauma
2. An "intensity and tirelessness" of traumatic memories that affect experience continuously
3. Hypermnesia, or a particularly vivid and detailed recall of traumatic events, as I described before
4. Spotty amnesias and depression
5. Failure to habituate, or a tendency *not* to slowly disengage from trauma stimuli (the stimuli do not become less traumatizing over time, in other words)
6. A tendency to remember the trauma even when doing so makes little sense
7. "Indelible subcortical responses" or emotional reactions unaltered by later experiences, such that, in the words of one researcher, "emotional memory may be forever," one can't think one's way out of it

The brain forces the replaying of trauma. Artists don't choose to go back to it again and again. It chooses itself. It's there, waving, saying write about me, paint about me, sing about me. It is perfectly dense, complicated, turbulent, confusing raw material. It won't take no for an answer.

The writer Patricia Highsmith was Capote's friend; he helped get her into Yaddo. She, too, made murder a theme, her most famous character the shape-changing, almost identityless "Mr. Ripley," for whom killing was a blasé game, one he tended to win. Other Highsmith books and stories focus on obsession and the hopelessness of relationships, most notably *The Price of Salt* (recently made into an Oscar-nominated film retitled *Carol*).

There almost was no Patricia Highsmith. Her parents, including a biological father she would not meet till she was 12, tried aborting her. To end the pregnancy, her mother drank turpentine.

Highsmith's childhood was "desperately unhappy," according to one of her biographers, and she felt it doomed her. Each of us, she said, "is forced to confront the fact that our personalities are largely formed by our childhood and adolescence and though one might try to change certain aspects or qualities, any substantial transformation of our character is impossible." She thought she had been sexually abused by a salesman. Four or five times a week up to the age of 7 she was plagued by a hallucinatory spot, a "grey blob that would dance and dart diagonally across the upper left-hand corner of her vision." This figure was lifelike. She was ashamed to tell anyone about it. "I was never able to control my shock," she wrote.

Highsmith's mother lied to her, rejected her by sending her off to Texas to live with her grandparents. She "never realized what a devastating betrayal of faith this was to me," said Highsmith. Her situation resembled Capote's. Her parents didn't want her. There was no explanation as to why.

Like Capote, Highsmith adopted defensive strategies. "If I have the steady thing [i.e., the promise of faithful love], I reject it," she wrote to a friend. "This has happened over and over—rather, I made it happen. I repeat the pattern, of course, of my mother's semi-rejection of me to my grandmother, when I was aged 12, when my mother took me to

Texas, with a promise she would divorce my stepfather. . . . I never got over it. Thus I seek out women who will hurt me in a similar manner."

Gradually, as her writing took shape, with its qualities of ominousness and incipient violence, she became more and more fascinated by deviance, how "each person carries around in himself a terrible other world of hell . . . an enormous pit reaching below the deepest crater of the earth. . . . But it is frightening and essentially unlike man as he knows himself familiarly, so we spend all our days living at the other antipodes of our self." These ruminations put her on the verge of suicide. She couldn't understand why she wasn't better, more successful, more creative. In a notebook she says, "Passed my first suicide test this evening. It comes when one is confronted with work, empty sheets of paper all about, and inside one's head, shame and confusion." She figured creative people like her were born without protective barriers. Her depression, then, came from being blown about, beaten and broken "and trampled underfoot." The blackness, the despair she felt, was mirrored in her work. She would never be able, she said, "to write about apple-blossom faces, Valentine cards, roaring kitchen fires and old-fashioned bedsteads, and there was little point in creating work which affirmed man's status quo." Instead, her approach was to "dismantle and subvert normality until the comfortable and the conventional took on a more sinister, dangerous edge."

Loss of love gave rise to violent fictions. You could twist yourself into someone lovable, someone not yourself, but finally you'd be found out, exposed, like Ripley was again and again. An option, then, was one Highsmith imagined and wrote about with frighteningly bland ferocity: You killed who you tried to be loved by. You murdered the rejecter.

7

The Myth of the Mentally Ill Artist

If I walk over to the bookcases in my dining room, here are some of the names I see: Flannery O'Connor, James Baldwin, Iris Murdoch, Alberto Moravia, Ken Kesey, Kingsley Amis, Muriel Spark, Martin Amis, Philip Larkin, Gabriel Garcia Marquez, Adrienne Rich, Wallace Stevens, and John Kennedy Toole, to name a few. With the exception of Toole, who killed himself (agonized because publisher after publisher had rejected his novel *A Confederacy of Dunces*), none of these writers can be called "mentally ill." It would make no sense to give them a disease label. They had their quirks, and they wrote great works.

Now, if I sit and think of iconic artists from across the last century, these are names that spring to mind (for me, at least): Sylvia Plath. Van Gogh. Kurt Cobain. Michael Jackson. Marilyn Monroe. Edgar Allen Poe. Picasso. Jackson Pollock. Diane Arbus. Hemingway. It's not a list that means anything special. You can daydream your own list, and it would differ from mine. At any rate, in my list, just names off the top of my head, everyone seems to be tortured. There are six suicides. There are six with serious addiction problems. Van Gogh was psychotic. Several were clearly depressed. Some say Hemingway was bipolar.

My books argue for no link between great artistic creativity and mental illness. My free associations say a link is there, and it's obvious. I'd bet the second position represents the common view. Most people believe art and insanity are connected. It's the idea of the "mad genius."

But think it over. The names that spring to mind aren't representative. They are more available, more salient, and more easily accessed, yet because of those things, misleading. We make these kinds of cognitive errors all the time. We seize on stereotypes and elevate them. Because stereotypes come so readily to mind, we assume they capture something real. Even people acutely aware of thinking biases fall prey to them over and over. It's the system 1 thinking I described before. It's quick, but sometimes wrong.

The Mind of the Artist. William Todd Schultz, Oxford University Press. © Oxford University Press 2022.
DOI: 10.1093/oso/9780197611098.003.0008

There's another question that's more complicated, and it has to do with causality. Apart from simple statistics, why do we care that more great artists suffer from mental problems? Because we want to assign causality. We want to explore how disorders shaped the art or made it necessary. We want to see the labels as formative. There are two serious problems with this.

Number one, the *life* of the artist might be crazy-making. The crazy, then, may be an effect. It's a chicken-and-egg conundrum. What came first, the madness or the art? In any single case it can be hard to say. The second point is this: Labels can't be, and never are, explanatory. They are names, *only names*, for sets of feelings and behaviors. In fact, if we try to make labels causal, they collapse. How so? Let's say person A asks, Why was Marilyn Monroe so vulnerable, so needy, so insecure, and why did she resort to taking drugs, and why did she kill herself? Expert B answers: because she had borderline personality disorder. Then let's say person A replies: How do you know she had borderline personality disorder? Expert B can only answer: because she was so needy, so vulnerable, so insecure, and so forth. The explanation seems to go somewhere; in fact, it goes nowhere. Labels are seductive. We use them all the time, whether it's calling someone a narcissist, a sociopath, bipolar, or an asshole. Labels appear to offer an answer, and we find it hard to believe they don't, but they can't, and they never do.

So attempts to link art and madness in order to get at causality are specious. It's a misspent, misguided enterprise. It's logically fallacious.

Why take up the question at all, then? To get at the truth (brace yourself; it isn't easy). And to explore the real nature of the "torment" great artists seem to be thrown into. In the end, we may know what we don't know. But that's preferable to thinking we know something we don't.

As my bookcase/free-association exercise made clear, getting at links between art and mental illness can't begin and end with lists of famous artists. The selection of who to include is nonrandom, biased. Also, there is no matched control group with which to compare. So, to arrive at valid conclusions, it's essential to look to science. What do the studies show? And more to the point, are the studies any good? The second question precedes the first. If its answer is "no good at all," then the studies show nothing or, at best, leave the question undecided.

Before we explore the nitty gritty of the studies and what they do, and mostly don't, show, let's review where we are in order to set up a clear contrast. What this book argues, based on scores of scientific findings, is that high openness predicts high creativity. There is no doubt about this. It's a truth beyond dispute. Openness also predicts states of mind—cognitive disinhibition, schizotypy—that themselves correlate with creative activity. There's no dispute about this, either. Finally, there's a need in artists to narrate, or make up stories about, challenging personal experiences such as loss, which is twice as common in eminent creators. None of this has anything to do with mental illness. We need to be clear on that. I'm arguing something very different from the art–madness equation. *Art is rooted not in disorder but in variations of personality. It's personality that's predictive, not emotional disturbance.*

The studies we are about to look at do not focus on personality. They focus on disorders. What they attempt to prove is that artists disproportionately suffer from mental illness. I think we are right and they are wrong. What I want to do—mainly because the general public seems to buy the art–madness myth—is put the facts in order. Studies rise or fall based on how they get conducted, the quality of the research. We need to look closely at this quality question.

Famous Studies of Art and Mental Illness

Andreason

What some refer to as the landmark study began in 1972 but wasn't published until 1987, in the *American Journal of Psychiatry*. It was conducted by brain scientist and schizophrenia researcher Nancy Andreason, and it focused on 30 faculty members from the Iowa Writers Workshop, who were compared with 30 matched control subjects.

Here's what Andreason found. There were no differences between the groups in relation to schizophrenia, drug abuse, suicide, any specific bipolar disorder, or major depressive disorder. A negative result all around. But she then lumps the findings together, creating broader groups. This adjustment of categories reveals differences. Writers are more likely to suffer from "*any* affective disorder," depression or bipolar mania (24/30 vs. 9/30). They are also more likely to show signs, across their entire lifetime, of "*any* bipolar disorder" (13/30 vs. 3/30) and, additionally, of alcoholism (9/30 vs. 2/30). Results, then, reduce to two associated problems in writers—mood disturbance and a tendency to abuse alcohol.

Onto the second question. Is the study any good? Here it's hard to say yes. Andreason herself refers to "recognized limitations."

To start with, the numbers are small. Thirty subjects isn't a lot, not for scientific studies. Almost all the subjects are men (27/30) and likely white (though she does not say). That's a serious problem. All the subjects are writers, too, so there's no way to generalize to different artistic media. Finally, all the subjects are part of a faculty group in Iowa. Let's say I decided to study Democrats in rural Mississippi. Could I then say anything true about Democrats in general? No.

There's more. Andreason conducted the interviews herself, a basic design flaw since it leaves room for experimenter bias. We don't even know what the interview questions were. She made use of an instrument she designed herself, but she doesn't include it in the paper.

Andreason's article is titled "Creativity and Mental Illness." It ought to have been called "Descriptions of About Two Dozen (White?) Male Writers in Iowa Who Have Problems With Mood and Drink." It's always important to go back to original sources. Often they are more iffy than believed. When they get reported on, the untidy details tend to get set aside.

Ludwig

Next is Arnold Ludwig, whose research "draws inspiration" from Andreason's. Andreason included only males; Ludwig, as if to finish an unfinished picture, includes only females, 59 total, all volunteers from a national women's writers conference held at the University of Kentucky. Ludwig compares his writer group with 59 nonwriters from homeowners' associations, medical auxiliaries, and a university women's club. He doesn't interview the women himself—an improvement over Andreason. Instead, subjects complete psychological tests and inventories—sensation-seeking scales, coping scales, questionnaires targeting psychiatric syndromes, personality measures, and lifetime creativity scales.

Ludwig's findings are startling for the range of disorders that turn up. This is a seriously disturbed group of female writers. Statistically significant differences are shown with respect to depression (33/59 vs. 8/59), suicide attempts (9/59 vs. 2/59), mania (11/59 vs. 2/59), panic attacks (13/59 vs. 3/59), generalized anxiety disorder (8/59 vs. 1/59), drug abuse (10/59 vs. 3/59), and eating disorder (7/59 vs. 1/59). The writers were also more likely to have been sexually or physically abused (23/59 vs. 7/59). Finally, and less pathologically, the writers really were more creative than controls, according to lifetime creativity scales. Oddly, Ludwig does not report findings for some of the tests he lists. We don't hear about results on, nor are there any tables for, sensation-seeking, coping, attribution, or personality. This is an unusual omission for a scientific article.

Ludwig says "caution is necessary" when interpreting his results. The writers are all female, and "there is no way to determine how representative these female writers are of all female writers (those who participate in writers' workshops and those who do not)." He adds, in reference to Andreason, "observations made on female writers neither confirm nor disconfirm those made previously on a group of writers, most of whom were male." Also, we're talking only of writers at workshops. The findings therefore can't be extended to female artists who paint, take photographs, compose songs, and so forth.

There's another problem Ludwig mentions without spelling out its significance: He takes the writers at their word. Now, we always take subjects at their word when they answer questionnaires and checklists. We don't contest their answers. But here, there may be more of an issue. Writers might simply endorse more stuff, disclose to a degree the control group did not. After all, that's what writers do. They repress less, they tend to be more open about what's going on inside them. Ludwig admits his research "cannot resolve this issue." He thinks his results are reliable, but he can't say for sure.

Ludwig includes an additional analysis of special interest, especially because he goes on to propose extraordinary motives for art based on it. He looks into factors predictive of creative activity, those correlating with scores on the Lifetime Creativity Scales. Four are said to account for 26% of the variance (a modest amount). These are (1) cumulative psychopathology scores, (2) presence of mental illness in mothers, (3) reporting of sexual or physical abuse before age 13, and (4) levels of creativity in parents. An interesting list, for sure. We can say these four factors appear to be *associated* with creativity; we can't say they *cause* it. But Ludwig feels they "invite interpretation," so he has a go at what they might mean. "These emotional difficulties," he speculates, "seem to become enmeshed with [the writers'] work, not only fueling their motivation for expression, but also providing them with the basic ingredients for their art, much like the paints on an artist's palette. . . . Their writing seems to represent an important way of unburdening themselves. By imposing a narrative structure on their experiences, many writers seem able to satisfy their needs for communication and to establish order in their otherwise chaotic emotional world."

These ideas are a leap. Ludwig has no clue what these women write about, so it is impossible to say, as he does, that their difficulties get enmeshed with their work. He hasn't read their work. Nor, for the same reason, is he in any position to assert their work orders chaos, or represents an unburdening, or contains themes related to disturbance. Let's suppose—and that's all we can do, *suppose*—some of these women wrote stories centered on sexual abuse. Does that mean the stories were cathartic? No. Does it mean they were curative? No. Besides, one of the factors Ludwig lists has no relevance for his conjectures: Creativity was greater in those whose parents were creative. If we isolate this last fact, simple modeling stands as a reasonable possibility. Maybe the writers wrote because their parents did. It's a boring explanation, but maybe more true. In any case, we can't say. We don't know.

Jamison

Most everyone looking into questions of creativity and mental illness cite the studies by Andreason and Ludwig. They don't prove a lot, but they get reported as if they did, most likely because people have not read or scrutinized the original articles. But when it comes to links between mood and art specifically, no one generates more appeal, or meets with more prostrate respect, than the writer Kay Redfield Jamison, who has cornered the market on bipolar mania—or its more muted form, hypomania—and creativity. Reading her, it's impossible to escape the conclusion that art minus serious mental illness simply doesn't exist. Put differently, if you aren't manic, you aren't an artist.

Jamison first weighed in on this subject in 1989, 2 years after Andreason. Before that, her writing focused on medication compliance and physician attitudes toward, say, lithium as a mood stabilizer. But she developed opinions on what she called "positive experiences associated with primary affective disorder," so it was no major leap to explore these "positive experiences" in the realm of art. Artists famously tend to be moody; the question becomes: What role do these moods play in the creative process, if any? Do they help or hinder?

Jamison herself selected 47 poets, playwrights, novelists, biographers, and artists to examine, based on their having won prestigious prizes. This is suspect, right off the bat. More than 47 artists win prizes. Jamison lists some of the qualifying awards, but not all. So why and how did she choose her particular 47? And what makes a prize prestigious exactly? It's not clear.

Almost all the artists were British subjects (87%), and as with Andreason, almost all were men (also 87%). These facts limit possible conclusions, just as Andreason and Ludwig were limited by their unrepresentative samples. There's another, more serious problem: Jamison includes no control group. She can't compare rates of mental disorder in artists and nonartists because there are no nonartists. In short, Jamison can't test a hypothesis. Her study cannot answer the question of whether artists are more psychologically disturbed.

Here's what Jamison found: 38% of the total sample of artists had been treated for a mood disorder; 33% of poets (there were 18 poets total) had used medication for their depression. Playwrights had the highest rate of affective illness (63%; there were just eight playwrights), though the treatment they received tended to be "psychotherapy alone." Not a single playwright, novelist, biographer, or artist had been treated for bipolar disorder—so, within those groups, no sign of serious manic episodes. Poets showed more evidence of bipolar illness, but at a rate of only 17%.

Such are the findings. They show an absence of bipolarity generally. But Jamison is undeterred. She says 89% of subjects reported "intense, highly productive and creative episodes." What's that mean? More "enthusiasm, energy, self-confidence, speed of mental associations, fluency of thoughts, elevated mood, and sense of well-being." She quotes one artist as saying, "I have a fever to write, and throw myself energetically into new projects." Another reports "elation together with some gloominess."

These changes in mental state occurring during intense creativity seem like positives. They seem like a good thing. Who wouldn't want to feel more energy and enthusiasm, more confidence, more well-being? In fact, the list of characteristics sounds like openness—*productive creativity*—combined with cognitive disinhibition—*fluency of thought, speed of associations*. But Jamison sees them pathologically; she sees them as disease, specifically hypomania (a muted form of full-blown mania) and/or cyclothymia (mood fluctuation without high highs or low lows). The artists weren't treated for these disorders, they rarely sought help for them, but Jamison diagnoses them anyway (despite the fact that "specific diagnostic criteria were not used in the study").

Hypomania turns out to be a tricky diagnosis. The person seems especially happy, energized, enthusiastic, productive. Symptoms include pressure to talk, low need for sleep, flights of ideas, impulsivity, increased activity, restlessness, and mild euphoria. Those with hypomania don't typically lose control, don't become delusional, and don't engage in the sorts of outrageously reckless behaviors one meets with in full-blown manic psychoses. Even the American Psychological Association's *Diagnostic and Statistical Manual of Mental Disorders*, the *DSM*, acknowledges this. It states that hypomania does *not* include deteriorations in social or occupational functioning. It doesn't cause harmful dysfunction. On one hand, Jamison's subjects may not even have hypomania—they may just be more open. In fact, that's how it sounds to me. On the other, if they *do* have hypomania, it isn't a mental disorder. It's a subclinical form of bipolar disorder. It describes people who seem incongruently happy and productive.

What Jamison really discovers in these 47 artists is creativity. It may come with special energy, some euphoria, some gloominess, more motivation, more enthusiasm, more overall output—but these are par for the course. She takes what Nietzsche called creative frenzy and twists it into madness. Her study finds little evidence of bipolarity in the 47 subjects, so she digs deeper, on the lookout for signs of soft disease. These are there, so Jamison says, and she implies they play some causal role, that mood disturbance sparks artistic quality and production.

In a meticulous and scathing 2009 article by Judith Schlesinger ("Creative Mythconceptions: A Closer Look at Evidence for the 'Mad Genius' Hypothesis"), Jamison's *Touched With Fire: Manic-Depressive Illness and the Artistic Temperament* comes in for the lion's share of critique. The book's chock full of thick descriptions of creative states, with special focus on Lord Byron, who serves as a lynchpin. It's also filled with lists of eminent creators Jamison scrutinizes for signs of illness. For instance, in a table titled, "Mood Disorders and Suicide in British and Irish Poets Born 1705–1805," Jamison includes 35 individuals. Only seven are judged to be free of sickness. She bullet-points reasons for her judgments, but as Schlesinger notes, "she leaves them unreferenced," referring readers to a text note. This note is 10 pages long, "but it provides no details beyond the basics of title, author, publisher, and date." In other words, there's little or nothing in the way of argument or persuasive marshalling of biographical evidence.

Another table lists bipolar creatives: 166 dead writers, artists, and composers. Here we get more of the same. Jamison sees them all as afflicted with "probable" cyclothymia, major depression, or manic-depressive illness. But as Schlesinger points out, it's "virtually impossible to analyze the strength of each case for oneself." There's no specific guidance provided as to exactly "whether, how, or how well" precise diagnostic criteria were "actually met," Schlesinger says.

By way of illustration, Schlesinger isolates the case of Ralph Waldo Emerson, a writer included on the mood-disordered list. She checks the index to see what evidence gets provided for Emerson's pathology and finds four pages where his name appears. On one page Jamison names Emerson as someone with "at least one seriously-affected first-degree relative" suffering from disorder. Two other pages quote Emerson on the subject of writer's block. The fourth page is simply Emerson placed on the list. As Schlesinger concludes, reasonably, "none of this would seem to qualify Emerson as a mad creative." Other artists get equally short shrift. Whitman's on Jamison's list because he shared Coleridge's "cosmic temperament." Handel makes the list, though Jamison notes a "relative lack of autobiographical materials and reliable contemporary medical accounts." People like Michelangelo, Irving Berlin, and Noel Coward appear just once in the index—and the entry is for the list itself. So, no justifying rationale for why they are on the list in the first place. What Jamison seems to be doing in *Touched With Fire* is what I did at the start of this chapter. She's compiling names of artists she believes to be mood-disordered. Putting a list like that together is easier than putting together a list of non–messed-up artists, but that doesn't prove anything. Could someone name 166 writers, artists, and composers who seem to be, for the most part, psychologically healthy? Probably. Would that prove anything either? No.

German composer Robert Schumann is an artist Jamison dwells on. He was troubled, there's no doubt. He saw visions—angelic and demonic. He feared being poisoned. He suffered from depressive episodes, one in 1833 after the deaths of his brother and sister-in-law from cholera. In 1854 he tried suicide by throwing himself off a bridge (boatmen rescued him). His problems appeared to be phasic—there were melancholic periods and euphoric periods. This last detail suggests mood spectrum difficulties, but opinion is divided when it comes to what, exactly, caused his instability. Some say his symptoms were syphilis-related, products of the poisonous mercury used to treat it. He also had a gelatinous tumor at the base of his skull. It could have been, some suggest, a meningioma, generally benign. But meningiomas cause auditory hallucinations, which Schumann reported. Toward the end of his life he heard an "A" note that he found annoying; he also had longer musical hallucinations beyond just the single "A." Other possibilities are psychiatric. Perhaps Schumann was schizophrenic. Perhaps his symptoms reveal a psychotic depression—for instance, demonic visions and fear of being poisoned. Jamison prefers to see Schumann as bipolar, chiefly because he was sometimes depressed, sometimes euphoric. But bipolars don't typically hallucinate. They also tend to be grandiose; they don't fear things like poisoning. Inconsistencies aside, Jamison tracks Schumann's work patterns. She reduces his productive periods to mania or hypomania, his less productive periods to depression. Again, the notion is that manic thought facilitates creative work—it quickens it, enhances it, "fires" it. More mania (or hypomania), more and, maybe, better art.

But there's a question here, complex and significant. Assuming Schumann was bipolar (that's not a safe assumption), did the mania enhance just the *quantity* of his output, or *both quantity and quality*? The former possibility isn't all that spectacular. A "more mania, more production" formula leaves quality out of the picture. Manics, for instance, tend to write a lot, a symptom called hypergraphia. They fill lined notebooks effortlessly (I've seen this myself many times on psych units). But if what they write is uncreative, then the mania isn't enhancing artistry. It's just pushing out word after word after word; it's garrulousness absent creative bite.

Creativity researcher Robert Weisberg looked into this question by exploring not only Schumann's productivity but also the quality of his compositions. This sort of quasi-experimental approach takes the inquiry to a higher, more refined level. One question, admittedly dicey, is how to define quality. What makes a composition good? Weisberg uses the Schwann and Penguin Guides—the number of recordings of a composition listed in those catalogues. This, he argues, represents "the combined judgments of musicians, recording companies, and the record-buying public." He determines, for each year of Schumann's career, the absolute number and the relative proportion of high-quality compositions produced. These facts are then used to assess whether a particular year—depressed versus manic or hypomanic—was a "good" one.

These are the results. Schumann's total number of compositions increased over his lifespan, but the proportion of high-quality work, the *relative quality*, was not higher when Schumann seemed to be manic/hypomanic. That is, the "proportion of high-quality compositions was essentially constant over the years of Schumann's career." It made no difference (to quality) whether Schumann made the work when he was depressed or when he was euphoric. He was more motivated, more productive when euphoric, but what he churned out wasn't disproportionately wonderful. As Weisberg puts it, "in this case, genius and madness are not causally linked, although the [more mundane] correlation between Schumann's productivity and mood has been interpreted as supporting the claim that mania increased the creativity of his compositional processes."

If we take stock of Jamison's investigations, here's what we end up with. In the original study, she finds no solid evidence for bipolar mania in the lives of artists. She then spins descriptions of creative states into hypomanic symptoms, a questionably tendentious interpretive gambit. The sense is, she manages to find what she's looking for. In *Touched With Fire*, Jamison assembles lists of mood-disordered creatives with, in many instances, scant supportive evidence. "At this point," Schlesinger muses, "the question becomes: How many of the list selections rest on Jamison's say-so?" Maybe all of them? But no matter. As Schlesinger sees it, "given [Jamison's] prominence and the common expectation that all great artists are wired for psychopathology, for most people her opinion alone will suffice."

The truth when it comes to links between bipolar mania and great art is actually rather simple. Anyone with clinical or hospital psychiatric unit experience knows it, but it's regularly elided. If you are in a full-blown manic state, there's no chance for great art. You're deluded, rambling, unable to stop talking, hyperkinetic, impulsive, prone to risky behavior, hypersexual, disorganized, and full of irrational grandiose plans. A patient of mine flew to the United Kingdom thinking she had a tea date with the Queen. Another wrote a symphony complete with musical score sheets—yet zero musicality. People in manic episodes are out of control. Great art requires discipline. Manics lack discipline. Their mind kicks them off onto one tangent after another.

Hypomania is a different story. It comes in all shapes and forms, impossible, really, to place on a continuum. But as I mentioned before, it's a turned-down manic state. Hypomania *can* facilitate creativity, unless it veers into full-blown mania. Yet it's not a mental illness. One can live with it. It doesn't take full control of the personality. Any link, then, between hypomania and creativity does not prove links between *mental illness* and creativity. Suggesting otherwise is either conceptually unsound or a disingenuous sleight of hand. A friend of mine has a saying: Stop picking fly shit out of pepper. But this is one instance when picking fly shit out of pepper is warranted. The minutia make a big difference.

There are two more studies worth looking into, mainly because they tend to be cited approvingly. One is "Mind and Mood in Modern Art II," and it appeared in 1994 in the *American Journal of Psychiatry*. Here the focus is on 15 abstract expressionist painters, such as Pollock, Gorky, de Kooning, Rothko, and Motherwell. (Again, no females.) How was the list compiled? "Somewhat arbitrarily," the authors explain, from a book on the New York School. More arbitrariness: They decide to exclude Hans Hoffman (too old), and they add David Smith, a sculptor, who also happened to be (according to the authors) depressed and alcoholic.

Once again, who gets put on the list, and why, is everything. The Met website includes abstract expressionists not explored in the study. Also, if one simply searches under the New York School on Wikipedia, it's a heterogeneous hodgepodge of poets, dancers, and composers, as well as 97 painters, men and women. Why not include every single one? Why not include an equal number of women?

The authors say they collected information from biographies, letters, and diaries contained in the Archives of American Art. There's no attempt to be objective, no measure of interrater reliability (a standard practice). They refer to "problems and pitfalls"; they say they lacked "specific details of clinical history"; they say retrospective diagnoses are "problematic"; they admit terms like "melancholia" can be used in romantic or nostalgic senses. Yet they plunge ahead, finding that eight of the 15 men may have been depressed, seven of the 15 were alcoholic, six of the 15 sought psychiatric treatment, and four of the 15 died young. At each point they qualify the findings. They link drinking to the social context of the time and to a "romantic identification with one or more heavy drinkers important in the art world." About psychiatric treatment, they say, "one must be cautious about drawing inferences concerning possible psychopathology" because of a "romance with psychotherapy and psychoanalysis in New York." About mood states, they refer to possible hypomanias, but warn, smartly, that "creative furor may not be identical with hypomanic excitement." Such provisos don't appear to have been chastening. They don't dampen any speculative spirit. For as the authors finally conclude: "In bringing the Abstract Expressionist artists [or, at least, 15 hand-selected ones] into direct and lonely confrontation with the ultimate existential question, whether to live or to die, depression may have put them in touch with the inexplicable mystery that lies at the very heart of the 'tragic and timeless' art that they aspired to produce." It's a sweeping, fulsome conclusion. Maybe it's even true, but the study itself doesn't show it to be. It's more of the same. Handpicked artists. No matched controls. Only 15 subjects. Possibly biased diagnoses by researchers who know what they are looking for, know what they hope to find. No check on interrater reliability. All male subjects.

A final study makes at least some attempt to be objective with ratings, and also explores the link between art and mental illness, speculating as to art's (or, some art's) lack of automatic therapeutic value. It's on the "Sylvia Plath Effect," a melodramatic name for a psychological variable, since it implies Plath herself causes something terrible to happen.

James Kaufman begins by surveying the work of Andreason, Ludwig, Jamison, and others and finds it "not always methodologically perfect"—a demurely worded conclusion—and "murky at best." So far, so good. He sees the flaws; he realizes that "most review articles tend to claim a positive link, even if the evidence itself is more mixed."

What Kaufman does is comb through biographical entries in reader's guides. He analyzes 1629 writers: 1210 are male, 419 are female. He looks for "setback variables," which come in the form of three categories: signs of mental illness, lingering physical illness, and the experience of significant personal tragedy. Lingering physical illness is never defined. We aren't given examples. We also aren't told what amounts to "lingering." It's the same for personal tragedy. Kaufman lists one possible example—losing a child—but that's it. Apparently, tragedies are judgment calls made by Kaufman alone. This is a problem. It introduces bias. As for mental illness, "some judgment calls" were made there, too, Kaufman says, but he does (to his credit) reduce subjectivity. He has another rater judge the mental illness variable, too, and finds acceptable levels of agreement, or interrater reliability. He does *not* do this for personal tragedy. It's unexplained why.

The findings are these: Female poets show more mental illness than any other type of writer, even when compared only to other female writers; and male nonfiction writers are less likely to experience personal tragedy. In a second study of 520 eminent women (as profiled in *Webster's Dictionary of American Women*), Kaufman again looks at female poets, whom he compares with female fiction writers, playwrights, nonfiction writers, journalists, visual artists (painters, sculptors, photographers), politicians, and actresses. He finds that the poets are more likely to suffer from mental illness (actresses come in second). They are also more likely to experience personal tragedy (politicians come in second).

The message is clear: Female poets are damaged and traumatized. The question is why and how. Can one arrive at valid conclusions based on short dictionary entries? Kaufman pulls back a bit, calling the judgments "dangerous." He goes on:

> The problem is that it's possible to extrapolate too much. Biographies about incredibly normal and boring creative folks are rare (who'd read one?). So, if researchers claim this or that percentage of famous people show signs of mental illness and the general population only shows this (smaller) percentage, then it's comparing apples and oranges. We learn about the illness rates of famous people through biographies (which is not always a safe or accurate method), and we learn about the illness rates of the general population through much more rigorous testing. If researchers provide long lists of famous folks who suffered from mental illness (and they do) . . . well, here's another list: Shannon Doherty, Dwight Eisenhower, Ogden Nash, and Beth Orton. They all have Crohn's Disease. So what?

This critique applies to all the studies reviewed before, but it applies to Kaufman, too. He used dictionaries. These likely overemphasize tragic details. Or, to be fair, some may, some may not, depending on the dictionary chosen. In either case, what you get is a slanted portrait, and if this slanted portrait is the source for broad conclusions, the conclusions are suspect.

Toward the end of his essay Kaufman asks why Plath's writing, or the writing of any female poet, would have a "deleterious effect on mental health." The problem here is that causality hasn't been established. In fact, it's reasonable to assume, based on her biography, that Plath's mental illness *preceded* her poetry writing. The better question would be why Plath's writing did not make her better, did not cure her, under the assumption that writing about emotional experiences is good for people. She started out unstable; she did not write herself out of it. The answers Kaufman offers seem grasping. He says, "poets are more likely to put a negative spin on traumatic life events." Really? Plenty of counterexamples spring to mind—Wallace Stevens, Gary Snyder, Marianne Moore. He also says poems lack narrative, and that poets may be more inclined toward rumination. The first idea just isn't true. Poems, or a lot of them, do not lack narrative at all. Do poets ruminate? Who knows, and what would that mean compared to photographers, painters, or fiction writers, all obsessed with idiosyncratic ideas, themes, and images?

One last thing: Kaufman is silent as to which mental illness female poets are more likely to have. The *DSM* includes about 400 disorders. Were the poets more anxious, narcissistic, sociopathic, compulsive, psychotic, depressed, addicted? There is no breakdown by type. We don't know, and it's a critical question. Kaufman ballparked the judgments of psychopathology; he could have been more specific because finding that female poets are more likely to be psychotic implies different meanings than finding that female poets are more likely to be anxious.

***

Now, what can we say for sure about links between art and mental illness? The studies that made the case are flawed, their methodologies unsound. And conclusions based on unsound methodologies are suspect. Put simply, the crazy genius idea is unproved, and in most cases, untested, because the research was not properly conducted.

I'm not sure it's possible to pinpoint links between great art and mental illness because so many great artists, the ones we'd want to include as subjects, are dead. So, biographies—or dictionaries, or encyclopedias—are the main source material. Cases exist in which evidence is clear—say Plath or Van Gogh. But most of the time, it's unclear. Too much judgment is required, too much inference.

Most of the suspect findings converge on mood disorder. If we (charitably) assume these findings to be valid, how would "affective illness" logically fuel great art? Depression slows thought, turns it sluggish. One can't make decisions, calculate, solve problems, count backward from 100 by sevens. Memory deteriorates. Nothing gets done. There is loss of energy. The person can seem catatonic. Depression, then, does not or would not set the stage for artistic accomplishment. The idea makes no sense. Major depression is deadening. Major depression is uncreative.

Seeing how hypomania might charge-up creativity is easier, but again, nothing is gained by pathologizing creative states. Why artists get hot, why they trail off or stop—these are complex processes. They sometimes involve *responses* to the art, not the creator him or herself (people stop buying your records or books). Reducing either *quality* or *output* to fluctuating mood cycles is misleadingly one-dimensional.

The truth about creativity is subtler and, in many ways, more complicated than static links between art and madness. We know what the true truth is. We've worked it out. We've outlined the key elements, beginning with openness. We don't need to qualify. We don't need to equivocate or recommend caution. There's a reason for this, a reason to believe in what we know: it's based on decades of quality science. It's rock solid. It's an answer.

I said before that what Jamison really discovered in artists was not mania but creativity. Let's work out the meaning of that observation because it is critical to everything in this book.

High openness gives rise to a turbulent but very fecund inner world. That's what openness is: fecund turbulence. There's less repressing, so more mental contents to deal with. There's a wider range of feeling, a receptivity to feelings, a built-in moodiness, in the sense that moods are felt rather than suppressed, avowed rather than disavowed. There's a higher chance of depression, less need to deny sadness. Behavior is unconventional, rule-rejecting, for two reasons: high boredom and high need for experience. If you're open, you are closure-averse, the opposite of a black-and-white thinker. Sometimes you seem to be all over the map mentally (in a good way). You want complexity, ambiguity, uncertainty, mystery.

We've gone over these things. You can take them in and call them madness, mental illness, disorder, disease. But that is a category error. They aren't madness. They are personality. They are the personality of the artist. And they make for great art, we know that, too.

Let's add to this something else we know. Openness sets the stage for ways of experiencing the world, fecund ways, including unusual perceptions, weird beliefs, lowered filters, chaotic thinking, and cognitive disinhibition. These go into creative process. These are the real "fire" creatives are touched with. Again, one might corner this chaos with mental illness labels, call it mania or hypomania or schizophrenia. It's not. In those who use the chaos, it's a foundation for art, a stimulant for creativity.

There is support for what I'm saying here. One point is obvious by now. It's the theme of this book. More than any other factor that has ever been identified, openness predicts creativity. It is the single indispensable element, bar none. But we can look to additional studies, as well. Two in particular compare and contrast openness traits in creatives with signs of mental disorder. What they show is highly instructive.

The first is by David Nettle. It appeared in 2006, in the *Journal of Research in Personality*. Nettle examined several groups—poets, visual artists, mathematicians, psychiatric patients, and control subjects. First off, he found no differences in treated psychopathology between the artists and controls. In other words, zero evidence of higher rates of mental illness among creatives. Then, he explored trait-based factors. Poets and visual artists reported more unusual experiences than nonartists. Poets also reported more cognitive disorganization, difficulties with attention and concentration. Both poets and visual artists were more impulsively nonconforming. Artists were not more depressed. In fact, in some instances, they were less depressed than controls. All these are expectable. All are in line with the ideas we've been tracking.

Nettle also found something else: Professional artists showed more self-control, not less. They made use of their disorganized mind. They didn't get lost in it. They shifted to a crazy mode, then shifted back out again, as demands for creativity dictated. The "craziness" of their thinking was a choice. Remember Kerouac, for instance. He adopted a method of spontaneous prose, and he did so because he knew it worked.

A second study from 2008 explored everyday creativity in 17-year-old schoolchildren, a roughly equal mixture of males (67) and females

(61). They were given tests of personality, hypomania, intelligence, and creativity. They were asked, for instance, to come up with as many uses as they could for three inanimate objects—a paperclip, a blanket, and a barrel. They completed inventories of creative behaviors and rated their creative capacities. Combining the creativity measures, the measure of hypomanic traits, the IQ measure, and the measures of personality, 10 different variables were examined in total. The question was how they correlated. Would IQ predict creativity? Would hypomania? Would personality? Of all correlations, the strongest was between openness and hypomania, which raises the question, Are these two variables or one? Hypomania predicted divergent thinking, but so did personality measures (chiefly openness and disagreeableness). Interestingly, the factor significant across all main analyses was hypomania. This sounds like a confirmation of the art–madness formula, but it's not. In a final analysis including all three sets of variables—IQ, hypomania, personality—personality traits possessed the most predictive validity. As the authors explain, "It seemed that the overlap between traits with hypomania meant *it was those personality traits which accounted for all the variance*."

There's one last question that's been floating in the margins of this discussion: Why is it that we seem to need to think of artists as mentally ill? What makes that idea so attractive?

Several answers come to mind, but one especially: Great art is dangerous. And great artists are dangerous. What they do is provoke, challenge, incite. They see the world differently, they redefine it. They flout boundaries and convention. They problematize what we take for granted. They are enemies of the status quo. They make things harder, not easier.

Not only are artists, a lot of them, dangerous, but they are also inscrutable, confusing; they live chaotic, contradictory lives. It's hard to make sense of what they do. And some of the things they do are disturbing. There is an alienness to them. They are, as many have noted across the ages, outsiders.

Writer James Agee explored this subject in his masterpiece, *Let Us Now Praise Famous Men*. "A good artist is a deadly enemy of society," he says. "No society, no matter how good, could be mature enough to support a real artist without mortal danger to that artist." Every "fury on earth" has been absorbed in time, he argues. "Swift, Blake, Beethoven, Christ, Joyce, Kafka, name me a one who has not been thus castrated." Fighting off effects of fury's "castrating" cultural absorption requires reconnecting with art's intrinsic danger.

> Get a radio or a phonograph capable of the most extreme loudness possible. . . . Sit down to listen to a performance of Beethoven's Seventh Symphony. . . . But I don't mean just sit down and listen. I mean this: turn it on as loud as you can get it. Then get down on the floor and jam your ear as close to the loudspeaker as you can get it and stay there. . . . You won't hear it nicely. If it hurts you, be glad of it. . . . Is what you hear pretty? or beautiful? or legal? or acceptable? It is beyond any calculation savage and dangerous and murderous to all equilibrium in human life as human life is; and nothing can equal the rape it does on all that death; nothing except anything, anything in existence or dream, perceived anywhere remotely towards its true dimension.

Acceptance nullifies art, says Agee. So does reductionistic labeling. What we do these days, when faced with people we can't understand, people who disturb and frighten us, people who say things that don't make instant, conventional sense, is call them mentally ill. It's a social pacifier. It seems to explain something away. But it's not, in fact, an act of understanding. It's an act of fear, helplessness, and confusion.

8
Art and Suicide

I got a call a couple of years ago, from someone I don't know, who wanted to talk to me about the photographer Diane Arbus. I don't remember the caller's name. She was an artist herself, apparently, and a professor of some kind back East. It was a strange, "Deep Throat" exchange, a little Socratic too, as if the idea was to set me straight, correct my errors of fact and reasoning.

"You know the real reason Diane Arbus committed suicide, right?" This was said with very few preliminaries.

"Well. I wrote a book about her."

"But, you know the real reason, correct?"

"What real reason?"

Some vague Socratics: "She kept a notebook."

"I know. I wrote a book about her."

"What was the final entry?"

"I know the final entry."

"But what was it?"

"I know it!"

"Say it."

"OK. I'll play along. It was 'Last Supper.'"

"Right. What does 'Last Supper' refer to?"

"Are you going to tell me what you want to tell me or is this some sort of test?"

"Betrayal. Judas, remember? The Judas kiss? It's a Bible reference."

It went on like this. The idea was to tell me what the caller believed I did not know: the exact single reason why Arbus had killed herself, the cause, the solution to the puzzle. My caller spoke with the assurance that such a thing was knowable, that there was no obscurity in it, nothing mysterious or contestable. In fact, most of what she said I did know. Arbus had been having a strange and obsessive affair with the artist Marvin Israel, who was also a kind of mentor or advisor to her.

The Mind of the Artist. William Todd Schultz, Oxford University Press. © Oxford University Press 2022.
DOI: 10.1093/oso/9780197611098.003.0009

He had been taking steps to end it, or he had ended it. This "enraged" her, in the words of her therapist, Helen Boigon. What I didn't know, and what the caller said members of the "inner circle" did, was that Arbus had discovered Israel was also having an affair with a person exceptionally close to her, a betrayer—hence, the "Last Supper" entry. It was this revelation, the caller suggested, that sealed Arbus' doom. Not only was Israel ending things, but he was involved with someone else whom Arbus loved and trusted deeply. The suicide was a kind of punishment delivered to the two of them, betrayers both, it would appear.

How many reasons for suicide suffice, in great artists or in anyone? Is there ever just one? And if, instead, there are many, even limitless reasons, when we add them together, do they really thoroughly account for the act, or is some degree of variance always left unexplained? Is it possible for suicide to be almost random? The philosopher Ludwig Wittgenstein, a kind of philosopher-artist, actually, feared that he would take himself "by surprise." Can such a thing occur? Might anyone ever, as does a Kafka's character in the short story, "The Judgment," impulsively jump off a bridge to death? Or, can a person, one of sound mind and body, sanely kill himself? Is suicide *ipso facto* mental illness?

When it comes to making sense of people, especially complex people, and the question of why they do what they do, the best rule of thumb, one I've always adopted, is "overdetermination"—that is, everything happens for a chorus of reasons, each contributing some motive force. This goes for writing a book, reading a book, marrying, divorcing—and it certainly goes for suicide or, for that matter, creating art. Motives are confederacies. No one reason alone suffices. Multiplicity is the thing. Just as there isn't likely to be any single reason why poets write poetry, there isn't likely to be any single reason why poets commit suicide, when they do. To search for one, to believe in one, is a fool's angle. Simplification is a form of misunderstanding.

There's also the matter of intent. Famous suicides, in particular, elicit a well-intentioned but also sometimes semi-delusional protective impulse. It was a mistake, people insist. She did not mean to die. This was Boigon's position on Arbus. The real goal, Boigon told me, was to punish those who had hurt her. Arbus wanted to be found; she did not want to die. Others have said the same about poet Sylvia Plath. Plath only wanted to come close. She expected to be discovered. Her death was a miscalculation. In extreme versions, this impulse veers toward nefarious, desperate monomanias. It wasn't suicide at all; it was murder. By far the best example of this particular mindset is Kurt Cobain, the subject of an industry of clotted, irrational, illogical speculation, in which every stray fact is accorded a superabundance of malevolent meaning. There's handwriting not his on the suicide note. He was too high on heroin to pull the trigger. He had plans for the future; he was starting to get his life together. Then the final, inevitable salvo: Courtney did it, the evil harpy, the hateful female.

What we don't like to admit, and what seems somehow wrong or unacceptable, is the fact that, in many ways, suicide is boring. It happens for all the same reasons anything else happens. It's just a lot more sad and scary, a lot more consequential. And probably most important of all: It forces introspection. Do I, too, have it in me? Could I do the same? For Camus, this was the fundamental ethical question: Why not kill yourself? Why continue to live in absurdity?

In Chapter 7 we saw that research on the link between art and mental illness was flawed, so to take the position that suicide in artists is a function of artists disproportionately suffering from mood disorders like depression or mania/hypomania is risky. That foundation is anything but firm. Besides, less than 5% of people admitted to a hospital for mood disorder die by suicide anyway. Most people with a psychiatric disorder "will not die by suicide, nor will they experience suicidal behavior," according to one review. More to the point, "although the presence and accumulation of psychiatric disorders are risk factors for suicidal behavior, they have little predictive power and perhaps more importantly do not account for why people try to kill themselves." Research on artists and suicide, specifically, is sparse. We know as little about any artist's reasons as we do about anyone else's, and again, it's not as if their reasons must be more complex, more inventive, or more difficult to survey. But a few studies are out there. And at least actuarially, in relation to level of overall risk, the good ones provide some helpful grounding.

For instance, in 1996 in the *Journal of Suicide and Life-Threatening Behavior*, Steven Stack gathered facts on suicide from 21 states reporting occupational data in the National Mortality Data File. Artists were identified using standard federal occupational codes, including authors (code 183), musicians and composers (code 186), actors and directors (code 187), painters and sculptors (code 188), and dancers (code 193). Stack found 33.30 artist suicides per 100,000 artists—three times the national average. Controlling for gender (males are more likely to kill themselves) and other sociodemographic correlates, artists remained at "an elevated risk of suicide amounting to 125%." Musicians' risk was exceptionally high. The percentage of suicide in all who die is 1.5%; the rate for musicians, 2.1%—hardly overwhelming, but significant all the same.

As for how to account for the findings, Stack focuses on artist labor markets. "As an occupational group," he says, "artists are more likely than others to experience labor market strains. These include unemployment, underemployment, client dependency (in a quest after gigs/contracts), multiple job holding, and low incomes. Some work at menial jobs by day and do art at night." Another reality, known with painful clarity to creatives, is that most artistic products get rejected—usually summarily, and thus, apparently totally. And artistic products aren't like other products, or at least not many. They are personal; they come with added vulnerability; they express secrets, intimacies, yearnings. The stakes are high. As Stack puts it dryly, "such rejections are often difficult to deal with."

No one likes rejection. It's never easy. But for artists, the pain is magnified. Art lives closer to the self, closer to the core than, say, accounting or roof repair. There's no dearth of cases fitting this dreadful recipe, but an especially poignant one is John Kennedy Toole (mentioned briefly before). His desperately personal comic novel (is any novel not desperately personal?), *A Confederacy of Dunces*, which he wrote with a feeling of total certitude, was rejected by editors as "pointless," "about nothing." He was advised to start over, to set it aside and begin again. He couldn't. He believed in it, it was all he had, it was unbetrayable, and except in minor details, unalterable. He kept going back to publishers, pleading his case, explaining his position, yet nothing changed. He got the same response, over and over: The manuscript was flawed, possibly hopelessly so; and if it was flawed, so was he, his vision, his genius, his sense of his own ability. He drove his car to California, then, from there, to Milledgeville, Georgia, to find the home of Flannery O'Connor. He may have felt like one of her characters. A deluded true believer in the God of his art. He poisoned himself with carbon monoxide. Crushingly, 11 years later his "merely amusing" novel appeared, through the intervention of writer Walker Percy, who fought for it. The book won a posthumous Pulitzer.

In the broadest sense, maybe it all comes down to that "wound" Norman Mailer said artists possess: no wound, no great art. This wound animates, but it also claws. You want it when you want it—it's your gently melancholic soundtrack—but you also wish it would go away when it's no longer needed. Edvard Munch, the Norwegian painter famous for "The Scream," saw things this way: "I would not be without suffering. I owe so much of my art to suffering." The cost, then, was acceptable. Or the poet Rilke: "Don't take my devils away because my angels may flee too," both (devils and angels) issuing from the same tangled source. Or Kafka: "Art for the artist is only suffering, through which he releases himself for further suffering." You suffer to make it, and you suffer in its wake to make it again.

There's little hope for success in any artist–suicide algorithm, that much is obvious. There's the abiding wound, but not a lot more to go on. So, to get at a range of possible dynamics, none universal, what I want to do, completely speculatively, is inspect particular cases and see what they tell us. I also stop to take the measure of one special feature or determinant: how suicide sometimes comes at the end of a process of artistic redefinition. The artist tries something new, in terms of form or content, apparatus or theme, and the product, so unlike anything he or she has attempted before, seems at first outrageously right and satisfying. Sometimes that feeling lasts, sometimes it doesn't. But either way, the new development occasions a risky and not necessarily valid reassessment, or devaluing, of all prior artistic activity.

Diane Arbus

Arbus wasn't famous in her lifetime, and she came to photography late—around age 35—taking all her pictures over only a little more than a decade. From very early on she decided she would be a "great sad artist." For her, the sadness preceded any intuition of greatness, so she joined the two together. The sadness was there first. It was a master narrative. There did not seem to be any other kind of artist to try for. The sadness had to be accommodated. In school she painted; she also wrote. The writing continued alongside the photo-making, but painting revolted her; brushes sounded distastefully squishy. She also got sick of hearing how great she was, how anything she did was flawless, an annoying habit of teachers at the elite school she attended. She didn't trust the feedback. If everything was so great there seemed to be no point.

Her family was rich, and it made her feel like a "privileged exile." She found it humiliating. She was the "princess" in a loathsome Transylvanian movie. What she suffered from, she said, was the feeling of "immunity and exemption" afforded by the family's money. Her mother went through long depressive episodes borne of narcissism and fragile self-absorption in which she felt unloving and unlovable. Her father Arbus saw as all front and money-mad, a phony whose one talent seemed to be "giving advice." So there wasn't any secure base to count on. It was a family of silences. You were on your own. Arbus' response to the sickness was to get sicker, intentional exposure therapy. She'd defeat it by magnification. She'd identify to nullify.

Her first big show was "New Documents" in 1967. From the start she wasn't settled about it. It was the typical artist dilemma: She wanted it desperately, but she didn't like how desperately she wanted it, she didn't feel ready. She told *Newsweek*, "I always thought I'd wait till I was 90 to have a show or a book because I figured I was good for only one shot. . . . I wanted to wait until I had it all done." All the same, she prepped for the opening with uncharacteristic self-regard. She cut her hair, she got a perm, she bought a dress, she asked a friend to help with makeup. It was the junior prom she never had. Friends called her "very radiant but studied." She could not "just come and have a good time," like other artists in the show. She lingered for hours, "watching people watch the pictures and listening to what they said," veering from laughter to tears. The night was splendid, she said in the end, "but too many calls and letters and people thinking I am an expert or incredibly lovable." "I need to be forlorn and anonymous," she realized, "in order to be truly happy."

In July she's in San Francisco but feels "queasy and repudiated" by California. She starts to believe her pictures are changing, like she's making people instead of photographs. She doesn't want her subjects to look at her anymore. She sees "odd new things" in the photos that strike her as either necessary or exciting. "I want to make order and begin again," she says, "in obscurity."

Through 1968, everything is the same and different, there's stasis and change, though with Arbus the sameness always seems most salient of all. Internally, she's all over the map. Her work goes on "oddly and obsessively." She thinks she'd like to shoot criminals, whores, returned runaways—her standard freak subject matter. She looks forward "like a bride" to what she still calls her "new beginning," but she feels no less "queasy and strange" to herself, her incompetence looming "like a middle name." There's a new energy coming from somewhere. It's more than she knows what to do with. She wants to dam it; she's not sure she can aim it anywhere. She calls it a "subterranean revolution." Signs erupt that seem portentous but also vague and probably pointless. The energy's no good, she says, if all it does is make her feel elated.

Whatever this energy was, whatever message it carried, it didn't last, because by July 1968, 3 years before Arbus' suicide, she found she couldn't walk up the stairs. She's hospitalized for evaluation and testing. Her liver is biopsied, and the finding is hepatitis. What's remarkable, at this point, is the use to which Arbus put her hospitalization. Forced to rest, unable to chase obsessions, physically cut off from her cameras and equipment and all the creepy, dark places she compulsively took herself to as a way of seeing what she was never allowed to see as a child, there wasn't much to do but reflect, take stock of who she was and what it all meant, or might mean, in the near future. Writing letters as a way to pass time, she reaches several challenging conclusions, most of them uprooting. "No state of being is intrinsic," she finds. The possibilities are endless. You don't have to be anything. You don't have any built-in purpose. Also, "oneself is dispensable"—this being less a wish to die than a feeling that you could throw it all away if you wished to. In fact, there is no self. It's more just moment-to-moment existence. When she was most sick and scared, she says, "I was no longer a photographer"—her art, and the identity bound up with it, disappeared. For the first time in a long time, it came to seem inessential. She goes on: "I am still not [a photographer] and something about realizing that I don't have to photograph was terribly good for me. . . . I lost my curiosity . . . but learned that was OK." What comes through is the feeling of relief. Her frantic, chaotic need to shoot, to make pictures, she begins to see, momentarily, as ego-dystonic—at odds with who she is, an accident. The burden of art and art-making drops off during her convalescence, and she's grateful for this, she finds it OK. She doesn't have to be *that thing*; "what if I'm no longer a photographer," she wonders. Part of her seems to want it to stop. She doesn't say this outright, as far as anyone knows, but it's likely she began to wonder why she took photos in the first place. If no state of being is intrinsic, then it's alright not to be what she believed she had to. Anybody who is great at anything entertains such thoughts now and then. Should I keep at it, should I try again, or have I done enough, is there more to say or do, at what point should I stop? Arbus saw that she could stop. She didn't, as it turns out. But the realization turned her around to face deep questions about who she really was.

By September she's back at work but she misses being sick. It was no doubt a lot easier than generating ideas and carrying them out, or working with magazine editors who sometimes seemed to be putting her off, as if she were, she says, "too big for my britches." The energy is back too. This time she feels it as rage, appearing every night at 4 AM "like a werewolf." She doesn't try making sense of it, she doesn't touch on its aboutness—who or what it has to do with—but wonders once more how to turn it into energy that could serve the work. More thoughts surface about the nature of her art—its function, its origins. She decides, now, that "photography is a sort of private sin of mine. As a virtue I find it really hard to sustain." On other occasions she uses similar words. She calls her photography "very perverse." From the beginning it seemed "a naughty thing to do." This isn't a passing sentiment. Arbus repeated it across years. It's the secret behind what she was up to. She can't see what she does as virtuous. It's not positive. It's not well-intentioned. If it were, she'd have no interest. It's unclear whether she ever really understood what she was driving at, or even wanted to, and she's not positioning herself as an outsider, or her art as a form of protest. The sin, the perversion, is personal. She calls it "a mysterious body thing." More specifically, "it had a lot to do with not believing what I was told. . . . I had tried to do everything right, and then suddenly it was a kind of license to go wherever I wanted to go and to see what it really seemed like, and do exactly what I wanted to do." She compares the feeling to going into the kitchen in the middle of the night. An impulse drives you; you don't know what. "There's something you want and there's a lot of things you don't want," but before setting out, you have no idea which is which. Then you find what you like, and you like it "sort of obsessively." If it's Oreo cookies—Arbus' example—you "keep eating them," you can't stop.

What's striking is how adolescent this is. The art is misbehavior, not doing what you've been told, a sneaky sort of "acting out." It's "naughty." It's also not under your control. You follow "the mysterious body thing," and it takes you someplace unknown. At the end of it all, the photograph is the "proof." You went and saw. "Undeniably something was there," Arbus says, "and it left this stain"—an interesting word, as stains are unpretty and unwanted, like a lot of her sitters.

In December 1968 she first gets the idea for a series that would occupy the rest of her life. She says, without explanation as to why—she never thought in terms of why—that she wants to shoot "mentally retarded people, idiots, imbeciles, and morons, especially the cheerful ones." She imagines a book, which she sees lying at the end of a rainbow, and despite her sense that she's "not as good a photographer as people think," the "only thing is to go to the limit with it." To "excel."

On assignment she's off to London, but can't find anything "sordid" enough to shoot. Nobody seems sufficiently "miserable, drunk, crippled, mad, or desperate." In a development that's been in the works for some time, she finally legally divorces her husband Allan, an official end to a relationship already over. It's amicable—in fact, maybe too amicable, Arbus feels. She wonders if there needs to be more of a "total severance." In the beginning, Allan had been her "Swami." He's still an important confidant and sounding-board. Now and then he also helps out with money, a constant source of stress.

There are times she feels paranoid and besieged. People want to see her and show her pictures they believe resemble hers. Her own work strikes her as "junk." She considers abandoning the square format, which seems a great artistic leap.

It's in September 1969, roughly 2 years prior to her suicide, that Arbus, for the first time, goes into therapy. It's not clear what led her to do this. Perhaps the rage, perhaps her depressions, her questions about her work, her divorce, the realizations she came to during her convalescence. Therapy was unnatural to Arbus. She never seemed hopeful about its prospects. But she was making various small, to this point, artistic leaps, and therapy was a personal leap. The pain, whatever it was, apparently provided just enough motivation.

The therapy itself seemed to stumble along without clear goals. Never was the art discussed. Nor was Arbus' family, a subject she ruled out of bounds—she was "sick of talking about them," Boigon told me. The two women didn't even seem to like each other all that much. Arbus' art did nothing for Boigon. It "stirred no longing"; it left her with a feeling of "faint sadness"; it seemed to speak of "the regrettable part of life experience." Boigon says, "We just accepted the phenomena as they evolved. Not to be explained—that was Diane."

The phenomena evolving were twofold, and connected: sex and rage. Arbus "sexualized everything," Boigon says, and she wasn't alone in this observation. Around the same time—1970—photographer Stephen Frank attended one of Arbus' lectures at the Rhode Island School of Design. The pictures she showed were fresh and unknown to most—twins, nudists, transvestites, a thin boy with a hand grenade, a deranged-looking man holding a small American flag. What resonated more than the shots was Arbus herself. What Frank has to say is surprising but it speaks to Arbus' talent for seduction. "She was very sexy. She told stories about each of her photographs, and she had a great sexual anecdote for every picture, and by the time she was finished we were all in love with her." "There were no taboos," he said. "You just felt like you could tell her whatever your sexual fantasy was, and she would understand." In therapy it was the same. Arbus delighted in cataloguing her "sexual exploits with total strangers who struck her as bizarre in their appearance," Boigon said. Freaks enthralled her from day one—her first subject—but to Boigon, she was "just as much obsessed with sex." In a book of his own, Arbus' brother, the poet Howard Nemerov, about whom she rarely spoke, noted "sexual experimentation" with Diane when they were kids. This emerged in therapy. Arbus saw Howard as one of her "more intriguing sexual playmates," says Boigon. She seemed, Boigon believed, to be referring to more than innocent childhood games. The suggestion was that she and her brother had sex. But there was no elaboration, and Boigon never pushed it.

Whatever the case, incest was a real possibility. (Other accounts, recently published, claim Arbus had sex with her brother just 2 weeks before her suicide.)

Unsurprisingly, Arbus came on to Boigon, too. The therapy space had a couch and chair, but Arbus rarely used either. Boigon says she "sashayed." She'd look at objects on the shelves. She'd peer out the window. She studied the stuff on the table Boigon used as a desk. Sometimes she would "fling herself on the floor beside my stool," says Boigon, on which she kept her feet elevated because of a medical condition. Once, after "plunking herself down" like this, Arbus tried caressing Boigon's legs with what Boigon calls "a slimy expression on her face; she postured and grimaced frequently." Boigon said, "I don't like that." She told her she could say whatever she pleased, but she couldn't, under any circumstances, "touch my person." Arbus did stop, and there was no repeat.

The rage revolved around Marvin Israel, a major focus of discussion. Israel was an art director and graphic designer whom Arbus met in 1959, and whose importance in her life skyrocketed with Allan Arbus' departure for California and the subsequent divorce. Israel was also a painter, his work disturbing and sexually themed, with one piece, "Hanging Dog," depicting either erotic asphyxiation or a bizarre suicide scenario. Boigon says Israel was a sex-games partner for Arbus. She counted on him to concoct scenarios including various self-made dildos. But he began to refuse, Boigon claims. She says he was "slacking off," not providing the accustomed "sexual stimulus." This is what came to enrage Arbus. The rage was ongoing, and it dominated the therapy. Artist Mary Frank knew Israel and Arbus independently. "Marvin," she says, "could not have given Diane that feeling of being cared for. He was a very complicated person, and interested in his own powers." Though at times capable of kindness, "there was always this explosive aspect" in him. When Frank saw Arbus despondent, "it definitely had to do with Marvin." Boigon's feeling was the same. The rage didn't abate.

In January 1970 Arbus moved to Westbeth, a living and working space for artists. She thinks of trying an antidepressant—her regular doctor had recommended one—but says Boigon "doesn't believe in them." Money is a constant pain. She takes assignments but feels, at times, that it's "too arduous to go on," she finds freedom "a bit eerie."

Something in her "pretends" she can't deal with it. She wins an award from the American Society of Magazine Photographers but calls it a "booby prize." "It just depressed me so," she says. The idea of giving a speech freaks her out; she tells everyone not to come. She wakes up at night obsessed with the idea of buying a new camera, a Pentax with which she is smitten. "What it could do," she imagines, "to make the pictures more narrative and temporal, less fixed and single and complete and isolated, more dynamics, more things happening." By the end of the year, her last, she declares "I have so much to learn about how to live. What have I been doing lo these 47 years?"

Through all this, she'd continued to visit institutions for the retarded (her word for them) for special events, and to take photographs. These shots bewitched and unnerved her. They weren't like anything she'd ever done. Before, with all her other work, two reactions set the tone, as she saw it: recognition and identification. These were missing now. She wasn't sure what she was seeing anymore, it wasn't any kind of metaphorical re-seeing, as it had been before. She also could not easily identify with her subjects, although she tried. In letters, she wrote little accounts of some of these people, described them, imagined their thoughts, zeroed in on gestures. But she couldn't unmask or expose them—they were already unmasked, they were guileless. She couldn't go at them aggressively, as she'd done with other sitters so many times before. She couldn't, as she used to put it, shoot the gap between intention and effect, because there was no high-order intention. These people just were who they were. They weren't trying to be something else. Arbus was no humanist. Her pictures, especially those of "normal" people, were editorials. The façade needed to be blown up. In the image, she interpreted her subject's efforts at self-presentation; in the process, her subjects felt "Arbused." It was a seduction and a swindle. Arbus asserted her power; the image belonged to *her*, it was about her reaction. I don't think Arbus ever recognized this, but the shots at institutions exposed her. She disappeared; she was erased. Her method had always been search and destroy. Now she was really giving everything up. The pictures were about something she didn't understand. What they *weren't* about was her.

Initially, none of this mattered. Arbus' response was ecstatic. She told Allan, "FINALLY what I've been searching for," as if the shots were a long-desired culmination, a visitation. She didn't understand it at all. She wasn't sure if the strobe even fired or if it did as a sort of strange fill in. She says she's discovered sunlight, late afternoon early winter sunlight. She tells Allan, who had introduced her to photography, "I seem to have perverted your brilliant technique all the way round, bending it over backwards you might say till it's JUST like snapshots but better." The list of adjectives she tosses out is virtually endless: gorgeous, terrific, marvelous, lyric, tender, pretty. "It's the first time I've encountered a subject," she says, "where the multiplicity is the thing. I mean I am not just looking for the BEST picture of them. I want to do lots."

Doon Arbus, Diane's daughter, who became her posthumous interpreter, saw things much the same. Diane, she says, recognized in these pictures something new, something she'd been searching for. It "must have felt like a foreign country," she says. To keep pursuing what she'd seen in the shots, Doon says, "entailed giving up certain elements of a style and technique that had become identified with her work . . . and seemed responsible for its unique character." "She knew the value of what she was giving up and the value of what she was gaining in return." Her presence goes all but unnoticed. "The collaborator has become a witness . . . The discovery set her free." To me, the key insight, the key difference, is this. Doon writes: "No one else had ever posed for her so unself-consciously, with such abandon, such equanimity about their own sense of identity. . . . That's why none of her other photographs looks quite like these do."

It's worth repeating: Before, Arbus wrestled the image away from sitters. If it was a collaboration, it didn't include much compromise, much negotiation. She got what she wanted; she chose the shot, the moment confirming her perception. Her method, most of the time, was to stir up and shoot the agitation, the sadness, the anxiety, the awkwardness. She worked from awkwardness, she said. When she pressed the shutter, she felt "gently clobbered," and so, after the fact, did her subjects, although probably a lot less gently. In the residents of the institution there was nothing to steal or distort. They didn't pose at all. They just were. And by being, as Doon says, unself-conscious, they robbed Arbus of what had been her constant motivation. These shots weren't naughty or sordid. They weren't a private sin. They weren't perverse. They weren't, as she used to say about her pictures, "a secret about a secret." There weren't any secrets. It was all out in the open, utterly unguarded. I don't think this discovery set her free. I think it exposed her, to herself. The difference she felt and saw in the pictures undermined her prior working methods. Maybe for the first time, she understood what she had been about, what she had been up to. The "discovery" became an indictment. If you finally find what you've been searching for, what does such a finding mean for everything that has come before?

What makes these ideas a little less speculative is that over time, in the months preceding her suicide, Arbus began to hate the pictures. She did an about-face. She was less sure of them. She started telling friends that her art wasn't doing it for her anymore. She wasn't getting anything out of it. It had stopped delivering. She keeps waking at 4 AM, feeling jittery, talking to herself. She conjures new ideas for series, one on love, one on S&M. To make money she offers a class, but her students' pictures bore her. She isn't sure what's wrong with them, but she doesn't want to look at them, as if the boringness "might be catching." The worst, she says, is that she's "literally scared of getting depressed." Energy "leaks out" and she finds herself "lacking the confidence even to cross the street."

In the words of the Arbus Estate, Arbus' suicide in late July 1971 was "neither inevitable nor spontaneous, neither perplexing nor intelligible," both understandable and un-understandable. She was found by Marvin Israel, crunched up in the bathtub, on her left side, in a red shirt and blue denim shorts. The "Last Supper" notation was made on July 26 in an appointment book, but according to the Estate, that page, along with the next two, were "meticulously excised," no one knows by whom, and the pages were never recovered. Would they solve anything? Maybe. Were they excised to conceal motive or, more to the point, blame? Maybe. Whatever the case, the fact that the pages were clipped—"meticulously"—and never found seems difficult to explain. It makes no sense. As judged by the medical examiner, whom the Estate suggests may have taken the pages—an unlikely possibility, it seems—cause of death was doubly determined: acute secobarbital poisoning and "incised wounds" of both wrists. She had cut herself and overdosed.

Going back over this history, it seems nearly impossible to perform any sort of clarifying calculation. It's a mess of motives. Some suicide risk factors are present, it's true. There were money problems. She was in ill health with hepatitis, the reason for her hospitalization. She was depressed. She felt a rage that she never knew how or where to direct. She seemed to have difficulty sleeping, waking often at 4 AM. There was also the divorce, which, though a long time coming, felt like a major loss. And the therapy, continuing on up to her death, failed to provide any serious relief. It meandered; Arbus never seemed clear on what she got out of it. Or, for that matter, what to put into it. Finally, there was the end of the affair with Israel, which left her desperate and flagrantly needy. And maybe, as the caller phoned to tell me, a revelation of betrayal, a final sickening straw.

But beside all this, there were the reassessments of the art. It started as acting out. She was born rich and immune; the art was a sickness of her choosing. She said she photographed what was evil. Yet it's not as if photographing evil made her feel less evil inside—or perverse, or sinful, or naughty. It's not as if the pictures purified her, or even helped her figure anything out (not that she ever wanted to). They were just more evil. Evil was why Arbus did photography. And it's why the series taken at institutions proved uprooting. Those shots were *good*—pure and innocent. She loved this; then she decided she didn't. Her art wasn't doing it for her anymore because she wasn't doing it in the way she needed to. The new pictures stopped repeating trauma. They weren't about feeling like an exile. It's not that this revelation killed her. But at the same time, it made her see things about herself that she found hard to live with. Arbus was her art; she had said, once, she couldn't kill herself because the work needed to go on. Once the work shifted, the need for it to go on started to seem less worth living for. As she said, if the work wasn't a private sin, it was unsustainable.

Kurt Cobain

Arbus wasn't famous in her lifetime. Cobain was, very, and to his last day, as evidenced by a suicide note, he never stopped love-hating it. To

Cobain, being famous was like being popular in high school. He didn't want to be liked by the people who liked him. He wanted to be liked by someone else. Maybe, fundamentally, himself.

Cobain grew up in Washington State between Aberdeen and Montesano, towns about 20 miles apart. This was the wet, green Pacific Northwest, the kind of place Ken Kesey rhapsodized about in *Sometimes a Great Notion*: moss-covered, moldy, endlessly drizzling. Every basement smelled like a forest. Boys wore Carhartt jackets over wife-beaters and drove pickup trucks. You started drinking around age 12, stealing booze from your parents or your neighbor's open garage. Girls were hard and tough and smoked and played Foosball in parlors. Cobain felt like a "scapegoat," although no one really picked on him, he says. He was so withdrawn, so antisocial and isolated "that I was almost insane." He liked to draw, "do artistic things and listen to music," but he couldn't find friends he was fond of or whom he believed to be compatible. "I felt so different and so crazy that people just left me alone," he says. "I wouldn't have been surprised if they had voted me Most Likely to Kill Everyone at a High School Dance"—"but I'm sure I would opt to kill myself first," he adds.

Cobain's "origin story," one he grew more and more tired of, though it was he who posited it and kept coming back to it, centered on divorce. His parents split up when he was 7, and it left him feeling ashamed and resentful. He kept up a relationship with his more affectionate mother, but for long periods of time, one lasting more than 10 years, he did not speak to his dad, who finally sought him out backstage at a show. "I was happy to see him because I always wanted him to know I didn't hate him anymore. On the other hand, I didn't want to encourage our relationship because I just didn't have anything to say to him. My father is incapable of showing much affection, or even of carrying on a conversation. I didn't want to have a relationship with him just because he's my blood relative. It would bore me." Cobain always dismissed efforts to find any deep or personal meaning in his lyrics, which were cut-ups of poetry and journal entries, but in the song "Serve the Servants" he writes about trying hard to have a father; he also calls the "legendary divorce" a bore. He'd "hardly ever written anything that obviously personal," he said. "It's the first time I've ever really dealt with parental issues."

Donald Cobain was an auto mechanic; Kurt was, in his words, a sickly, feminine person, more drawn to girls as friends than to Aberdeen's legion of "big redneck jocks." Kurt called himself "gay in spirit," and for a time he figured he could actually be gay: "I thought that might be a solution to my problem." He sometimes pretended to be gay as a way of being more simply and conventionally isolated and alone. "People just thought I was weird at first, just some fucked up kid," he recalls. "But once I got the gay tag, it gave me the freedom to be able to be a freak and let people know they should just stay away from me, instead of having to explain to someone that they should just stay the fuck away from me." Fake gayness made apartness easier.

For a long time there was nothing but apartness. No one wanted Kurt, and for good reason—he didn't want anyone either. He was too active; his mind never stopped. He was prescribed Ritalin, inevitably, but it had no positive effect. He bounced from home to home; he hung out with losers under bridges. He could have easily gone nowhere. That's where he was headed—a talented, sensitive, arty kid dosed with messages of worthlessness, at total odds with his depressing surroundings, seduced early on by the prospect of suicide as a sort of last resort escape clause. But one day a friend passed along a punk compilation tape—Black Flag, Flipper—and it blew him away—"I'd finally found my calling; it expressed the anger that I felt, the alienation." He cut his hair. He lip-synced to the tunes. He'd started playing guitar already; now he played faster, and he added distortion.

Just like a lot of musically inclined kids did back in the early 80s, especially those who tracked down alternative vinyl and watched new wave bands like Oingo Boingo on MTV, at some point Cobain made a four-track demo at his aunt's house. He carried it around for a year or so. He'd foist it on friends he wanted to start a band with. By this time, Cobain had known Nirvana bassist Krist Novoselic for several years—he'd moved to Aberdeen in 1979, from California. Krist hear the cassette, decided it was at least OK, and what Kurt called his "imaginary band," Fecal Matter, was born. Gigs were any random party they could manage to play at, and what they did, for the most part, was run through the songs on the Fecal Matter tape—"our seven songs," Cobain said. A first performance was out in the woods, somewhere between Aberdeen and Montesano, which is pretty close to nowhere.

It was Halloween night, the typical kegger. "We were really drunk," Cobain says, "and we had some fake Halloween blood and we smeared it all over ourselves. We alienated the entire crowd. . . . Locals who hated our guts. . . . The entire party moved into the kitchen, just left us there in the front room." One song was "Buffy's Pregnant," and it starts out like a chainsaw (it is on YouTube, as is the entire demo). It's obvious satire. Guys get drunk and vomit, and notice women's asses, and fantasize beating up "punk rock faggots," one of whom would have been Kurt. The chorus ends with the word "clone" repeated three times. But it's good. It's actually good.

Sub Pop noticed, and the band signed, releasing a cover of Shocking Blue's "Love Buzz"—the label's idea. The first record, *Bleach*, appeared in 1989. Initially, Cobain wanted to re-record the Fecal Matter tunes because "that was a period of our band, that was part of our progression. We were really into experimental, noisy." The label had other ideas, as usual—"there was a little bit of major label attitude going on," Cobain recalls. So a batch of new tunes got written, dashed off in less than 2 weeks, sets of lyrics completed the night before recording. This wasn't anything new. For Cobain, the words usually came last, they seemed almost inconsequential, mostly a matter of filling and phrasing. About *Bleach* specifically, he says, "When I write a song the lyrics are the least important thing. I can go through two or three different subjects in a song and the title can mean absolutely nothing at all. Sometimes I try to make things harder for myself, just to try to make myself a bit more angry. I try out a few subconscious things I suppose, like conflicts with other people. Most of the lyrics on the *Bleach* album are about my life in Aberdeen." If there's any sort of theme on the record, it's emotional. The words don't coalesce into meaning. Shame figures frequently; there's constant mistreatment—Floyd the Barber ties him to a chair, cuts him up; a girl hangs him out to dry, "in your eyes I'm not worth it." He feels lobotomized; he even resents the lack of recess in high school; he's a "negative creep." The record is angry. Cobain says he wrote a lot of it when he was feeling particularly pissed off. Most likely, anger was what the label wanted, what it expected; but it's personal, too, a stored-up encyclopedia of bitterness, distrust, resentment, and rejection. The wound was capacious, and Cobain channeled it because, very simply, there wasn't a lot else there. It was the atmosphere he moved in.

What happened next is almost impossible to fathom. Sub Pop didn't see it coming, nor did anyone else, including Nirvana. It has to be one of the strangest success stories ever, and one of the most improbable, discontinuous artistic leaps. *Bleach* (recorded for $606.15) had its moments, as did the Fecal Matter tape. But melody was almost nonexistent. There was nowhere to latch on—on purpose. The songs weren't songs, per se, so much as migrainous aural assaults befitting the punk Cobain was enchanted with at the time.

Then came *Nevermind*, preceded by a signing with Geffen. And "Smells Like Teen Spirit." And "Come as You Are." And "Lithium." And "Something in the Way." It sold astronomically; the videos were spectacular, especially "Smells Like Teen Spirit," filmed in a smoky gymnasium, with tattooed cheerleaders in anarchy gear, and Cobain looking like he'd just eloped from a psych unit. Even the onlookers, this time, in fantasy, fit the image of the people Cobain wanted to play for—they head bang and crowd surf. It's a psychotic riotous Jailhouse Rock. It ends with a janitor sweeping up in front of a bow-tied, tied-up teacher in a dunce cap. Now the misfit loser nerds were mainstream, and still pissed off, even when the record hit number one—ousting U2, Metallica, and Michael Jackson. Every record exec in the world headed to the Pacific Northwest to headlock and sign the next "grunge" commodity. As "Smells Like Teen Spirit" took off, Nirvana was touring in Europe. Reports starting reaching them—they'd hit the top 40—but no one believed it. Cobain says, "We thought everyone was pulling our legs." When at last they got back, it was Nirvanamania. MTV asked if Cobain was surprised. "Shocked is a good word," he says. "How long did it take me to get used to it? Three years." It was "the right record at the right time," he figured. "I mean, I'm sure there was a collective consciousness. People were tired of Warrant. It just got old." As for the music, "we have no regrets. It was definitely an album we wanted to make. Other than maybe the production was too slick. I don't think it's as raw as it could have been. And that's our fault." Not that rawness wasn't there. It obviously was, but prettied up, folded into melody. Producer Butch Vig says, "even though you couldn't quite tell what Cobain was singing about, you knew it was intense as hell." Asking people to "load up on guns" and bring your friends hardly qualifies as demure; it's the perfect violent fantasy of loser revenge .

The band responded to it all by going into whatever degree of hiding they could manage. An unusual but, given the history, unsurprising dynamic emerged. Cobain famously hated fame—distrusted it, felt a need to disavow it, ridiculed it. He wanted it, of course. He had worked for it. But it didn't fit. It was incongruent with his inner experience—he was never wanted, now he was colossally wanted. He was temperamentally unsuited for fanfare and accolades. But beyond just this, he and the other band members, Grohl and Novoselic, spent "unhealthy amounts of time," in the words of one write-up, "deriding their new audience, dismissing them as jock meatheads." In Cobain's words, "I was upset about finding myself having to play in front of really rude, sexist jerks. I'd never really had any desire to play to people like that and I never expected to have to." In liner notes he even called them out, ordering them not to buy Nirvana records. No doubt this bravado increased the band's street cred, their alt bona fides, their anti-corporate posturing; on the other hand, no artist gets to hand-select his audience. The fans weren't only the kids in the "Smells Like Teen Spirit" video. A lot of them didn't want to riot, they'd never heard of the Butthole Surfers; they just thought Kurt was cute.

And he hated that. He didn't want to be the prom king of the rock world. He was "anti." There was no way he could ever become "pro." He was the whining, complaining, unsatisfiable jerk, as he saw it, or as he imagined others to see it. "Wait! I've got a new complaint," he wrote in "Heart-Shaped Box." Nothing was ever going to be good enough. His script featured him as the scapegoat. The undesirable. The castoff. His vibe was a sort of metaphysical homelessness. So when it came time for a follow-up, the aim was to break what wasn't broken. Novoselic saw it as a "litmus test" for their audience. No "glossiness." No "mainstream appeal." Cobain claimed he never listened to *Nevermind*, and "that says something. I can't stand that kind of production and I don't listen to bands that do that kind of production, no matter how good their songs are." As if speaking to his parents, or the Aberdeen hordes, he said the record company was going to "eat my shit. Of course, they want another *Nevermind*, but I'd rather die than do that." The band signed with the notoriously uncompromising Steve Albini to produce, who told them, "I think the very best thing you could do at this point is exactly what you are talking about doing: bang a record out in a couple of days with high quality but minimal production, no interference from the front-office bulletheads. . . . If a record takes more than a week to make, somebody's fucking up."

It took 2 weeks—more than Albini thought necessary, but far less than the label might have wished for. The fallout has passed into legend. And like all legend, it's hard separating hyperbole from historical fact. But Cobain said the "grown-ups" hated it. Apparently, the label pronounced it "unlistenable"—hard to fathom, since so many of the songs—"Heart-Shaped Box," for instance—are anything but. Even "Rape Me" is perversely hummable. Whatever the case, the idea—and it was very deliberate—was to blow everything up or, less explosively, to be true to a more desirable and honestly self-defining aesthetic; to get back to something that felt more like what the band was and in drummer Dave Grohl's words, "what the band sounded like." *Nevermind* wasn't it. The record that popped, that accounted for the fame, wasn't it. Success was, therefore, in some kind of basic sense for Cobain, fraudulent. *In Utero* was contamination, undoing, what media called "artistic suicide." Themes are sickness—visceral—and brutalization. Gruesome, almost psychotically incongruous images show up in almost every tune—Cobain's childhood and adolescent drawings in verbal form. He kisses open sores, he eats cancer, "her milk is my shit," he's his own parasite, choking on the ashes in a nest of salt, dangling from umbilical nooses. It's very dark and very bizarre. Cobain's head gets unloaded with zero secondary elaboration, and as one reviewer said, you might want to visit but you would not care to stay for long. There's brutalization in "Rape Me"—which Cobain flips into a request, as if to say he's asking for it, it's what he knows—and in a tune about movie star Frances Farmer, a victim of psychiatric abuse. Farmer was from Seattle; Cobain and his wife Courtney Love had read a book about her. The ghastly tale of her life clicked. In a sense she was Courtney, no doubt—radical, loud, opinionated, reckless, formidable, creative—but more broadly she's yet another artist punished—via coma and lobotomy—for being herself, for refusing the persona foisted on her, refusing to behave, just like Cobain.

The record was made in the middle of nowhere, in isolation, with no outside presence except for one visit from Courtney Love, who apparently did not like the look of things (or the sound or process).

Cobain's chronic stomach ailments, which he believed to be idiopathic and poorly understood by the different GI doctors he saw, and which he attributed to his angry screaming on songs, led to a semi-logical—in terms of how Cobain explained it—addiction to heroin. A child arrived, and Kurt and Courtney named her "Frances." There were ODs, media attacks—an article in *Vanity Fair* was particularly eviscerating—and a massively successful unplugged appearance on MTV, in which Cobain's eerie self-possession—a combination of confidence and complete ennui—looks like either mastery or despair. Or maybe, somehow, both. Cobain had been saying he was feeling thoroughly positive for the first time in his life—he'd found a life partner he loved, and he'd had a child. His message was that he was getting it together. A bit like Arbus, "FINALLY what I've been searching for" seems to have been the rally cry. But then, full of heroin, in flight from detox, in the wake of a difficult record that he had first considered calling "I Hate Myself and Want to Die," he was dead, of a gunshot wound to the head. No one believed it. Everyone believed it. It was shocking. It was totally predictable.

Just like Arbus, just like so many of the fiery creatives in this book, Cobain was the "great sad artist," the sadness was the content. Just like Arbus, there was rage that needed to be put to use. There was also the untreatable, irreversible feeling of being unwanted, unloved. Arbus was a freak who made her work freaks; Cobain was, too, and it "paid off well"—teen angst—a fact he realized and deplored. It was a cliché. It was too easy. Both fought off the grind of physical illness—a constant sapping, a constant preoccupation. These weren't illnesses that went away. They flared, they waxed and waned, but they were chronic, the body turning against itself. Arbus' fame was the work on freaks, Cobain's the adolescent anarchy of "Smells Like Teen Spirit." When they died, they were both moving on artistically. They were restarting. They were redefining. They were in process. The work that got them to the mountain top they began to find insincere, insufficient, illegitimately motivated. Everyone loved it, but they didn't buy it. On one hand, this is fear of success, with an added twist of repudiation. You get what you always wanted but it's not what you imagined, it's not you; you want something different, you want something more, something that feels right, and maybe, no matter what you do, no matter who weighs in, you find the result unsatisfying. You are being told you made it, but all you want to do is remake. And every remaking, especially when it seems like a path toward greater truth, occasions the death of a previous way of being.

Sylvia Plath

On the surface, Sylvia Plath is the flawless embodiment of the process I've been talking about. Wading into writing about her is like wading into the most debris-filled inlet imaginable. It's a bit like writing about Hitler, in that seemingly everyone under the sun has had his or her say. Some of the draw has to do with disparity. In Janet Malcolm's words, here, on one hand, reposes this "vacuous girl of the fifties, with dark lipstick and blond hair"; she's "highly self-involved and confused, unstable, driven, perfectionistic, rather humorless." On the other, we have the jarringly surrealistic, deeply spooky last poems of *Ariel*, like nothing else she had ever done, a complete departure into genius, as Plath clearly recognized herself. She "doesn't add up," Malcolm says. I agree. The effort is always to somehow make her add up. How does one get from A to B?

The simplest narrative is provided by Plath's poet-husband Ted Hughes, who, a little surprisingly, saw things in blandly one-dimensional terms—terms that, for others, might come wrapped in decent amounts of postmodern irony. For Hughes it was a movement from false self to true self, from a falseness she could live with, barely, to a truth she couldn't. Over years, Hughes claims, Plath labored conventionally, throwing off various artistic "impurities." She wrote stories and bloodless poems, she wrote the novel *The Bell Jar*. Like almost all first novels, it was transparently autobiographical. It included an accurate account of her initial serious and potentially lethal suicide attempt; it chronicled her attempts to get well, which included ECT or shock therapy. Then, inconceivably, via some alchemical process, in the fall of 1962 and winter of 1963, the impure got pure. The persona, which Plath had perfected so successfully from virtually the day she was born, dropped off, bone by bone. This carapace, gone at last, had been crushing a realer inner life that, now making up for lost time, grabbed the poetry by the hair and dragged it into dark, psychotic imagery, a move from form to formlessness. Plath went from sort of nice to not-nice. She got what she always wanted, but it took her to a place she couldn't get out of.

The core drama of Plath's existence, one I've touched on already, and one she preferred to understand in mythical terms, or really any terms that magnified its impact, was the loss of her beekeeper father Otto when she was 8. This is the kind of trauma most people slowly get over. It fades; one detaches in time. One moves on. Not Plath. She never could or would let go. She pulled Otto into her inner world—what psychologists call "introjection." She made him an indissoluble part of her, she caressed and finessed his image. This "dead father" is "somewhere in you," she tells her journal, "interwoven in the cellular system of your long body." "I brought my love to bear and then you died," she writes in her poem "Electra on Azalea Path"—"it was my love that did us both to death." She realizes, "the guilt, the need for punishment is absurd." It does no good talking about her father, she finds. Any catharsis lasts a day or two, but no real insights emerge. She needs a "catalyst." The answers are in her, but she can't locate them on her own. And of course, as always, they must transform the art: "What inner decision, what inner murder or prison-break must I commit if I want to speak from my true deep voice in writing?" Hughes knew her true voice had not yet emerged; Plath confirms his hypothesis.

This idea of "inner murder" is no accident. It's a canny choice of words. And she seems to know, as well, that the prison she must break out of is entirely her own invention. She's the jailed and the jailer. Like Arbus, Plath was in therapy, dissecting her various stuck points, and journaling her findings. Somewhere along the way, and a little improbably, she read Freud's difficult essay, "Mourning and Melancholia," a jargon-filled exploration of the roots of melancholia and what Freud called "narcissistic object-choice." Plath found it to be an "exact" description of her reasons for suicide. Except, she misses the point; she misreads the essay. What Freud said was this: Certain people, maybe even most people, have a difficult time relinquishing love objects—in Plath's case, a father who has died and is gone. They take them inside, and continue relating to them in fantasy. This internal version of the lost person is restless, it agitates. It won't sit still. It can become, in time, an object of hatred; or if one loves it, the love is always ambivalent—there's resentment, anger, and disappointment aimed its way. To deal with this, Freud said the anger must be accessed; the image of the dead person must be hated into valuelessness. This can be tricky because hating the image is also hating oneself, as the image is inside, not outside. Freud linked this with suicide. To Freud, suicide was a form of murder—or, murder-suicide. What we want to kill is the image; but in killing it, we kill the container, which is us. Plath seems to have registered all this. She keeps asking in her journal, What am I angry at? Why do I keep punishing myself? What part do I want to kill? Initially, though, she connects all this not to her dead father—what Freud would have been describing—but to her mother Aurelia. She calls her a "walking vampire," an "enemy." She realizes she needs to "grab my life from out under her hot itchy hands. . . . She's a killer. Watch out. . . . She wants to be me; she wants me to be her; she wants to crawl into my stomach and be my baby and ride along." Journaling in bed, Plath thinks what a luxury it would be to "kill her, to strangle her skinny veined throat."

It's as if Plath took Freud deadly literally; she uncorked her fury and let it fly, at least in private. She set about the business of hating her tormenters, exactly as Freud advised. First was her mother, and her mother became the target. But the rage extended, as she knew it had to. She would drain it entirely, as if it existed in exhaustible supply. She'd protected her father; she saw her mother as his killer, a "murderer of maleness." Then she went after daddy, too. Within 4 days of each other, as if on self-assignment, she wrote the poems "Daddy" and "Medusa." The timing is meaningful; the intent is obvious. In one—an "awful little allegory" she has to "act out" in order to "be free of it"—she kills her father in poetic effigy; in the other, she kills her mother. With "Daddy," she says she knew what she had to do. She makes a model of Otto—a fantasy facsimile. She stabs his "fat black heart," then tells him, "Daddy, daddy, you bastard, I'm through." In "Medusa," her mother is a "barnacled umbilicus" steaming across the Atlantic, keeping itself in "miraculous repair." "Off, off, eely tentacle," she writes. "There is nothing between us."

This was deliberate, imaginary, poetical murder. It was fine in theory; it had come out of theory. It was like a project Plath expected to get an A on. She knew she had violence in her "hot as death-blood." "I can kill myself—I know it now," she said, "even kill another." But just like Kerouac never moved past Gerard, like Lennon never moved past Julia, Plath never moved past her parent introjects. This was her "true self," the one Hughes stipulated; it was nasty and ravenous. She'd always been, in the words of her Cambridge professor, "neat and fresh, wearing charming, girlish clothes . . . hair so neatly brushed and combed." Now, to poet friend A. Alvarez, she carried a "curiously desolate, rapt air, like a priestess emptied out by the rites of her cult. . . . Her hair gave off a strong smell. Sharp as an animal's." She writes to her friend, "I kept telling myself I was the sort who could only write when peaceful at heart, but that is not so." At times she felt "a gag in my throat." Yet now, "the muse has come to live here. . . . I am like a Spartan, producing free stuff I had locked in me for years." Finally, to her mother no less, came the definitive realization: "I am a genius of a writer; I have it in me. I am writing the best poems of my life; they will make my name."

What's maybe most thrilling about Plath, disturbingly thrilling, shamefully thrilling, is the sense, argued for by Hughes, and implied by Plath herself, that she paid the ultimate price, that she died for genius. In the poem, "In Plaster," she contrasts her two selves—a tidy, clean, polite white "saint" with a "slave mentality," and an ugly, hairy alter—rude, dirty, disorderly. I used to think we might make a go of it together, she writes. After all, it was a kind of marriage. Then she sees "it must be one or the other." I'm collecting my strength, she explains. "One day I shall manage without her"—and she'll perish with emptiness. The truth is, Plath wasn't able to manage either side of the equation. She wasn't the good girl everyone told her she was, nor was she as bad as she hoped to be. Her badness was something she acted at. She kindled it, stoked it, blew hard on the embers. It did catch fire; she disappeared into the role; it was a sort of compensation, a correction for saintly lopsidedness, but it was just as limiting, just as one-dimensional. Mental health, as many have said, is a blending, an integration of split-off parts into turbulent unity. Plath didn't try this. She tried killing the bits she felt she could do without. She fastened onto one side of the ledger. It inspired and ignited her. The bad-self method-acting got her to the words she had sought and failed to find from the other side. But she couldn't resurface. Alone, both sides were empty. There was nothing except poetry to grab hold of. The words outlived her, but they were just words. No one who loved her could have recommended she die for them. The narrative is, she died to live; the fact is, she died.

In those last weeks of early, frigid 1963, these facts start adding up terrifyingly. Ted had had an affair; he and Sylvia were living apart. She felt she had lost her heart and wouldn't get it back. Plath was alone with her two small children. Off and on she was running fevers, about which she wrote a poem. She was an American, a kind of uber-American, coming to terms with England and its ways. She was writing poems romancing suicide, many in the early morning hours before her children woke, feeling herself metaphorically unkillable, a "Lady Lazarus," rising with her red hair. If the account of an eccentric painter and actor living in the flat below Plath can be believed—and parts of it have been shown to be wrong—two spooky encounters suggest she may have become psychotic. In one, just days before her suicide, she arrives at his door sobbing, with red swollen eyes: "I am going to die. Who will take care of my children?" Why she felt she needed to make this confession to a man she did not know in the least is a mystery. At minimum it highlights her total aloneness. It also speaks to a loss of judgment. The man, Thomas, says her sadness quickly turned to fury. He invited Plath in for a drink, and she tore into Hughes and his new lover, Assia Wevill. Thomas tries making a joke to distract her, "but as on previous occasions," he says, "she was wholly and intensely concerned only with her troubles." (Thomas, throughout his account, brands Plath a narcissist, a trait he finds to be common among artists.)

The second encounter is even stranger and more frightening. On the very eve of Plath's death, she showed up at Thomas's door again, asking for stamps. She takes out a small purse to reimburse him, but he tells her, weirdly, "I never take money for stamps." She replies: "But I must pay you or I won't be right with my conscience before God, will I?" Upon closing his door and returning to his room, Thomas realizes Plath has not yet left. He returns, and finds her "head raised with a kind of seraphic expression." To Thomas she looks ill; he says he can call a doctor (it is 11:45 PM). She answers, "No, please, don't do that. I'm just having a marvelous dream, a most wonderful vision." She doesn't report on the vision's contents.

The next morning, the morning of her suicide, she leaves milk and bread at her sleeping children's bedsides, seals their room, turns on the gas taps in the oven, and lays her head on a folded cloth to die. The little folded cloth seems to be the final act of assistance of the discarded saintly self. In its mundanity, it's a deeply odd detail, a terrifying note of bland specificity. She was going to be tidy about it. The fact that the children were present is also horrifying. It seems to show that Plath was out of her mind. She sealed them off against the gas, but of course there would have been no way of knowing, no way of being truly certain, that this sealing was effective. In other words, the children might have died with her. That they didn't is surprising, especially since Thomas, below, was knocked unconscious by gas that seeped into his flat. He would not awaken till the afternoon.

As usual, and with evidence from the poems and from Plath's prior attempts, there were efforts to rescue her from her own intentions. Most famously, A. Alvarez pressed the case that Plath did not mean to die. She expected to be saved, either from Thomas, or from a nurse who was scheduled to arrive at her room in the morning hours. This seems unlikely. Thomas had never even been to her room, nor did he have any real interest in her. He found her irritating. He wasn't looking out for her. And the nurse would have been too late, in any event. According to one biographer, had the girl found her, Plath's brain would have been long destroyed. Besides, getting no answer from inside the room, it's just as likely the nurse would have wandered off as it is that she'd have found some way to knock the door in. If Plath gambled, she must have known, with sureness, that the odds were stacked against her. She must not have cared either way. Living or dying must have been equally acceptable outcomes. That's how it often is with suicide. You do not care if you live or die, but mainly, you want to die.

It's interesting how, in all these cases, intimates and nonintimates alike seem hard-pressed to accept the suicide. Boigon claimed Arbus only aimed to punish, not to die. Like Plath—in Alvarez's view—she expected to be found alive, Boigon says. Then with Cobain, of course, a confederacy of monomaniacs assert murder, this in respect to a man who was a drug addict in flight, who had been suicidal most of his life, and who contemplated calling his last record, "I Hate Myself and Want to Die." As I said before, suicide is the ultimate affront to all systems of ethics. As philosopher Ludwig Wittgenstein put it, "If suicide is allowed then everything is allowed. If anything is not allowed then suicide is not allowed. . . . Suicide is, so to speak, the elementary sin." To kill yourself is to be judged guilty. This is likely why those left behind go to such extremes to render a finding of not guilty. They feel as if they are freeing the dead prisoner.

***

If we step back from these cases and try to sift through their features, there are commonalities, though most don't seem especially glaring. All three had been depressed, most obviously—Plath and Cobain for most of a lifetime, Arbus more recently (although even as a child, she harbored that "great sad artist" fantasy). All three were in the throes of what suicidologist Edwin Shneidman calls "psychache"—intense, agonizing emotional pain. This is obvious for Arbus and Plath—both betrayed by a lover, both inconsolably angry and hurt. Cobain's psychache had mostly to do with heroin use. He'd essentially eloped from treatment. He was on the run and feeling, one guesses, desperate, maybe hopeless. All three were cut off, isolated. Cobain was in hiding; Plath was alone in her flat, Ted away with his lover; Arbus had finally realized the relationship with Israel was over, her ex-husband, whom she still could have turned to, was in California, and her daughters were away. All three had problems with physical illness. For Arbus and Cobain, these were chronic issues (hepatitis and stomach pain); for Plath, there had been ongoing fevers. Fever may seem triflingly minor, but it certainly alters consciousness and impairs one's ability to cope. At minimum, it's a stressor. All three were very angry. For Cobain and Plath, this seems to have been dispositional. It was part of who they were. It was a major feature of their art. For Arbus, the rage was more new, a recent development, but it seized her in the middle of the night, and it was a focus of her therapy. All three had serious conflicts with parents. Plath had just metaphorically murdered hers; Cobain resented his, and spoke not at all to his father; Arbus saw her dad as a "phony," power- and money-obsessed, and her mother either self-involved or depressed—feeling like, in her words, a "zombie," "unloving and unlovable." For some people parents can be a source of support; they can be turned to in times of need, and they deliver. Not so for Arbus, Plath, and Cobain.

All three were involved in conflicted, difficult love relationships. Arbus and Plath had been rejected and abandoned. For Cobain, there was Courtney Love. In interviews, he spoke glowingly of his love for her, he defended her, he said he saw her as a life partner, someone he'd always been searching for. But by any measure she was a human tornado, a chaotic force, unstable, emotionally reactive. Sonic Youth's Kim Gordon co-produced Love's band's debut record, "Pretty on the Inside." To her, Love was a borderline personality. She says, "No one ever questions the disorder behind her tarantula LA glamour—sociopathy, narcissism—because it's good rock and roll, good entertainment. I have a low tolerance for manipulative, egomaniacal behavior, and usually have to remind myself that the person might be mentally ill." Whatever the case, Love was anything but stabilizing for Cobain. She wasn't a secure base he could turn to, and in his final hours, he didn't turn to her, she wasn't an option. One last detail, less clearly true for Arbus than for Plath and Cobain, is this: an extremely high degree of what might be called suicide preparedness. Plath and Cobain both constructed a personal myth, a life story, in which suicide came to assume chilling prominence. It was a fate they seriously entertained. If it wasn't exactly inevitable, it was at least likely—not just to others, but to them. To Cobain, suicide was a final angry rebuke, a world-murder. His choice of method makes this plain. To prepare, he shot up; then he blew his head off. Plath is almost scarier. She'd tried killing herself before, and came very close at least once. She played with suicide, she romanced it; it was a talent, like juggling or piano. Her lines "Dying is an art / Like everything else / I do it exceptionally well" fairly clearly capture her attitude. She was, in her mind, skilled at coming close. It made her "feel real." Destruction, or near destruction, was something she required, to *feel*. When she was dead inside, or empty, or blank, self-harm shored her up, it restarted the system. It was a remedy for nothingness that finally worked too well.

In terms of the art, there are a few jarring, shared features specific to these three cases, but also characteristic of the particular artist profile I've been constructing. In her book on Plath, *The Silent Woman*, Janet Malcolm sizes up the "not-niceness" of Plath's art. It's not just an ambient element. It's central, it's pervading, it's temperamental, and it's the reason for the art's existence. You read Plath to be disturbed. It's the bargain you accept. The poems are not pretty, uplifting, or comforting. They repel. Like crime scene photos, you look reluctantly. Arbus' pictures were maybe even more "not-nice." She shot evil, sin, perversity—the inner freak externalized. She knew this; it was also the reason for the art's existence—to create a world that matched her interior. Same for Cobain. His music mirrored the sound of his mind—melody interrupted by noise, angry screaming that ruined his stomach. For all three, the art was an affront. It was a protest. It didn't say yes; it said no, over and over. Art that's fueled by pain, by trauma, that exists to express that pain and trauma, that literally, by the fact of its existence, creates more pain and trauma, leaves little room for escape. It affirms negation. In one specific respect, Plath and Arbus may have had it easier. They didn't need to play their art for massive crowds who came for the sound of pain. They could read it and see it, but they didn't have to enact it.

Then, in the end, there is one more baffling reality. In the days before her suicide, Plath had finally achieved genius. In the months before her suicide, Arbus had finally found what she was searching for in the shots taken at institutions. For Cobain, it was a little different. His final record was a return to form, a reassertion of the sound he wanted, but also a fuck you to convention, to the mainstream, to the industry, to success. Unlike Plath and Arbus, he didn't see *In Utero* as genius, or at least he never said so. On the other hand, by default it was the best thing he'd ever done. *Bleach* was juvenilia, *Nevermind* a sell-out he could not listen to, it didn't sound, to him, like him. So, what to make of this? Maybe it's a red herring. Maybe the art itself had nothing to do with these suicides. Maybe it was a mitigating factor—to me, a long-shot possibility. An alternate reading takes us back to the possibility of art as a destabilizer. Even when it seems to be perfect, or genius, what it is, for this sort of artist, is a crystallization of suffering. It shows you who you are. It exposes your needs and obsessions. It might be a culminating dangerous truth, as with Plath. It might, in its difference, complicate the sureness and the basic validity of what was produced before, as with Arbus. It might express insoluble ambivalences, as with Cobain. He wanted the fame that came with *Nevermind*, but he also hated it. He wanted the love, but he wasn't willing to sell out to get it. He wanted goodness, but his instinct was to contaminate. To reach an artistic apex would seem to be total confirmation, total celebration, total satisfaction, a healing. But it's probably not that simple. If the top is the bad self, as Plath saw it in her poem, "In Plaster," what can that mean, how does one live with that? For Arbus the top was an implicit rejection of much of her prior work, the top was unsustainable, it threw her back to questions of why she even photographed at all. No wonder she finally felt the art stopped delivering for her. There's one last challenge about getting to the top. What's next? Is there another top? Can you get there again, and how?

We like to think of success as an unqualified reward. It's got to be good. But it also sometimes tells you what you didn't want to know. Then what?

Epilogue

I was talking to a Grammy-winning singer-songwriter in a suite atop the El Cortez with a balcony view of downtown Vegas—Fremont Street, not the Strip. She'd just performed for Believer Fest, an art/writing celebration put on annually by the Black Mountain Institute, where years before I had been lucky enough to serve as a Shearing Fellow. My hometown came up, Portland, Oregon, a place I lived still. I asked if she knew Portland. I was trying to describe a location. She said she'd been a few times, but only "for my job."

The comment struck me. She didn't say "while on tour." She didn't say "to perform." She said, "for my job."

It was refreshing, this blunt stripping away of bullshit, the implicit refusal to glamorize or romanticize. As I wrote earlier, art is a job. Art is hard. Performing your art is hard. It is work. It is an occupation (if you're lucky). To be sure, it's regarded by most as an exotic, cool occupation, but not necessarily to the person who does it. It's labor, hard labor, just like poetry, painting, playwriting, movie-making, or novel-writing. This is one of the main things that gets missed or distorted about art—how tough it is to do. Lots of jobs are tough, of course, and art may not be high on the list of toughness, but it is up there. I'm always hearing from people that they are, or want to be, writing a book. To them book-writing is exciting and fun. To me, having done it a lot, it's a grind. It has its fun, exciting moments, but those tend to come in the margins. The day to day is lonely, doubt-filled, frustrating, often dispiriting. I'd suggest that no one who has written a book looks forward to the next one gleefully. The vibe is more ominousness.

Because the job of the artist is to make something out of nothing, out of one's own head, it can seem like magic, a conjuring, achieved invisibly through a process inscrutable. This leads to the notion that art products—songs, poems, paintings—arrive by magic, too, as if dropped from the sky, a package you receive and have next to nothing to do with, a serendipitous delivery. Some artists talk this way. Dylan likes to refer to destiny. As we saw—and in a way that's not unique—he claims not to know where songs come from or how he'd go about writing them again in the same way. It's a mystery. Novelist Philip Roth makes a similar point. Each time he starts out understanding nothing. He's lost. He has no idea what to do. He's not sure how to proceed. Past experience is no good guide. Then, word by word, sentence by tortured sentence, a book settles in, a groove emerges, a voice, a point of view, a style.

This set of circumstances is bizarre. Art is work, but unlike with other professions, each next time you undertake it you have no clue how to do it. This isn't what car mechanics or plane pilots say. The last thing we want to hear from a pilot is that she has no idea how to fly the plane we are on. But artists say this a lot. It's like every day is a starting from scratch. You don't profit from past attempts. Or you do, but you can't describe how. Something obscure grabs you, a mood, an atmosphere, and you feel yourself carried along, and in the end, you've made something, and others like what you've made (again, if you are lucky). If, from scratch, you were designing an occupation guaranteed to be crazy-making, art would be it. You're good at it, but it comes when it wants. It controls you as much as you control it. You're riding high in April, shot down in May. That's life, and that's art.

Part of the appeal of art, and part of its allure, is the otherness of the artist. It's the outsider concept. We demand it. It's why, most likely, we are eager to see artists as mentally ill. "Mad genius" quenches a thirst for artist exceptionality. We can't do what they do. We wouldn't know how. We find it inconceivable. They find it inconceivable. You can't even really teach writing, lots of writers say. It's in you or it's not, and if it's not, you can only go so far. In a word, it's a gift. The package that fell from the sky. What we can't easily understand we like to call crazy, so artists are crazy. Only crazy, many instinctively feel, could account for the miracle of creation.

To write about the artist mind is to demystify the miracle which the miracle-maker himself finds miraculous. It's translating a language spoken in tongues. For this reason, some say don't translate at all. Not only is it not possible, it's unnecessary. Avoid it, or perish trying.

This is the position taken by Susan Sontag in her essay, "Against Interpretation," a thrilling work whose thrill is attributable to the cogency of its wrongness. The aim, it seems, is to declare a moral position. The essay's less a how-to than a how-not-to, a "thou shalt not" of art criticism.

We react to art in stages. I don't suggest these are sacrosanct. I derive them half from common sense, half from introspection. First, we respond—standing in a gallery, hearing a song, reading a poem. This response is probably, as they say, subcortical, or wordless, preconscious. Then we perform a valuing—we like it, we don't like it, we are indifferent (indifference is a form of benign not-liking). Lastly, we respond to our response. We think about it, we analyze it, we dissect it, we locate reasons in the art itself—in short, we ask why we like it, why we don't. Here's an example. I show my "Mind of the Artist" students photographs by Francesca Woodman. In most cases they have not seen them before. They tend to find them dark, eerie, haunting, strange. They decide, then, whether or not they like them, and what it means to like them, how to judge them as good or bad. Finally, they interpret. What were Woodman's intentions? Was she trying to be eerie? Was she provocative on purpose? Why did she use herself as a subject? To what extent do the pictures derive from life experience? No doubt our responses alter over time; there is a time element. As we learn more about Woodman, we might find we like the photos less. As we inspect the photos, we might like them more. Or, as with the rereading of a beloved book, we might come to question the salience of first impressions. This is likely how most anything works, whether we happen to be talking about a new toaster or a new play. We respond, we respond to our responses, and we revise as needed. Film is an excellent example. We are sutured to the screen, we leave the theater, then we analyze what we saw—plot, script, characters, acting, soundtrack.

Sontag's moral is "leave the work of art alone." She's fine with the initial jolt, the subcortical response, what she calls, effectively, an "erotics of perception." But she detests the notion of content, aboutness, motive. She rejects subtext. She calls our response to responses "revenge of the intellect," its aim to "impoverish," "deplete." Interpretation, for Sontag a stain, is aggressive and contemptuous. What art criticism needs, then, its antidote, is silence. It's fine, Sontag says, to produce new, loving, sensuous vocabularies of form; what is not fine is fetishization of content, any discussion of what art or an artist is "trying to say." In fact, message-driven art is axiomatically bad art, as in unnatural, overdetermined, unfree.

To cite just one example, the art of Jackson Pollock would seem to be not against interpretation but beyond it, a triumph of form over content, process over meaning. Pollock said many different things at different times about what he was up to. But about motive, he was consistent. He put himself in service of unconscious drives, he said, splattering ancient energies. Like Freud, he rejected accident, in effect declaring irrational purpose and intentionality. And he called technique "just a means of arriving at a statement." In other words, he was trying to say something, and if he was, we are justified in efforts to figure out what it was.

Yet taking Sontag at her word, we'd cease parsing possible statements. There's a Zen aspect to what she's implying: If you eat, just eat; if you sleep, just sleep. Nothing added. (But even Buddha sought the source of his suffering, the result of which was the Four Noble Truths.) This notion that nothing is needed to prop art up—no context, no artist biography—Janet Malcolm called "breathtakingly silly." Yet it's not so much a matter of what's needed. In fact, we do not need to think about art. We can take it in and leave it at that. Sontag is more about what we should not do. She's against thinking. She wants to rescue art from interpretation.

How can we be Sontagian about art, though? What would that mean? I'm not sure. We look at or read or hear art and we think, automatically, what is it saying? We begin with an assumption: Art is expression. It comes out of a person, it needs a person behind it. It's a communication. It's meant to show us something we would not otherwise see, tell us something we would not otherwise know. There seems no other way to relate to art products. We take them in and think about them. We critique, analyze, parse, find meaning. Of course, to Sontag, art need not justify itself. It need not say anything. Less "hermeneutics," more "erotics" (she tells us). I agree, art perception could use more erotics. Can intellect interfere? Yes. We don't need piles of language about language—poetry criticism, for instance—to feel more deeply, or to know what or why we feel. But the thing is, when it is good, writing about art is art. It's more art, not less. I'm not the first to say this. It goes back at least to Oscar Wilde, his critic as artist essay. Covertly, what Sontag objects to, in her extraordinarily artful essay, is artless thinking about art. I object to that, too. Probably, you do, as well. Then the question becomes: What is or is not art? Can writing about art be art? I say yes.

Another buried point has to do with the relation between hermeneutics and erotics, addition versus subtraction. Sontag sees the former as interference, a degradation. For several reasons, that's plainly ridiculous. Admittedly, there are times when we avoid knowing about things we love. We want to keep on loving. We resist clouding of judgment. It's a sort of protective impulse. If I love Dali's painting, I may prefer not knowing about Dali's psychology (more on this later). Personally, however, I've not found my enjoyment ruined by knowledge. I like Plath's poems; I've read lots of bad Plath interpretations; I don't thereby like Plath's poems less. At least, the equation isn't axiomatic. Likewise, if I discover that Paul played drums on "Dear Prudence," or that "She Said, She Said" was written about a "he," Peter Fonda, or that "Get Back" may have been Paul's concealed dig at Yoko, or that Joni Mitchell wrote "Circle Game" as a reply to Neil Young's "Sugar Mountain," I experience no depletion, no impoverishment of liking. The effect, at worst, is neutral. It's the same in cases of deep interpretation (for me it is, at least). I edited a book by Tim Kasser arguing that Lucy of "Lucy in the Sky With Diamonds" stood, in terms of remote motivations, for Lennon's mother Julia. Both had a habit of appearing only to disappear. Being shown this subtextual connection put no "stain" on my feel for the song.

Then there is Sontag herself, her own interpretations (though she might label them differently). She's written at length about photographer Diane Arbus, her analysis focused on Arbus' undeclared or elided intentions, intentions Sontag sees as "truer" than those offered up by others. That is, Sontag suggests she knows what Arbus was *really* doing. In substance, she's telling us how Arbus' pictures ought to be *viewed*. She does something similar with Artaud; she recommends better ways of *reading* him. So, it turns out Sontag isn't all that Sontagian. This is fine; it's what I meant by the cogency of her wrongness. Figuring out the senses in which she's wrong has a salutary impact. In the best of cases, hermeneutics *increases* the erotics of perception. We see better when we understand more.

Hermeneutics—interpretation—can be an addition, not a subtraction. There's another type of knowledge to explore, as well. This concerns the life of the artist—her character, possibly—and how knowing about character complicates art appreciation. George Orwell takes up this subject in a wonderful essay on Dali, titled "Benefit of Clergy." He starts with Dali's childhood, replete with tales of violence. He gives his sister a "terrible kick in the head," as if it "had been a ball" and feels "delirious joy." He flings a boy off a suspension bridge. He bites a dead, ant-covered bat in half. He kisses and caresses a girl on a "five-year plan," leading her on and "enjoying her humiliation." He luxuriates in his sexual perversity, his excretory fixations, his necrophilia. Of Dali's 1942 autobiography, Orwell says, finally, "it is a book that stinks. If it were possible for a book to give a physical stink off its pages, this one would." Yet against all this, Orwell notes Dali's exceptional draughtsmanship, the minuteness and sureness of his drawings, his capacity for hard artistic work. "He has fifty times more talent than most of those who would denounce his morals and jeer at his [often disturbing] paintings," says Orwell. It's these combined facts Orwell is most concerned with. Namely, the fact of Dali's artistic abilities contrasted with his "antisocial" and "undesirable" character. How, in other words, ought one respond to the art of an artist who is, as Orwell sees Dali, personally detestable?

The two most common answers Orwell rejects. First, artists don't deserve the benefit of clergy. They are *not* exempt from moral laws, any more than surgeons or presidents or college professors. So, Orwell concludes, "art for art's sake alone" fails. On the other hand, a refusal to admit that "what is morally degraded can be aesthetically right" makes no sense either, says Orwell. It's a category conflation. Character is independent of merit. I can *choose* not to look at Dali's art because I find him despicable; I can do the same for, say, Michael Jackson's music. But this is a moral stance, not an aesthetic one. My refusal means nothing in terms of the relative goodness of the work itself. A societal decision might be made, too. Imagine a gorgeous wall encircling a concentration camp (Orwell's analogy). We might elect to tear it down, destroy the beauty. But again, the beauty is the beauty. It stands apart.

So, what to do? Orwell's answer is sociological. "The important thing is not to denounce Dali as a cad who ought to be horsewhipped," he says, "or to defend him as a genius who ought not to be questioned," but to find out why he is like he is, how he came to be "*a symptom of the world's illness*." The rich, after all, clamor to buy such pictures as "Mannequins Rotting in a Taxicab," pictures Orwell calls "diseased and disgusting." This, he tells us, is where to start any investigation. How did the world make Dali, and why does the world reward him? In a like fashion, we enjoy suicidal art, psychotic art. We find the poignancy arresting. Why? What makes it so? What are the origins of this thrill?

This takes us back to where we started: the expectation, the presupposition of artist torture and the effect this presumption has on our consumption of the art itself. Art as torture symptom. Art as, in John Lennon's terms, "expression of pain." Orwell reaches similar conclusions. The "wickedness" of Dali must be diagnosed, he says (it's in him and it's in his admirers). He says it ought to be discoverable in the art itself, even the art's less obvious margins. On one hand, this is a factual matter. On the other, the side Orwell is most focused on, it is social, sick art for a sick world. These questions need to be separated.

Huxley said the sign of top-quality art is sincerity. You have to mean it. It has to be true. It's something one cannot fake. Orwell said essentially the same: "For a creative writer possession of the 'truth' is less important than emotional sincerity. . . . It is the difference between genuine despair and despair that is at least partly a pretense." Suffering is one kind of seal. It is seen, automatically, as sincerity proof. It shows the artist meant it, it shows he/she paid a price, sometimes the highest possible price, dying for genius, genius vouchsafed by dying. Orwell implies he doubts Dali's detestable childhood stories. Are they fact or fiction? If fact, so be it. If fiction, which seems likely, the motive's more interesting. One possibility: Dali could not abide ordinariness. A benign backstory was unacceptable. So, he set about making himself vile, despicable, crude, sadistic. This, to Dali's way of thinking, anchored the art in turmoil. The art had its origin myth: blunt, unapologetic wickedness. The wicked artist made wicked art. The art was sincere. It wasn't disgusting gratuitously. It was *sincerely* disgusting.

We anticipate torture, we look for signs; to prove the price of the art, the artist may also fabricate it, as with (possibly) Dali and others. This can seem required. It's not enough for the making of art to be hard. The atmosphere of its creation must scar. In cases where there is no price, the art is delegitimized, insincerely expressed. These are ways in which the *myth* of torture is advanced. The process is sociological, and also psychological. The world demands it, the artist obliges. The world buys the myth and the artist, as part of that world, does, too. Nirvana's Kurt Cobain apparently invented a homelessness backstory according to which for months he lived under bridges outside Aberdeen, Washington. He may also have exaggerated the targeting he experienced from loathsome jock rednecks in school. Contemporaneous friends sometimes say of these disclosures, "That's impossible" or "That didn't happen" or "That's a lie." We invent episodes that match the degree of pain we feel. It's a function of autobiographical memory. It also, in this case, makes the art emotionally piquant, more "sincere." We experience the art differently when made aware of its torture-based origins.

I said Orwell's questions had to be separated. What I meant was this: Apart from the sociological elements, what do the facts say? In this matter, we know the answer. For complicated reasons, artists may exaggerate their torture; the art must be seen as justified. But generally, *artists really are more tortured*. It's one of this book's key points. The torture is a product of personality organization, a set of tendencies I've described, each a direct outgrowth of high openness. The crux of the torture is qualities of mind the openness trait makes more likely, not events in the life. The outer life may be relatively ordinary; the inner life usually is not. Constructing a trauma-filled history, then, is an effort to make the outer fit the inner. It's an attempt at an explanation. In reality, no explanation is required. But the mind does not work that way. It needs its answers. It needs its stories. Its job is to identify causes. The real cause, however, is largely intrinsic personality-based structures. Whatever Dali may or may not have done as a child, his need to embellish, to darken experiences, his self-presentations aimed at certifying bizarreness and wickedness—these stand apart from an original inner world.

A last auxiliary portion of the myth has to do with art's redemptive promise. To many, art is seen as therapy, not first and foremost, but as a salutary side effect. It's important to ask why. Let's start with other occupations. People bake astonishing, intricately designed cakes; they build ornate, finely wrought fences; they design spectacular homes; they teach carefully curated classes. All these creations come with the imprint of personality. They contain idiosyncratic stylings, the aesthetics of their maker. We will say, "That's clearly a Frank Lloyd Wright," and so on. Yet these jobs are not, or rarely, regarded as therapeutic: We do not see the making as *ipso facto* solving emotional problems. We often do in the case of art, however, and the reason might relate to ingrained, leftover Freudian-type assumptions about the basic uniqueness of artistic processes strictly defined. Art, or high art at least, is regarded as reenactment. Conflicts unconsciously surface and get reworked symbolically, resulting in problem-solving and emotion regulation. If I write about my toxic family, I come to a new understanding and thereby move beyond stuckness. Or, more complexly, I "sublimate," I harness and channel sexual energy to the point where it becomes functionally autonomous, that is, released from its infantile origins. The energy is put in the healthier service of creative productions. I don't try to do this, it just happens. I don't even always know it is happening.

People will sometimes say their gardening is therapeutic, or their model train-track building, or their sewing of masks. The question, then, can become semantic, at least partly. What is it people mean by this? Possibly that they enjoy doing it. It fills their time. It brings them pleasure. They feel excited and effective as their skills increase and their creations, whatever they are, grow more appealing, to them or to others. I do not discount any of this, it seems sensible, but therapy, properly defined, includes, at minimum, increased self-awareness and lasting change. This fact shifts the conversation. Therapy is more than enjoyment, more than positive-feeling accompanying a task.

Making something—a cake, a fence, a song—is sometimes thrilling. There can even occur a momentary catharsis. But to say this making is *therapeutic* goes beyond these mean outcomes, and it sets aside another Freudian concept that's particularly apposite: the requirement, in therapy, of "working through." Recollection and repetition are not enough; they set the stage, but no more. One must also work through what's come up: dissect, analyze, reconnect, feel the bottled-up feelings. As a rule, artists don't do this. In fact, many superstitiously avoid it, in the belief that knowing too much about the art's sources might calcify a process that is better left alone. Photographer Diane Arbus is a good example. In her therapy she rejected all "why's." She had no interest in explanations. Her photos never came up. Nor would she have wanted them to. What the photos meant, how they related to her life history, the ways in which they may have constituted projections of inner experience—all this was out of bounds.

The truth is that art is allusion. It contains and points to traumas and conflicts; it does not automatically solve them. It is an uninterpreted dream. In one sense, it is more trauma and conflict, symbolically repackaged. The contrary idea that art is therapy accepts suspect premises—of uniqueness, transcendence, superhumanness. Seeing art as work and a job is a different, liberating starting point. It's a way of clearing out mythical mystifications. At times, it can seem as if two options alone exist: artist as mad and artist as incomprehensible genius. Or, artist as genius *because* mad. These don't work for the reason that they are not true. With what, then, can we replace the myth? Factors that ground us in simpler, less mystical realities. Hard, grueling, often thankless work. A devotion to perfecting craft. Talent, of course. And a serendipitous personality structure making creative responses in general more likely. Art precipitates problems, aesthetic problems, and the most fine, effective artists solve those on a path to beauty. All other, global matters, those in the parallel universe called life itself, stand quietly by, used, shaped, ordered, yet not necessarily dispatched.

Further Reading

Acar, S., & Runco, M. (2012). Psychoticism and creativity: A meta-analytic review. *Psychology of Aesthetics, Creativity, and the Arts,* 6, 341–350.

Agid, O., Shapira, B., Zislin, J., Ritsner, M., Hanin, B., Murad, H., Troudart, T., Bloch, M., Heresco-Levy, U., & Lerer, B. (1999). Environment and vulnerability to major psychiatric illness: A case control study of early parental loss in major depression, bipolar disorder, and schizophrenia. *Molecular Psychiatry,* 4, 163–172.

Aluja, A., Garcia, O., & Garcia, L. F. (2003). Relationships among extraversion, openness-to-experience, and sensation seeking. *Personality and Individual Differences,* 35, 671–680.

Ando, V., Claridge, G., & Clark, K. (2014). Psychotic traits in comedians. *British Journal of Psychiatry,* 204, 341–345.

Andreasen, N. C. (1987). Creativity and mental illness: Prevalence rates in writers and their first-degree relatives. *American Journal of Psychiatry,* 144, 1288–1292.

Andrews, P. W., & Thomson, Jr., J. A. (2009). The bright side of being blue: Depression as an adaptation for analyzing complex problems. *Psychological Review,* 116, 620–654.

Antinori, A., Carter, O. L., & Smillie, L. D. (2017). Seeing it both ways: Openness to experience and binocular rivalry suppression. *Journal of Research in Personality,* 68, 15–22.

Ashton, M. C., Lee, K., & Goldberg, L. R. (2006). The IPIP-HEXACO scales: An alternative, public-domain measure of personality constructs in the HEXACO model. *Personality and Individual Differences,* 42, 1515–1526.

Beaussart, M. L., Andrews, C. J., & Kaufman, J. C. (2013). Creative liars: The relationship between creativity and integrity. *Thinking Skills and Creativity,* 9, 129–134.

Brent, D., Melhem, N., Donohoe, M. B., & Walker, M. (2009). The incidence and course of depression in bereaved youth 21 months after the loss of a parent to suicide, accident, or sudden natural death. *American Journal of Psychiatry,* 166, 786–794.

Buckley, D. (2005). *Strange fascination: Bowie, the definitive story*. New York, NY: Virgin Books.Carson, S. H. (2011).

Creativity and psychopathology: A shared vulnerability model. *Canadian Journal of Psychiatry,* 56, 144–153.

Carson, S. H. (2014). Cognitive disinhibition, creativity, and psychopathology. In D. K. Simonton (Ed.), Handbook of genius (pp. 198–221). New York: NY: Wiley-Blackwell.

Carson, S. H., Peterson, J. B., & Higgins, D. M. (2003). Decreased latent inhibition is associated with increased creative achievement in high functioning individuals. *Personality Processes and Individual Differences,* 85, 499–506.

DeYoung, C. G., Grazioplene, R. G., & Peterson, J. B. (2012). From madness to genius: The openness/intellect trait domain as a paradoxical simplex. *Journal of Research in Personality,* 46, 63–78.

Dorpat, T. L, Jackson, J. K., & Ripley, H. S. (1965). Broken homes and attempted and completed suicide. *Archives of General Psychiatry,* 12, 213–216.

Duberstein, P. R. (2001). Are closed-minded people more open to the idea of killing themselves? *Suicide and Life Threatening Behavior,* 31, 9–14.

Eisenstadt, J. M. (1978). Parental loss and genius. *American Psychologist,* 33, 211–223.

Elms, A. C., & Heller, B. (2005). Twelve ways to say "lonesome": Assessing error and control in the music of Elvis Presley. In W. T. Schultz (Ed.), Handbook of psychobiography (pp. 142–157). New York, NY: Oxford University Press.

Fiest, G. J. (1998). A meta-analysis of personality in scientific and artistic creativity. *Personality and Social Psychology Review,* 2, 290–309.

Furnham, A., Batey, M., Anand, K., & Mansfield, J. (2007). Personality, hypomania, intelligence and creativity. *Personality and Individual Differences,* 44, 1060–1069.

Herrera, H. (2002). Frida: A biography of Frida Kahlo. New York, NY: Harper Perennial.

Irwing, P., Cook, C., Pollet, T. V., & Hughes, D. J. (2020). Comedians' trait level and stage personalities: Evidence for goal-directed personality adaptation. *Personality and Social Psychology Bulletin,* 46, 590–602.

Isaacson, W. (2011). Steve Jobs. New York, NY: Simon & Schuster.

Jamison, K. R. (1989). Mood disorders and patterns of creativity in British writers and artists. *Psychiatry,* 52, 125–134.

Kanzer, M. (1953). Writers and the early loss of parents. *Journal of the Hillside Hospital,* 2, 148–151.

Kasser, T. (2013). Lucy in the mind of Lennon. New York, NY: Oxford University Press.

Kaufman, J. C. (2001); The Sylvia Plath effect: Mental illness in eminent creative writers. *Journal of Creative Behavior*, 35, 37–48.

Kaun, D. E. (1991). Writers die young: The impact of work and leisure on longevity. *Journal of Economic Psychology,* 12, 381–399.

Kendler, K., Neale, M. C., Kessler, R. C., Heath, A. C., & Eaves, L. J. (1992). Childhood parental loss and adult psychopathology in women: A twin study perspective. *Archives of General Psychiatry,* 49, 109–116.

Kensinger, E. A. (2009). Remembering the details: Effects of emotion. *Emotion Review,* 1, 99–113.

Kerouac, J. (1996). Selected letters: Volume I. New York, NY: Penguin Books.

Kyaga, S., Lichtenstein, P., Boman, M., Hultman, C., Langstrom, N., & Landen, M. (2011). Creativity and mental disorder: Family study of 300,000 people with severe mental disorder. *British Journal of Psychiatry,* 199, 373–379.

Leon, I. G. (1999). Bereavement and repair of the self: Poetic confrontations with self. *Psychoanalytic Review,* 86, 383–400.

Lester, D. (1989). Experience of parental loss and later suicide: Data from published biographies. *Acta Psychiatrica Scandinavia,* 79, 450–452.

Liu, S., Chow, H. M., Xu, Y., Erkkinen, M. G., Swett, K. E., Eagle, M. W., Rizik-Baer, D. A., & Braun, A. R. (2012). Neural correlates of lyrical improvisation: An fMRI study of freestyle rap. *Nature Scientific Reports,* 2, 1–8.

Ludwig, A. M. (1994). Mental illness and creative activity in female writers. *American Journal of Psychiatry,* 151, 1650–1656.

Luftig, S. (1997). The Paul Simon companion: Four decades of commentary. New York, NY: Schirmer Books.

MacLean, K. A., Johnson, M. W., & Griffiths, R. R. (2011). Mystical experiences occasioned by the hallucinogen Psilocybin lead to increases in the personality domain of openness. *Journal of Psychopharmacology,* 25, 1453–1461.

Martindale, C. (1972). Father's absence, psychopathology, and poetic eminence. *Psychological Reports,* 31, 843–847.

Mason, B. A. (2007). Elvis Presley: A life. New York, NY: Penguin Books.

McAdams, D. P. (1995). What do we know when we know a person? *Journal of Personality,* 63, 365–396.

McAdams, D. P. (2005). What psychobiographers might learn from personality psychology. In W. T. Schultz (Ed.), Handbook of psychobiography (pp. 64–83). New York: NY: Oxford University Press.

McAdams, D. P. (2006). A new big five: Fundamental principles for an integrative science of personality. *American Psychologist,* 61, 204–217.

McCrae, R., & Costa, P. (1997). Conceptions and correlates of openness to experience. In R. Hogan, J. A. Johnson, & S. R. Briggs (Eds.), Handbook of personality psychology (pp. 825–847). San Diego, CA: Academic Press.

McCrae, R., & Costa, P. (1999). A five-factor theory of personality. In O. John, R. Robins, & L. Pervin (Eds.), Handbook of personality (pp. 153–199). New York, NY: Guilford Press.

McCrae, R., & Greenberg, D. M. (2014). Openness to experience. In D. K. Simonton (Ed.), Handbook of genius (pp. 222–243). New York: NY: Wiley-Blackwell.

Miller, G. F., & Tal, I. R. (2007). Schizotypy versus openness and intelligence as predictors of creativity. *Schizophrenia Research,* 93, 317–324.

Mousavi, S. V., Sheakhli, N., & Rezaci, S. (2015). Role of the big five traits in chemical suicide attempt. *Journal of Practice in Clinical Psychology,* 3, 235–242.

Nettle, D. (2006). Schizotypy and mental health among poets, visual artists, and mathematicians. *Journal of Research in Personality*, 40, 876–890.

O'Connor, F. (1967). Jackson Pollock. New York, NY: Museum of Modern Art.

O'Connor, R. C., & Nock, M. K. (2014). The psychology of suicidal behavior. *Lancet Psychiatry*, 1, 73–85.

Ogden, T. H. (2000). Borges and the art of mourning. *Psychoanalytic Dialogues*, 10, 65–88.

Ogilvie, D. M. (2003). *Fantasies of flight*. New York, NY: Oxford University Press.

Orwell, G. (1946). *Dickens, Dali, & others: Studies in popular culture*. New York, NY: Reynal and Hitchcock.

Perkins A. H., Arnone, D., Smallwood, J., & Mobbs, D. (2015). Thinking too much: Self-generated thought as the engine of neuroticism. *Trends in Cognitive Sciences*, 19, 492–498.

Pickering, A. D., Smillie, L. D., & DeYoung, C. G. (2016). Neurotic individuals are not creative thinkers. *Trends in Cognitive Sciences*, 20, 1–2.

Piedmont, R. L., Sherman, M. F., & Sherman, N. C. (2012). Maladaptively high and low openness: The case for experiential permeability. *Journal of Personality*, 80, 1642–1668.

Post, F. (1994). Creativity and psychopathology: A study of 291 world-famous men. *British Journal of Psychiatry*, 165, 22–34.

Richards, R., Kinney, D. K., Lunde, I., Benet, M., & Merzel, A. P. C. (1988). Creativity in manic-depressives, cyclothymes, their normal relatives, and control subjects. *Journal of Abnormal Psychology*, 97, 281–288.

Robison, M. K, Grath, K. I., & Unsworth, N. (2017). The neurotic wandering mind: An individual difference investigation of neuroticism, mind-wandering, and executive control. *Quarterly Journal of Experimental Psychology*, 70, 649–663.

Roth, P. (2017). *Why write? Collected non-fiction: 1960–2014*. New York, NY: Library of America.

Schildkraut, J. J., Hirschfeld, A. J., & Murphy, J. M. (1994). Mind and mood in modern art II: Depressive disorders, spirituality, and early deaths in the Abstract Expressionist artists of the New York School. *American Journal of Psychiatry*, 151, 482–487.

Schlesinger, J. (2009). Creative mythconceptions: A closer look at the evidence for the "mad genius" *hypothesis. Psychology of Aesthetics, Creativity, and the Arts*, 3, 62–72.

Schultz, W. T. (1996). An Orpheus complex in two writers-of-loss. *Biography*, 19, 371–393.

Schultz, W. T. (1998). Finding fate's father: Some life-history influences on Roald Dahl's Charlie and the chocolate factory. *Biography*, 21, 463–481.

Schultz, W. T. (2005). Mourning, melancholia, and Sylvia Plath. In W. T. Schultz (Ed.), *Handbook of psychobiography* (pp. 158–174). New York, NY: Oxford University Press.

Schultz, W. T. (2011). *An emergency in slow motion: The inner life of Diane Arbus*. New York, NY: Bloomsbury.
Schultz, W. T. (2011). *Tiny terror: Why Truman Capote (almost) wrote Answered Prayers*. New York, NY: Oxford University Press.
Schultz, W. T. (2013). *Torment saint: The life of Elliott Smith*. New York, NY: Bloomsbury Publishing.
Schultz, W. T. (2014). Psychobiography of genius. In D. K. Simonton (Ed.), *Handbook of genius* (pp. 20–32). New York: NY: Wiley-Blackwell.
Schultz, W. T. (2016). Behind the masks. *Psychologist, 29*, 614–617.
Segal, D. L., Marty, M. A., Meyer, W. J., & Coolidge, F. L. (2012). Personality, suicidal ideation, and reasons for living among older adults. *Journals of Gerontology, Series B: Psychological Sciences and Social Sciences, 67*, 159–166.
Silvia, P. J., Kaufman, J. C., Reiter-Palmon, R., & Wigert, B. (2011). Cantankerous creativity: Honesty-humility, agreeableness, and the HEXACO structure of creative achievement. *Personality and Individual Differences, 51*, 687–689.
Simonton, D. K. (2004). *Greatness: Who makes history and why*. New York, NY: Guilford Press.
Soldz, S., & Vaillant, G. (1999). The Big Five personality traits and the life course: A 45-year longitudinal study. *Journal of Research in Personality, 33*, 208–232.
Sontag, S. (1966). *Against interpretation and other essays*. New York, NY: Farrar, Straus & Giroux.
Stack, S. (1996). Gender and suicide risk among artists: A multivariate analysis. *Suicide and Life Threatening Behavior, 26*, 374–379.
Stack, S., & Gundlach, J. (1992). The effect of country music on suicide. *Social Forces, 71*, 211–218.
Styron, W. (1992). *Darkness visible: A memoir of madness*. New York, NY: Vintage Books.
Sussman, A. (2007). Mental illness and creativity: A neurological view of the "tortured artist." *Stanford Journal of Neuroscience, 1*, 21–24.
Thomson, E. (1996). *The John Lennon companion: Twenty-five years of comment*. New York, NY: Simon and Schuster.
Tomkins, S. (1987). Script theory. In J. Aranoff, A. I Rabin, & R. A. Zucker (Eds.), *The emergence of personality* (pp. 147–216). New York, NY: Springer Publishing Company.
Van den Bergh, O., Brosschot, J., & Critchley, H. (2020). Better safe than sorry: A common signature of general vulnerability for psychopathology. *Perspectives in Psychological Science, 16*, 225–246.
Van der Kolk, B. A. (1994). The body keeps the score: Memory and the evolving psychobiology of posttraumatic stress. *Harvard Review of Psychiatry, 1*, 253–265.
Velting, D. (1999). Suicidal ideation and the five factor theory of personality. *Personality and Individual Differences, 27*, 943–952.

Wagner, A. M. (1993). Fictions: Krasner's presence, Pollock's absence. In W. Chadwick & I. de Courtivron (Eds.), *Significant others: Creativity and intimate partnership* (pp. 223–243). New York, NY: Thames and Hudson.

Wanamaker, M. C. (1999). William Styron and the literature of early maternal loss. *Psychoanalytic Review,* 86, 403–431.

Weisberg, R. W. (1994). A quasi-experimental test of the hypothesis that manic-depression increases creativity. *Psychological Science,* 5, 361–367.

Werman, D. S. (2000). The passing of creativity: Two histories: James Ensor and Arthur Rimbaud. *Journal of Applied Psychoanalytic Studies,* 2, 65–80.

Wink, P. (2021). *Prima donna: The psychology of Maria Callas.* New York, NY: Oxford University Press.

Artist interviews/online sources:

Jerry Seinfeld on Pop-Tarts:
https://www.openculture.com/2012/12/jerry_seinfeld_explains_how_to_write_a_joke.html

Joni Mitchell interview:
https://www.youtube.com/watch?v=pEJuiZN3jI8

Kanye West, Jimmy Kimmel interview transcript:
https://genius.com/Kanye-west-2013-jimmy-kimmel-interview-part-2-annotated

Bob Dylan, 60 Minutes, Ed Bradley interview:
https://borntolisten.com/2020/07/18/the-classic-bob-dylan-60-minutes-interview-with-ed-bradley/

David Bowie interviews:
https://faroutmagazine.co.uk/david-bowie-dick-cavett-cocaine-interview-1974/
https://www.loudersound.com/features/david-bowie-on-songwriting
https://www.bbc.co.uk/programmes/p03f5cyt
https://www.bbc.co.uk/programmes/b06wc64p

Duplass brothers interview:
https://www.npr.org/2018/05/08/609349238/duplass-brothers-on-working-together-and-growing-apart-we-are-ex-soulmates

Francesca Woodman documentary, "The Woodmans":
https://www.youtube.com/watch?v=5zqNUdtCwkU

"The World According to John Coltrane" documentary:
https://jazzonthetube.com/video/the-world-according-to-john-coltrane/

Index

For the benefit of digital users, indexed terms that span two pages (e.g., 52–53) may, on occasion, appear on only one of those pages.